INSTITUTIONALISM
AND
CHURCH UNITY

INSTITUTIONALISM

and

CHURCH UNITY

A SYMPOSIUM PREPARED BY THE
STUDY COMMISSION ON INSTITUTIONALISM,
COMMISSION ON FAITH AND ORDER,
WORLD COUNCIL OF CHURCHES

Edited by
NILS EHRENSTROM
and
WALTER G. MUELDER

ASSOCIATION PRESS   New York

INSTITUTIONALISM AND CHURCH UNITY

Copyright © 1963 by
National Board of Young Men's Christian Associations

Association Press, 291 Broadway, New York 7, N.Y.

Publisher's Stock Number: 1482

Library of Congress catalog card number: 63-8883

 72

PRINTED IN THE UNITED STATES OF AMERICA

PREFACE

Ecumenical conversation is a noisy gong unless it leads to ecumenical conversion. One of the dangers accompanying the ecumenical movement is to become so absorbed in theological dialogues, in fraternal fellowship, in practical co-operation (all of which of course are laudable and necessary activities), that the gaze is diverted from the radical changes which are required throughout the churches' life for them to become *uniting* churches. The tragic separations which have occurred in the history of Christianity have become consolidated not only in distinct mentalities and systems of belief but also in different institutional and organizational structures. The scandal of disunity has been institutionalized. And the pervasive influence of such institutional factors is all the more powerful and resistant to change since they are mostly ignored and unacknowledged.

If the ecumenical movement is to be realistic and down-to-earth, it must, therefore, challenge the churches to become more self-critically aware of the subtle ways in which their institutional structures and procedures obstruct or facilitate ecumenical advance. Unity, too, needs to find appropriate institutional expression.

It is considerations of this kind that have prompted the production of the present symposium. It brings to focus a longstanding though somewhat sporadic concern of the Faith and Order movement with the implications of social and cultural factors for unity. Among the preparatory material for the Edinburgh Conference in 1937 was a pioneering report on *The Non-theological Factors in the Making and Unmaking of Church Union.* The issue obtained renewed attention in connection with the next world conference at Lund (Sweden) in 1952, and the ensuing studies were summed up in a pamphlet entitled *Social and Cultural Factors in Church Divisions.* It is perhaps characteristic of the American religious scene that the first North American Faith and Order Conference, in 1957, devoted one third of its program to an exploration of the bearing of "cultural pressures" on Christian unity.

It became increasingly clear, however, that such occasional reconnaissance flights over the territory were insufficient; they needed to be supplemented by specialized explorations in depth. In 1955 the Commission on Faith and Order of the World Council of Churches established a study commission on Institutionalism with the following terms of reference:

> To make a study of institutionalism as it affects all churches, and in particular:
>
> 1. The self-criticism of churches by which they may see their own structures sociologically as well as theologically;
>
> 2. The relations both positive and negative of the churches to each other in the ecumenical conversation;
>
> 3. The pattern of church relations which is finding expression in the World Council of Churches as an institution.

Adopting an interdisciplinary theological and sociological approach, the Commission has pursued two lines of investigation: (a) Because of the unexplored nature of its subject matter, it has been carrying out a continuing discussion on such basic issues as the nature and function of institutions especially as they operate in the Christian community, the Church itself as *koinonia* (fellowship) and as institution, ecclesiastical bureaucracy, and the like. (b) At the same time it has undertaken a series of empirical case studies on the influence of institutional factors in actual church union projects.

In accordance with its mandate, the Commission has produced a joint report, published in the Faith and Order booklet, *The Old and the New in the Church,* and the present symposium which contains a selection of the material emanating from its work. Both the report and this symposium will be transmitted to the Churches at the Fourth World Conference on Faith and Order, to be held in Montreal in July, 1963. The essays here presented are, for the most part, the outcome of a long process of joint planning and the give-and-take of group discussion. There has been revision at each stage of the process. First, the authors have incorporated numerous suggestions; then the editors have made excisions and emendations; finally, the secretariat of Faith and Order has pruned various paragraphs and modified section-headings in the direction of greater consistency. The volume should, if possible, be studied in conjunction with the report. Since there may be readers who do not have access to the report, references to it have been included in the introductory chapter on "The Quest for Ecumenical Institutionalization."

As will be seen, the case histories in Part II of the volume all deal with relations between Protestant denominations. It is indicative of the complexity of these problems and of the existing lack of primary research, that the Commission has failed in its efforts to procure a number of other projected case studies, for instance, on Eastern Orthodox Churches and on conciliar organizations. Here awaits a vast and rewarding field of interdisciplinary research.

One of the projects initiated by the Commission has resulted in a separate volume, *Anglican-Methodist Relations: Some Institutional Factors,* edited by W.S.F. Pickering.

There remains the pleasant duty to express our gratitude to the

Council on Christian Unity of the Disciples of Christ, whose generous grant largely made it possible for the Commission to hold meetings and circulate documents; to various publishers who courteously granted permission to use quotations from their publications; to the loyal contributors of papers and critical comments; and above all to our colleagues who so admirably demonstrated that an ecumenical institution, such as this Commission has been, can be a true charisma of friendship and fellowship in Christ.

NILS EHRENSTROM
WALTER G. MUELDER

ABOUT THE CONTRIBUTORS

JOSEPH L. ALLEN

As assistant professor of social ethics at Perkins School of Theology, Southern Methodist University, Dallas, Texas, Joseph L. Allen teaches primarily in the field of theology and politics. He is a North Carolinian by birth, was graduated from Duke University, and then received his B.D. and Ph.D. degrees from Yale University. He is an ordained minister and member of the North Carolina Annual Conference in The Methodist Church.

WILLIAM B. CATE

William B. Cate is executive secretary of the Greater Portland Council of Churches, Portland, Oregon, having previously held a similar position with the Interchurch Council of New Bedford, Massachusetts. A minister of The Methodist Church, he took his S.T.B. and Ph.D. degrees from Boston University; his dissertation dealt with "Theoretical and Practical Aspects of Ecumenical Communication." He has also spent a year of study at the Ecumenical Institute, near Geneva, and the University of Basle. Currently he is chairman of the Studies Committee for the American Association of Council Secretaries.

HANS DOMBOIS

Hans Dombois received his LL.D. from the University of Göttingen and was for many years active in the judiciary. Since 1950 he is a member of the Institute of Protestant Studies, now located in Heidelberg, where he is responsible for research in the relations between theology, legal theory, and legislation. His special interest is ecclesiastical law, and the most recent of his publications is a massive historical and theoretical study in that field, *Das Recht der Gnade*. For the past decade he served as chairman of the Political Working Group of the Protestant *Kirchentag*.

NILS EHRENSTROM

Nils Ehrenstrom is professor of ecumenics at Boston University School of Theology. He has spent some twenty-five years in Geneva, first with the Research Department of the Universal Christian Council for Life and Work and subsequently as director of the Study Department of the World Council of Churches. Ordained in the Lutheran Church of Sweden, he received his theological degrees from the Universities of Uppsala and Lund. Contributor and co-editor of numerous ecumenical publications, he is the author of *Christian Faith and the Modern State: An Ecumenical Approach* and has been an associate editor of *The Ecumenical Review* since its inception. He is secretary of the Faith and Order Study Commission on Institutionalism.

JAMES M. GUSTAFSON

As associate professor of social ethics at Yale Divinity School, James M. Gustafson is responsible for teaching in theological ethics and sociology of religion. A minister of the United Church of Christ, U.S.A., he received his education at Northwestern University, the University of Chicago, and Yale University. He was assistant director of the Study of Theological Education in the United States and Canada, 1954-1955. Contributor to books and journals, he is the author of *Treasure in Earthen Vessels: The Church as a Human Community*.

BERNDT GUSTAFSSON

Berndt Gustafsson is assistant professor of church history at the University of Lund and since 1962 also head of the Institute of Sociology of Religion in Stockholm. A minister of the Church of Sweden, he has doctorates both in theology and sociology from the University of Lund. He is the author of numerous articles and books in the fields of modern church history and sociology of religion.

RICHARD P. C. HANSON

Since 1962 Lightfoot professor of divinity in the University of Durham, England, Richard P. C. Hanson taught previously at the Queen's College, Birmingham, and for ten years in the Department of Theology at the University of Nottingham. He has also been visiting lecturer at Seabury-Western Theological Seminary, Evanston, Illinois. Anglo-Irish by descent, he was educated at Trinity College, Dublin, in classics and theology. His publications include two books on Origen and a recent one on *Tradition in the Early Church*. For a period he served as secretary of the Faith and Order Department of the British Council of Churches.

KEN ISHIWARA

Ken Ishiwara, a member of the Commission on Faith and Order of the United Church of Christ in Japan, studied Greek philosophy and Christian thought at Tokyo Imperial University and in Heidelberg, Germany. In 1924 he was appointed professor of early and medieval philosophy at Tohoku Imperial University, Sendai. During the war he was president of Tokyo Woman's Christian College, later professor of church history at Aoyama-Gakuin University, and currently is guest professor of history of Christianity at several universities in Tokyo. He is the author of several books, including *Schleiermacher on Religion, History of Christian Thought*, and *Studies on Medieval Christianity*.

JOHN H. S. KENT

John H. S. Kent is tutor in church history at Hartley Victoria College, Manchester, England, and a lecturer in the history of doctrine at Manchester University. He was educated at Emmanuel College and Wesley House, Cambridge, taking his Ph.D. degree in 1950, and is an ordained Methodist minister. His special interest is in modern church history, especially the religious history of the nineteenth century. He has published studies of Jabez Bunting and of Elizabeth Fry, and is now working on a study of American revivalists in England in the nineteenth century.

W. EDWARD MANN

Born in Toronto, Edward Mann took his Ph.D. in sociology from the University of Toronto in 1953. He has taught sociology at various institutions in Canada and is now assistant professor of sociology at the University of Western Ontario. After studies at Trinity College, Toronto, he has served pastorates and was for five years executive secretary of the Diocesan Council for Social Service of the Anglican Church in Toronto. Among his publications are *Sect, Cult, and Church in Alberta*.

WOLF-DIETER MARSCH

Wolf-Dieter Marsch is professor of systematic theology at the Kirchliche Hochschule, Wuppertal; previously he served for a number of years as program director of the Evangelical Academy in Berlin and as student adviser in Göttingen. He wrote his Ph.D. dissertation at the University of Göttingen on the religious background of American democracy as illustrated in the life of Abraham Lincoln (published under the title *Christlicher Glaube und demokratisches Ethos*). He has published articles on Christian social ethics in its encounter with Marxist philosophy.

WALTER G. MUELDER

Walter G. Muelder is dean and professsor of social ethics in Boston University School of Theology. A minister of The Methodist Church, he holds S.T.B. and Ph.D. degrees from Boston University and has taught in Berea College, the University of Southern California, and the Ecumenical Institute near Geneva. He is chairman of the Board of the Ecumenical Institute, a member of the Commission on Faith and Order of the World Council of Churches, and chairman of its Study Commission on Institutionalism. His most recent books are *Foundations of the Responsible Society* and *Methodism and Society in the Twentieth Century*.

FRANKLIN E. RECTOR

Franklin E. Rector is professor of church and social structure and director of the Seminary Church Planning and Research Center at Christian Theological Seminary, Indianapolis. An ordained clergyman of the Disciples of Christ, he was graduated from Phillips University, and, following service as a chaplain during World War II, he earned his M.S. degree from Oklahoma State University and his Ph.D. degree from the University of Wisconsin. He has received the Faculty Research Fellowship grant from the American Association of Theological Schools, and he is a contributor to several magazines and religious journals, author and co-author of several religious and secular research studies, and a lecturer and consultant in church planning and development.

FREDERICK A. SHIPPEY

A native of New York, Frederick A. Shippey is professor of the sociology of religion in the Theological and Graduate Schools of Drew University. Educated at Syracuse University and Yale Divinity School, he holds a Ph.D. degree from Northwestern University. Recently he spent a sabbatical year at the Université de Paris. An ordained clergyman, he earlier served as director of the Department of Research and Surveys of The Methodist Church's Division of National Missions. Author of *Church Work in the City*, he has written numerous articles and lectured widely. He is editor of the *Review of Religious Research*.

EUGENE L. TEN BRINK

As a missionary of the Reformed Church in America, Eugene L. Ten Brink has been a presbyter of the Church of South India since its inauguration in 1947, and he now ministers to the faculty and students of the Christian Medical College and Hospital, Vellore, as presbyter of St. John's Church. He has served the C.S.I. as principal of the Agriculture Institute, Katpadi, and has been on the national staff of the Student Christian Movement of India. After graduation from Hope College and New Brunswick Theological Seminary, he earned his M.S. degree from Cornell University in psychology and sociology and his Ph.D. from Hartford Seminary Foundation in church history.

GIBSON WINTER

As associate professor of ethics and society at The Divinity School of the University of Chicago, Gibson Winter teaches and carries on research in the sociology of the churches and problems in the relationship of theology to the human sciences. He served in the parish ministry of the Protestant Episcopal Church in the U.S.A. after completing his B.D. at the Episcopal Theological School in Cambridge, Massachusetts. After serving in the United States Navy as a chaplain in World War II, he took a doctorate in the field of Social Relations at Harvard University, initially using this further study in the work with Francis Ayres of establishing a lay training center, Parishfield. He is the author of *Love and Conflict: New Patterns in Family Life* and *The Suburban Captivity of the Churches.*

Membership of the Faith and Order Study Commission on Institutionalism

Dean Walter G. Muelder, Chairman (Boston)

Professor Nils Ehrenstrom, Secretary (Boston)

Dr. Hans Dombois (Heidelberg)

Dean Charles R. Feilding (Toronto)

Professor James M. Gustafson (New Haven, Connecticut)

Professor Berndt Gustafsson (Lund)

Professor William Pickering (Winnipeg)

Professor Franklin E. Rector (Indianapolis, Indiana)

Professor Heinz-Horst Schrey (Berlin)

Professor Frederick A. Shippey (Madison, New Jersey)

CONTENTS

PART II: CASE STUDIES

PART I
Foundations

1.

THE QUEST FOR ECUMENICAL INSTITUTIONALIZATION

The quest of the ecumenical movement necessarily includes a quest for ecumenical institutionalization. This is perhaps the chief conclusion that can be drawn from the inquiry undertaken by the Faith and Order Study Commission on Institutionalism.

Traditional denominational structures and polities, originating in a pre-ecumenical age, are becoming increasingly obsolescent. The external reason for this is the revolution in the institutional dynamics of society which now is sweeping the globe with accelerating pace—a revolution accompanied by the rapid decline of the institutionalizing influence of a Western culture which once had shaped the life patterns of the Christian church, not only in the Western world itself but also, through the missionary enterprise, in Africa, Asia, and other parts of the world. The internal reason is, of course, the unprecedented surge of the ecumenical movement. The ecumenical dialogue in recent years has shown a remarkable growth of a common mind across denominational lines. But if the churches rest content with professions of their unity in Christ, while shirking any determined efforts to embody their maturing insights in new transconfessional patterns of life,

by NILS EHRENSTROM

they can hardly escape the charge of indulging in the comfortable heresy of ecumenical docetism.

A Faith and Order Conference has affirmed in a challenging sentence that "A faith in the one Church of Christ which is not implemented by acts of obedience is dead." * [1] It was this very same conference which laid the groundwork for the creation of a Study Commission on Institutionalism.[2] Those responsible for that decision may not have been fully aware of its implications; it nevertheless indicates a recognition that the struggle between Christian unity and unchristian disunity involves the total range of the Church's life—its forms of worship and witness, its polities and patterns of organization, its interaction with government and society, as well as the beliefs and the conduct of its members. What is at stake here is the incarnational character of the ecumenical faith. The proposed exploration of institutionalism, moreover, was not prompted by a purely academic interest in increased knowledge about the tangled ways in which institutional factors condition interdenominational relations and the search for unity. It was intended to serve a critical and constructive purpose: to evaluate these developments especially in the field of church unions, and to suggest criteria and guidelines for the manifold experiments in ecumenical institutionalization that are now being undertaken. The present volume and the previously published Report of the Commission [3] sum up the preliminary results of the inquiry.

The purpose of this introductory essay is not to present a summary or appraisal of those studies. It will be useful, however, to point up some of the major issues that have engaged the attention of the Commission in its work over the past few years.

Sociology and Theology in Dialogue

Does a study of institutionalism and church unity belong in a theological or a sociological frame of reference? Or is an integra-

* Notes for each essay appear at the end of the essay, followed by pertinent bibliography.

tion of the two perspectives called for and possible? A convenient answer would obviously be to assert that the Church as a religious reality belongs to the proper province of theology, whereas institutions as a social phenomenon belong to the province of sociology and "never the twain shall meet." There have been schools of thought which have tended to formulate the doctrine of the Church in such narrowly religious terms as to create the impression that its characteristics as a community of people living in society were theologically irrelevant. James M. Gustafson, a member of the Commission, speaks of a "doctrinal reductionism" which "refuses to take seriously the human elements in the Church's life, or if it acknowledges them it does not explore or explicate them except in doctrinal language." [4] Such a neat dichotomy between two discrete provinces of knowledge would doubtless be rejected by most theologians and sociologists today as based on false assumptions.

In keeping with the central thrust of contemporary ecclesiological thought, the present inquiry seeks to give full recognition to the divine *and* human nature of the Church "without confusion or separation." It takes seriously the truth that the Church is a unique community, the Body of Christ, and at the same time a human community displaying the same characteristics and the same institutional problems as do other social groups; and that these two sides of the Church subsist in a relationship of coinherence.

The methodological approach adopted in these studies is consistent with that basic conviction, at least in intention. Consequently we find here an attempt, articulated with varying degrees of balance, to integrate sociological and theological perspectives. Without committing itself to any particular school of thought, the Commission has freely used sociological insights and tools of analysis. It has drawn on the vast reservoir of knowledge that sociology and the sociology of religion contribute to our understanding of features in the Church's life which it shares with other social groups. But the social analysis is not conceived as an end in itself. It is here placed in the embracing frame of Christian interpretation and discrimination.

Where then are the standards of appraisal to be found? A sociology of institutions, apart from sharpening the awareness of often ignored and therefore uncontrolled forces in the Christian community, can furnish valuable subsidiary criteria of adequacy, efficiency, and the like. But it obviously leaves open the question of the determining norm system. Hence the Commission, along with its sociological and historical investigations, has also been grappling with the problem of a theology of institutions.[5] This attempt to mesh theological and sociological perspectives has raised a host of questions that will require further elucidation; they illustrate the perennial difficulty of giving a satisfactory explication of what it means that the Church is "in the world but not of the world." Do the theologians and the sociologists, while intending to study a common subject, the Church, in fact visualize different objects because of their diverse modes of thinking? If so, to what extent can their conclusions be made commensurable? Does the generalized notion of "religion," with which the sociology of religion operates, enable it to grasp the distinctive properties of the Christian community? How are sociological insights to be incorporated into a theological interpretation of the Church, so as to avoid the perils of arbitrariness and invalid generalizations? Are there certain ranges in the institutional life of the Church which are indifferent to theological values and where therefore such rational considerations as appropriateness, efficiency, technical competence, and prudence are of primary importance?

Institutions in the Church and the Church as an Institution

The subsequent essays will portray the wide gamut of meanings attached to the word "institution." [6] A glossary of definitions of the word to be found in American sociological literature alone lists no less than fifty such definitions. A similar diversity prevails in the theological usage of the concept. To make headway in spite of this confusion of tongues, the Commission has resorted to the device of using broad operational definitions. Thus it speaks, for instance, of institution as "a definite and established structure, built around and sustaining one or more social functions, and characterized by such traits as durability, persistence, and stability." Institution, in this sense, is obviously a phenomenon to be found virtually everywhere in the life of the Church. Preaching and administration of the sacraments, worship and ministry, creedal statements, missions and moral conduct, may thus be termed institutions or be said to possess institutional aspects. Churches are institutionalized both by their own functions and roles and by their response to stimuli of the environment. The radiance of a charismatic leader, the role of the presbytery in the Reformed tradition, the stereotyped Protestant images of the Roman Church, the tenacious influence of national origins in maintaining Lutheran divisions in the United States, the polarizing effects of the so-called East-West conflict on the polities of the world Christian community—these are familiar examples of institutionalizing agents. Today the ecumenical vision of the Church is another agent of growing strength, producing new patterns of institutionalization which are superimposed upon and which modify the existing denominational patterns.

To obtain a sharper focus for its own studies, the Commission has concentrated attention on such areas as church government, polity, administration, and bureaucracy in their bearing on unity. But, even within this limited area, the inquiry has hardly more than begun to map out the intricate network of institutional factors and patterns that express and mold the life of the churches —partly unitive, partly divisive, and frequently ambivalent.

Problems of a different order arise when the focus is shifted to the theological meaning of those phenomena. Which institutions, if any, are inherent in the very nature and mission of the Church? In what sense can the Church itself legitimately be called an institution? Does religious institutionalization perhaps represent a perversion of the freedom and spontaneity of a spiritual life in communion with God and with fellow believers? These questions are evidently crucial here; and the sharp conflict of opinions, stretching from a spiritualizing ultra-Protestantism to an ultra-Catholic legalism, does not admit any easy reconciliation. A step forward can be taken, however, by dissociating two elements in the confused debate.

The controversy partly reflects basic differences in the understanding of the Church; but it also partly reflects unclarified differences in the use of the term "institution," frequently associated in the Protestant mind with such emotion-charged ideas as lack of spirituality, impersonalism, and routinization. At this point, the sociological approach can helpfully contribute to a *rapprochement* by neutralizing such terminological and conceptual differences, thus paving the way for a grappling with genuine issues of ecclesiology; for here lies the root of the controversy. To clarify the matter it would no doubt be instructive to undertake a comparative study of the beliefs that are actually held by the several denominations about the nature and role of religious and social institutions in the Church. But its usefulness would be limited; though categorizing denominational differences and similarities, it would not transcend them. The Commission on Institutionalism has therefore adopted a different approach. It has taken its stance within the converging movement of thought about the ecumenical Church that is manifested, for example, in the work of the Faith and Order Commission on "Christ and His Church" and in the historic declaration on the goals of church unity emanating from the World Council of Churches Assembly at New Delhi in 1961.

On this basis, the theological problem of institution is analyzed in terms of "*koinonia* and institution" and "order and organization." [7] According to New Testament scholars, the term *koinonia* carries a double meaning: participation or sharing, with others, in divine realities and gifts; and derivatively, interpersonal fellowship of Christians. The distinction is pertinent here. The discussion of institutions in the Church is oftentimes vitiated by a conception of *koinonia* as being an exclusively personal fellowship in faith and love, along with a concomitant insistence that Christian unity is a spiritual and not an institutional or organizational unity. If, instead, due attention were paid to the primary meaning of *koinonia*, it would become more easily recognizable that it also implies a *structured* community for which institutional features are natural and necessary. Thus, interpersonal fellowship and institution are not opposed to each other; they are interactive and mutually supportive.

The following quotation illustrates the general position which has emerged in the Commission's deliberations:

> To assert that the Church possesses an institutional character and is articulated in a multiplicity of institutions, does in no way imply a derogation of the intensely personal quality of its *koinonia*. . . . Thus in the Church, in the community of the Spirit, the dichotomy of institution and *koinonia* is overcome. The institutional patterns of the Church provide an ordered structure for the common life, through which God imparts His gracious love to man and makes a personal existence in freedom and responsibility manifest.[8]

On this premise, how can we establish viable criteria for discriminating between institutional elements which are essential or appropriate for the Church and others which are not? More specifically: on what grounds can we judge whether the influence of a particular factor or set of factors is divisive or unitive? The complications of the question are patent. Yet it requires some kind of answer since upon it hinges the theological validity of any appraisal of church union schemes or other ecumenical endeavors.

In seeking an answer the Commission, developing the familiar distinction between "order and organization," [9] has identified a series of institutional manifestations, all of which possess theological dignity though in varying degrees.[10] The institutional structures and dynamics of the Church, it is asserted, are grounded in the primary fact that the Church itself is a God-given institution for the salvation of mankind. It is endowed with a determinate structure which ensures its continuity and identity as a community in history, namely, three dominical institutions: the Gospel, the Sacraments, and the Ministry through which these are administered. These essential institutions and the functions which they perform must, in turn, be distinguished from the varied and changing forms in which different denominations and different ages respond to them in faith and worship, in witness and service. In this manner a continuum is established which makes it possible to distinguish more clearly between institutional elements which are essential or derivative; which are permanent or contingent; which demand fixity or allow flexibility and diversity.

The question of "overseers" may illustrate this distinction between order and organization. Which are the essential elements in the institution of *episcopé*? Have perhaps certain traditions dogmatized their own historical forms of *episcopé*, thereby making it difficult for other traditions to recognize and accept its necessary function? Further, which are the functional equivalents of the episcopate in nonepiscopal churches? This question of course does not suggest that if the "overseer" functions in the various denominations were shown to be virtually the same, this would resolve the controverted problem of their ecclesiological status. But it would at least contribute to greater mutual understanding by placing the differences in a dynamic framework of common concerns and responsibilities. And it would challenge every denomination to reconsider what is essential and what is instrumental in its own ideas about leadership roles in the Church.

Ecumenical Guidelines

Ecumenical institutionalization is more than a postulate. One of the characteristics of current ecclesiological thought is the insistence on the givenness of unity, and the attendant conviction that the ecumenical task is not to create unity but to manifest and bear witness to it. Thus unity is interpreted in a threefold sense: as a gift of God inherent in the very nature and purpose of the Church; as a present reality which binds Christians together, in spite of the fact that it is obscured and distorted by sinful divisions; and as a demand to be obeyed and a goal to strive for.

The same holds true in regard to the institutional life of Christendom. Hence the quest for ecumenical institutionalization is, strictly speaking, no unprecedented innovation. It calls to mind the continual efforts of the Church, even in its processes of self-institutionalization, to remain faithful to its apostolic foundations, to relate its community life creatively to new societies, and to manifest its wholeness in the midst of its divisions. The unity movements of our time are a new, intensified phase of that continuing process. There is consequently much to be learned from a restudy of the interplay of unitive and disruptive elements in Christian institutions in the past.

The inquiry on institutionalism, in this concern to refocus the crisscross patterns of denominational institutional forms on a given wholeness, shows a close parallel to other current Faith and Order studies. The Commission on "Christ and His Church" seeks "to penetrate behind our divisions to a deeper and richer understanding of the mystery of the God-given unity of Christ with His Church." [11] The Commission on "Tradition and Traditions" speaks of a common Tradition from which all particular traditions derive their existence, and which affords the criteria for judging their Christian authenticity.[12] In the same vein a spokesman of the Commission on "Worship" has suggested that, behind the bewildering variety of forms of public worship in the churches, there can be traced a transconfessional pattern of worship congruent with the shape of the gospel message.[13] The lines are indeed remarkably convergent.

Having recognized that the problem of ecumenical institutionalization is, in fact, both old and new, we may well inquire whether the ecumenical movement of recent decades affords any specific reference points for our present reflection on the matter. It has admittedly been a neglected field; the initiation of a major inquiry on the subject does in itself indicate a felt need. There exist nonetheless several significant instances where representative conferences or agencies have made statements on some aspect or other of the subject. They will be briefly noted here, partly because of their general interest, partly because they have been formative elements in the thinking of the Commission on Institutionalism.

1. In the realm of polity, virtually every church union negotiation of interconfessional type has to come to grips with the familiar fact that in the history of Christendom there have emerged different systems of church government: episcopal, presbyteral, and congregational. Frequently, at least in the past, these have been presented with a claim for exclusive biblical warranty. At present, the actual practice of various Protestant denominations tends to blur those distinctions, displaying instead mixed forms of polity. The Faith and Order World Conference at Lausanne in 1927 issued a statement, endorsing the principle of a conflation of those three systems, which constitutes an early landmark in ecumenical thinking on the subject.

> In view of (1) the place which the episcopate, the councils of presbyters, and the congregation of the faithful, respectively, had in the constitution of the early Church, and (2) the fact that episcopal, presbyteral and congregational systems of government are each to-day, and have been for centuries, accepted by great communions in Christendom, and (3) the fact that episcopal, presbyteral and congregational systems are each believed by many to be essential to the good order of the Church, we therefore recognise that these several elements must all, under conditions which require further study, have an appropriate place in the order of life of a reunited Church, and that each separate communion, recalling the abundant blessing of God

vouchsafed to its ministry in the past, should gladly bring to the common life of the united Church its own spiritual treasures.[14]

This principle has found widespread recognition and forms part of the constitutional provisions of various church union plans. It is one of the foundation stones of the Church of South India.[15]

2. The first North American Faith and Order Conference, in 1957, devoted several of its reports to kindred issues: different ways of relating authority, power, and freedom in the American denominations, the relationship between church order and organizational forms, and so forth. Particularly its analysis of the latter problem (already referred to above) is a notable contribution, not least for the reason that it has opened the eyes of many Protestants to the fact that church order is not a "Catholic" idiosyncrasy, nor a matter of organizational pragmatism, but an organic aspect of the Christian faith.

3. The World Council of Churches and the Faith and Order movement have engendered an imposing volume of study and reflection on the nature of unity, climaxing thus far in the well-known statement from the New Delhi Assembly with its broad delineation of the shape of a reunited Church. The material contains few explicit references to problems of interchurch structures, with one notable exception which bears directly on our subject. In explaining its own nature as an instrument of the participating churches, the World Council of Churches has repeatedly repudiated the idea of "becoming a single unified church structure independent of the churches which have joined in constituting the Council, or a structure dominated by a centralized administrative authority." [16]

Although this particular statement refers to the World Council of Churches itself, it exemplifies an ecumenical principle of general import: unity in the essentials of the faith coupled with organizational and administrative diversity in differing historical and cultural circumstances.[17]

4. Councils of churches—local, national, and world—must be regarded as pilot laboratories of ecumenical institutionalization.[18] In a rapidly expanding range of co-operation and joint planning, they are not merely performing the difficult task of seeking to co-ordinate disparate denominational programs: they are also serving as catalysts of assimilative crossfertilization. Their constitutions, bylaws, and administrative regulations are source data of a nascent ecumenical church law. Their policy-shaping processes, their utterances and actions, are exercises in ecumenical church politics and statesmanship, no less valid and necessary (however imperfectly performed) than denominational and local church politics. To recognize this, straightforwardly and without emotional inhibitions, is a simple corollary of the Christian belief in the Incarnation.

In its own Report the Commission on Institutionalism has been bold enough to seek to distill, out of its discussion of principles and case studies, a series of suggested criteria and guidelines.[19] This is admittedly a hazardous undertaking, considering the exploratory stage of the discussion and the relatively limited range of the case studies. Yet the attempt must be made if study is to lead to self-scrutiny and action. These tentative projections have been set forth, therefore, in the hope that they will provoke further constructive reflection.

One thing is clear. There is need for a theological rehabilitation of the institutional, organizational, and administrative structures of the Church, based on the recognition that they, too, form part of the temple of the Spirit. To ignore the pervasive influence of such factors is a disservice to the cause of unity; for then they are left unprincipled, released from watchful scrutiny, and liable to control by forces which may run counter to their religious purpose. Today transversal movements of renewal are overleaping denominational boundaries, new ecumenical vitalities are bursting forth, which demand appropriate institutional expression. This demand is not met by grafting ecumenical organizations on to pre-ecumenical structures and patterns of operation. It requires

34

new forms of ecumenical institutionalization, more venturesome and future-directed, which will serve the upbuilding of the One Holy Catholic and Apostolic Church.

NOTES FOR ESSAY 1

1. *The Third World Conference on Faith and Order, Lund, 1952,* Oliver S. Tomkins, ed. (London: SCM Press, 1953), p. 16.

2. The actual decision to focus the projected study of the influence of social and cultural factors on the problem of institutionalism was prompted by a paper presented to the Working Committee of the Commission on Faith and Order in 1955 by Dean Walter G. Muelder, Boston. His paper entitled "Institutional Factors Affecting Unity and Disunity" was published in *The Ecumenical Review* VIII:2 (January, 1956), pp. 113-126.

3. "Institutionalism and Christian Unity," published in *The Old and the New in the Church* (London: SCM Press; Minneapolis: Augsburg Publishing House, 1961). Henceforth referred to as Report.

4. *Treasure in Earthen Vessels* (New York: Harper & Brothers, 1961), p. 105.

5. See Report, pp. 73ff., and Essays 2, 5 in the present volume. Further essay references below, which give no indication of sources, relate to this volume.

6. See Essays 2, 3, 6 and Report, pp. 56ff.

7. See Essays 3, 4, 5 in this volume and Report, pp. 76ff.

8. Report, p. 77. That this consensus does not exclude considerable variations of interpretation can be seen from two recent books whose authors are members of the Commission—Hans Dombois, *Das Recht der Gnade,* and James M. Gustafson, *Treasure in Earthen Vessels.* For Dombois see also his Essay 5 in this volume.

9. For a clarifying discussion of this distinction, see *The Nature of the Unity We Seek,* Paul S. Minear, ed. (St. Louis: The Bethany Press, 1958), pp. 229ff.

10. See Essays, 5, 7 and Report, pp. 78f.

11. *One Lord, One Baptism* (London: SCM Press; Minneapolis: Augsburg Publishing House, 1960), pp. 7f.

12. *The Old and the New in the Church,* pp. 20ff.

13. Joseph Sittler, "The Shape of the Church's Response in Worship," *The Nature of the Unity We Seek,* pp. 109ff.

14. *Faith and Order: Proceedings of the World Conference, Lausanne, August 3-21, 1927,* H. N. Bate, ed. (London: SCM Press, 1928), p. 469.

15. See Essay 10.

16. *The First Assembly of the World Council of Churches, 1948,* W. A. Visser't Hooft, ed. (London: SCM Press; New York: Harper & Brothers, 1949), p. 127.
17. The Anglican world communion and Eastern Orthodoxy illustrate that the principle is capable of realization. Their decentralized structure is telling counterevidence against the claim that church unity inevitably leads to governmental uniformity and top-heavy bureaucracy.
18. A professional study of, for instance, the structures and operational patterns of the World Council of Churches in its interaction with the member-churches, would be a highly instructive contribution to our understanding of the dynamics of ecumenical institutionalization.
19. Report, pp. 81ff.

2.

THE CONCEPT OF
INSTITUTION IN THE LIGHT
OF CONTINENTAL
SOCIOLOGY AND THEOLOGY

The ecumenical discussions on the Church have focused attention on a provocative question: Are the churches, as they live in ecumenical fellowship, not more determined by secular social forces and patterns than by the power of the Holy Spirit? Are they not to be regarded as social institutions among other social institutions? Must their institutional patterns not be viewed as mere "nontheological factors"? [1] Since these institutional factors exercise a profound influence on the structuring of the churches (for example, offices, hierarchies, status, role-sets),[2] as well as on their attitude toward one another (for example, co-operation, union, and reunion), it seems to be of some fundamental importance to ask *what the Church, as the Body of Christ and at the same time as an institution in society, really is.*[3]

We shall here discuss this issue with reference to certain trends of thought in Continental sociology and theology. Our intention, however, is to present not a descriptive survey but rather a personal critical interpretation. We hope to make clear that the question of the Church as a social institution is a significant theological issue. It is, speaking in a broader context, the question of

by WOLF-DIETER MARSCH

maintaining continuity and binding ties in a society which may be called "autonomous." [4] (Part I) Life in such a society, as we experience it in particular in the history of Western civilization since the Enlightenment period, is regarded as secular and as a self-fulfilling social process; man has taken the responsibility for his history and final destiny; his rational attitudes toward his environment and his shaping of inherited historical institutions have reinforced his autonomy. However, *even in this situation* man is inevitably confronted with the "ontological question": [5] the question of meaning, the question of the contingency of his history, the question of his *kairos* to act. This is to be one of the main concerns of contemporary Protestant ethics to ask for the will of God within such a changing, relative, and autonomous society. Against this background we then may discuss the problem of social institutions as it is seen in contemporary sociology: how do the social sciences deal with this question of continuity within a changing world? (Part II) Finally we apply the question to the Church: how can we speak about the Church as an institution—perhaps even as a "paradigmatic institution" [6]—in the processes of society, demonstrating by its very existence God's will to give continuity and stability in a changing history? (Part III)

The Theological Quest for Historical Order and Permanent Ties in Society

We may start with an evaluation of historical-genetic thinking as it evolved during the Enlightenment in the seventeenth and eighteenth centuries. A question of rising importance for this period was, What historical order in human society proves to be binding and permanent when metaphysical interpretations of such an order have lost their significance? When speaking of "historical order" we must, in defining the word historical, draw a distinction between at least three meanings of this word. (a) There is the experience of a general historical *relativity:* Order, characteristics, and ties within society may arise and disappear; they change and vary with the course of social history. (b) There is also the experience of a general *contingency* of order: Social order, characteristics, and ties make definite claims upon people who live according to them. But this claim appears to be somewhat accidental and contingent. It must constantly be asked, therefore, whether this or that social institution can make an unconditional claim upon man. (c) There is, finally, the experience of *being in process:* Order, characteristics, and ties are to be regarded in their very historical development. A universal teleology seems to be the only conceivable basis for understanding progress in history. Man regards himself and society as "being on the way" to final fulfillment. This enables and obliges him to transform and to reshape his institutions which he had hitherto regarded as eternal and unchangeable.

These three meanings may be summed up in the question: What is the permanently coherent force in a changing order of society? Analyzing its institutions, man discovered that he has always been creating them. He has been creating a "second world" of artifacts around him. And now these institutions impose claims and obligations upon man, even though he seems to be their creator and master. Obligation and existence seem to be synchronized in institutions, but their very essence, their quality of being, is felt as a highly problematic one. It is a "secondary" product, a "semitranscendent" being (A. Gehlen) which cannot be any more regarded as a God-given "higher order" and therefore requires continuous reflection and reconsideration. [7] This raises significant questions for Christian ethics. How can we possibly speak of God's eternal order and dominion in history? How does the Christian have to approach the ethical implications of a life bound up in secular social institutions? These questions may be related to three different modes by which Christians link the divine order and secular institutions.

• By appeal to the sole authority of the Scripture the Christian may take as God's order only what can be derived from the written commands in the Old and New Testaments. Puritans and Pietists, orthodox and liberal Christians, have all tried in different ways to deduce valid norms for the life of society from the

Scriptures. However, because of the immense variety of these social ties in the contemporary world as well as in the history of the Old and New Testaments themselves, it seems nearly impossible to reach a clear and universally acceptable norm. Thus we are in a situation where a simple recourse to the social order portrayed in the Scriptures does not solve our problem. This is particularly the case in ecumenical discussions, which must attempt to co-ordinate many different approaches to and interpretations of the Bible. These differ widely because the Bible is interpreted in very different historical and cultural environments. The biblical answer cannot be isolated from the human predicament. There have been times when, for example, the institution of slavery or the basic inequality of the rights of man and woman were defended with biblical arguments.

• Such permanent ties in society may also be taken as "orders given by God in creation" (*Schöpfungsordnungen*). These orders are regarded as rooted in an "original revelation" defined by God in the act of creation; or they may be understood as sustaining orders by which God sustains this world against chaos (*Erhaltungsordnungen*).[8] Or again we may say that it is simply incumbent upon man to accept the existing social ties and obligations in a given period in history as impenetrable forces of destiny, as manifestations of the "hidden God" (*Deus absconditus*).[9] Or such orders may be perceived only in exceptional cases when the Christian comes into conflict with them, as for example, when he lives in a tyrannical state or faces the power of totalitarian ideologies.[10] These are some of the ways in which German Lutheran theology in particular has sought, although not very effectively, to discern permanent and normative structures in a society in constant flux.

• Should not the Christian rather inquire about his own distinctive task in the changing processes of society? This raises the question of the concrete commandments of Jesus Christ, the risen Lord, who rules in His Church and His world. His dominion can be taken as the only stable structure in an unstable world, which is secular in its essence but at the same time is holy as a field of Christian discipleship. The Christian takes the ministry of Christ as a guide for his life—reconciliation, justification, and sanctification—and he is constantly transformed through the impact of Christ on his life. He experiences that secular, autonomous world as God's heritage, given to him for realization in history. Christian action in a particular social nexus, therefore, means accepting or rejecting the obligations of that situation as concrete opportunities for sanctification. The Christian does not ask about the essence of the social institutions in which he is bound to live, but he asks about the tasks set before him in the fulfillment of his Christian discipleship. The Christian who acknowledges the Lordship of Christ realizes that this social environment is a reality which belongs to God and which manifests itself in the faithful action of the believer.[11] The question is not what such an order or obligation *is* in itself (or in God's secret plan of salvation), but what those commitments are capable of *becoming* by human acceptance in faith.

This issue doubtless appears differently to Continental Christians than it does in an English or American perspective. Up to the nineteenth century the Continent lived under the strong influence of a "Christian" order of society, whose institutions were regarded as God-given, hierarchical, and authoritarian. England and the U.S.A. experienced more thoroughly what we might call with K. Mannheim a "fundamental democratization" of life. The resulting mode of thought has not been interested so much in establishing a *societas christiana* within a secular world (except for isolated experiments, such as Shakers or Mennonites), as in demonstrating how society at large can be molded and transformed, developed, and perfected in accordance with the principles of Christian ethics. The impulses which came from Puritan Protestantism led to an enlightened, democratic culture in which the Church found its place as a dynamic, evangelistic center, adapting the structure and patterns of other democratic institutions.[12] In their activities the churches are promoting a dynamic, flexible basis for institutional life in terms of justice and freedom. Christians are not so much interested in arguing about a theological basis for order and institutions in society as they are concerned to shape and transform society toward the coming of the "Kingdom at Hand," on the tacit assumption that God rules over this society and waits to be sanctified according to His will.[13]

Thus the question of the relation between God's will and autonomous human action in history is here answered in a fashion similar to the view stated above (under 3): God as the center and ultimate goal of society is already accepted as being in its midst; through Christian people, He will, under the guiding power of his Spirit, transform society.[14] Thus the quest for a Christian order of society seems to be replaced by the quest for Christian living in (sociologically interpreted) institutions, aiming at the establishment of a "responsible society." [15] It is taken for granted that these secular institutions have a bearing on God's will. Thus the relation between God and history does not offer to be such a perplexing and acute problem as in the Continental tradition, where the breakdown of a traditionally "Christian culture" has necessitated a rethinking of basic principles. Nevertheless, the very fact that the problem of institutions is now being discussed in the world ecumenical movement, in its relevance not only for Christian social ethics but also for the life of the Church itself, is an indication that the issue is increasingly felt to be of general importance.

The next step in our analysis will be to examine the question: what does it mean that the Church must be regarded as a social institution among other institutions?

Institutions as a Problem of Social Science

The rise of social science coincided with the crises and upheavals which became acute during the time when the issue discussed above arose. Society, having thrown off eternal orders and ties, appeared to become a problem to itself. Sociologists hoped to achieve an objective understanding of human activity in society by applying scientific "positive" laws to social life (J. Comte, *Physique sociale!*). Much contemporary sociology claims to be a "science of reality" (*Wirklichkeitswissenschaft*, H. Freyer), based more or less upon empirical findings, and aiming toward a "theory of social action" (T. Parsons) or at least toward a socio-philosophical evaluation of the process of culture (K. Marx, M. Weber, K. Mannheim). Thus, on this view, sociology gives us a chance to discover what basic foundations are conducive to improving and stabilizing social life within the stream of historical relativity. As controlling knowledge (*Herrschaftswissen*, M. Weber), sociology claims at least some of the tasks previously assumed by philosophical or theological ethics.

The interpretation of institutions as stable and stabilizing factors in society obviously varies in accordance with the basic assumptions and values accepted, or in accordance with the purpose of the sociological analysis presumed. By way of illustration, we shall examine here the analysis developed by three leading German scholars in this field. It will suggest a mode of approach by which the theological question of institutions in general and of the institutionality of the Church in particular may find a more appropriate formulation.

Theories about Freedom and Institutions

Continuing the tradition of German idealism and the crises through which it passed (Fichte, Hegel, Marx, Nietzsche), the German philosophers Hans Freyer (born 1887) and Arnold Gehlen (born 1904) connected a diagnosis of the contemporary situation of culture with an anthropological theory and a philosophy of institutions. They speak about man as an "unfathomed creature" (F. Nietzsche) or "the typical defective creature." What is meant by this is that man as the initiator of action in history is not able to manifest his own creative activity totally. He realizes himself as free, subjective creativity—he can do and he is allowed to do everything—but at the same time he experiences himself as preconditioned by laws and customs, by taboos and codes, in other words, by institutionally determined actions. In his freedom man realizes that he is not free; in his actions he realizes that he cannot act without being conditioned by institutions. Thus institutions belong to man's very historical existence. They demonstrate to him that his life is experienced as an "alienated" one. Alienation, as defined by Hegel and Marx, means the loss of creativity by living in the boundaries of a historically and economically defined society. This alienation can be overcome only by adapting to the existing institutions, by accepting the institutionality of human existence. Freyer in particular has developed this concept of alienation into a theory of a culture built of what he calls "secondary systems." Man has created a cosmos of institutional order around himself, which, however, in its turn becomes a cosmos of its own, with laws, customs, and cultural habits that govern man and limit him in his basic freedom. A "secondary" framework of human life has developed beside the "primary" one of spontaneous activity. Only in institutionalized form can human action become valid and effective.[16] As an influence which already shapes every free action, institutions are, therefore, on the one hand, essentially necessary in order to make alienated action possible at all; on the other hand, however, they are felt to be a constant stumbling block, preventing man from freely developing his creative forces of self-realization, and confronting him with the dilemma of choosing between adaptation or a critical attitude toward existing institutions.

Gehlen builds his analysis of institutions upon this dilemma of social action in general and connects it with certain socio-historical insights. In primitive civilizations man was relieved of the burden of personal free decision by accepting the mythical institutions in which he lived, such as taboo, custom, and cult. In highly differentiated civilizations, however, these institutions are looked upon as the products of man's own technical and cultural powers, which in their turn control man.[17] Man has increasingly thrown off his mythical and metaphysical ties, and is now being confronted with the necessity of constant choice and decision. He can either go on breaking down the inherited institutions and

thus live by uncontrolled impulses and unceasing intellectual reflection and personal engagement in contingent situations; or he
can accept existing patterns and institutions, but, being relieved
of the necessity to make continually new decisions, he then has
to accept a trend toward a gradual primitivization of the human
spirit. The gradual abolition of institutions inherited from earlier
generations, on the one hand, and the man-created influence of
powerful technical institutions, on the other, run concurrently
as two conflicting trends which determine human life in industrial society.

According to Gehlen this dilemma between free reflectivity and
conformist adaptation to institutions has been intensified by the
Christian theology of creation. Pre-Christian primitive man was
able to identify himself with the world around him. He found
himself bound by the powers of nature, the cosmos, by myths and
gods. The Christian view of creation as "creation out of nothing"
(*creatio ex nihilo*), however, has turned those natural or God-
given powers into pure objects of the sovereign, transcendent
will of God and at the same time into objects of human will, because man has been called to dominate this creation. Social institutions, thus, may be called "semitranscendental": they are half
sacred and half secular, partly given and prescribed, and partly
undergoing the process of human formation, half eternal law and
half malleable working material for the improvement of social
life. As Gehlen has put it in a pithy phrase, "God" (and hence also
the creative impulses of man as God's image) "and the machine
have survived the world of antiquity and now confront one another alone." [18] There is no longer a sacred world which can be
regarded as the framework for unquestioning acceptance by institutionalizing agents. Society with its institutions has become at
the same time the object and the foundation of human freedom.

The purpose of this analysis is to explain the "secondary" quality
of these social institutions today as "the great orders which at the
same time protect and swallow man, which will last far longer
than he does, and which he is accepting with his eyes open." [19]

It illustrates the point that man in industrial society suffers under a universal alienation. He is forced to live in institutions which are beyond his control; though realizing a relative freedom, he has no possibility critically to question the motive or purpose of these institutions.

Applied to the Church as an institution, this kind of social analysis would imply that there is no point in inquiring into the "motives" which lead to its institutional stabilization. Christians have to live in the Church and adapt to it as an institution, in order to live in the freedom of their faith. The question of the "true Church" (*ecclesia vera*) and of the "Church always being reformed" (*ecclesia semper reformanda*) seems simply unanswerable, and it even need not be asked as long as the existing ecclesiastical institution performs its functions. The question of expediency of church practices (for example, the organization of worship and of congregational life, the adaption to the structures presented by society) would replace the question of truth.[20] This would evidently mean the end altogether of questioning institutional phenomena in the churches. The Christian conviction that church life has to be the fruit of true faith, that the Body of Christ cannot live without constant recourse to Him, the Founder, would be put in doubt. The Church would share the fate of a universally alienated society.

Mention should also be made of Helmut Schelsky (born 1912). Though adopting some of the philosophical assumptions of Freyer and Gehlen, his approach is closely related to that of cultural anthropology. He sees the development and stability of institutions as resting upon the satisfaction of basic and derived needs in the sense of Malinowski, but at the same time he emphasizes the autonomous structure of institutions. These engender new artificial needs within society which must in their turn be satisfied by new institutions, building up a reality and a momentum of their own without relation to the functions originally to be satisfied. Hence the process of institutionalization must be regarded as a process of building up a "secondary" system, a framework of

FOUNDATIONS

artifacts in a sense reminiscent of the theories of Freyer and Gehlen.

Implications for Theology

To sum up, we may ask: what do these sociological theories about the interrelation of man and society imply for a theological study of institutions? Three points will be made:

• *Man* is thought of as a compound of impulses, actions, and needs. He has to satisfy these needs and their cultural reflection in society. He is living in order to survive, and to survive better and better in a structured cultural environment. Social integration is understood as a human achievement for the purpose of better survival. Man differs from animals because he is able to mold his life consciously, while animals live by the directives and certainty of their instincts and impulses.[21] Man must respond to certain functional imperatives to be capable of better self-realization. How do such statements square with biblical anthropology? According to the first chapters of the Bible man exists in a compound of institutionalized habits because he is living in society; he is not regarded as free individual subjectivity. Adam and Eve live in mutual encounter and dependence upon each other, not in free subjective self-realization. The imperatives of their lives are, on the one hand, to be interpreted as essentially functional ones, the function of sex and propagation; but there is, on the other hand, a different element which does not appear at all in functional sociological analysis: the element of mutual dependence in love as an image of God.

• *Society* as a whole may be regarded as a web of social relations which, according to their degree of continuity and formality, assume institutional forms. Society is always in the process of creating revised forms of institutional life. It is the process of culture itself which may be called the "structural movement of society" (R. Benedict). Society is defined as the process of integration of these different and differing individual impulses of life which become increasingly interdependent in the progress of history. There seems to be no *telos* of history conceivable behind or beside the continual integrating process of society itself. A fulfilled life equals to a socio-culturally integrated life. A biblical view of society, on the other hand, would question the validity of such conclusions in functional sociological theory. According to those passages of the Bible which affirm the eschatological thrust of history, society always points toward something beyond itself. It cannot be regarded as only a functioning and self-sustaining process, but must be seen as a process of permanent renewal in eschatological hope: the hope for a fulfillment and consummation of all history which transcends history itself. The historic dynamics of unconditional and unpredictable events as well as the thrust of Christian hope seem to be blocked by a theory of functional self-fulfillment of society.

• *Institutions* may be regarded as the mediating agents between man and society. They are necessary because man is in the process of self-realization in society: no isolated life is possible for the human being. They perform the function of regulating the abstract, fragmented, and pluralistic cultural and societal factors surrounding human life. In the light of the teachings of the Bible it does not seem necessary to abrogate such a functional analysis of institutional life. It must be placed, however, in the wider context of salvation history. The Christian must permanently ask what is the purpose of these functioning institutions and how he has to accept the conditions of institutionalized life. In the cultural environment of the Old and New Testaments the Bible shows human life to be bound by certain social conditions, that is, to be institutionalized in the sense described above. However, it shows in this very same view human life as instituted by the creative will of God. God's covenant provides the framework of every creative impulse in history. We shall therefore have to examine the interrelation between this act of divine *institution* and the process of human *institutionalization*. Is it possible to speak of a "vertical" as well as of a "horizontal" dimension in the institutions of society?

Before proceeding to this question, however, we shall briefly apply this sociological approach more specifically to institutionalism in the Church. We find in the Church, as well as in society, certain institutionalizing factors and agents. The Church as it enters history develops certain institutional structures because the individual impulses of the believers need to be sustained by generalized behavior patterns. The Church cannot live and prosper by relying on irregular, individual impulses. However, it seems impossible that the Church as the community of believers (contrary to Gehlen's thesis) could ever refrain from constantly reconsidering the "motives" (that is, the originating faith) of its institutional character. The traditional patterns of the Church cannot be so commanding as to relieve the believer from questioning the "motives" of the process of institutionalization. There may indeed be tendencies to consolidate the institutional framework of church life to such an extent that it becomes increasingly difficult to revitalize the historical forces which have formed the institutional life of present churches. Institutionalism becomes predominant in the Church when those petrified traditions become so all-powerful that no room seems left to ask for the "motive" of the life of the Church.

The Christian belief that the Church is both a creation of the Holy Spirit and a human community means in this connection that by the Cross of Christ man's freedom is at once condemned and confirmed. Through his failures, man experiences his freedom anew. It is therefore in the nature of the case that the Church is to be particularly alert to the problems posed by these institutional factors. The Church must not, and by its very nature even cannot, neglect the task of continually reconsidering the "motive" of its very existence: God's judgment and salvation. The Church may, therefore, perhaps be described as the "paradigmatic institution." [22] It is to proclaim the aim of all institutional life, recognizing alienation as a deep existential crisis which, however, cannot be thought of as the final fate of society, without hope for a rebirth grounded in the regenerating power of God who forever remains faithful to his covenant with mankind. [23]

Institutions as a Theological Problem

We can now attempt to draw some conclusions for a theology of institutions. In order to define the correlation of what we previously called the vertical and horizontal dimensions of institutions, it will be helpful to recall some of the historical meanings of the term. In the language of Roman jurisprudence, *institutio* was used in a pedagogical sense to denote an "introduction" to a subject; the term could also mean an instruction or teaching which helped the student to draw correct conclusions about a certain matter. In ecclesiastical Latin, *institutio* denotes an organization, a custom or tradition, which is either to be preserved (by fixing existing forms of life as good and permanent ones) or modified (by adapting those forms to new conditions of life) or even replaced by new institutions which serve the purpose of the common good. These different meanings may be summed up as follows: an existing order in human society is preserved or modified or replaced by divine *and* human action. Through and in institutions man realizes his position, his status; he is challenged to accept this personal status in society as a God-given one. In the dynamic process of society in history man becomes aware of this concrete institutionalized status. Believing this process to be at the same time the procedure of God's history of salvation, man is challenged to accept this.

Both the secular and the religious interpretation which we find mingled in the Latin use of the word contain dynamic and static elements. The dynamic element stems from the historicity of institutions which are regarded as parts of the historical process or as parts of God's history of salvation—God constantly challenging man to personal integration into his ongoing work of atonement. The static element is given by the fact that man lives under the contingent tutelage of the limiting and incommutable possibilities of self-realization in history. He sees himself as restricted by fixed structures of society or by the commandment of God who has placed man at a definite place in his created world. These two elements, dynamic and static, can be illustrated most clearly in the institution of marriage. A man and a woman take a free decision to marry one another, choosing this form of partnership out of the many possible forms of partnership as the one which befits them. They are then faced with the task of confirming this partnership afresh every day in this marriage. The institution proves to be capable of being renewed over and over, and it can take many forms of expression. This is the dynamic element. But at the same time the free choice of both partners restricts their opportunities for alternative self-expression. Even if the marriage comes to an end through separation, divorce, or the death of one of the partners, they cannot regain the freedom they had before marrying each other. The institution in its static element cannot be altered at will, it is irrevocable.

Under the auspices of the Evangelical Church in Germany, during the recent decade joint commissions of jurists and theologians have been engaged in long-range studies of the nature and religious significance of the institution of marriage [24] and also of the wider issue of the foundations of law.[25] Since 1955 a similar group, sponsored by the Evangelical Academies, has met in annual study conferences to investigate the interdisciplinary theological, sociological and legal problems of institutions.[26]

Although these studies are still of an exploratory nature, they have yielded illuminating insights. Among other things, they have indicated that it is possible to develop a theory of institutions without having recourse to concepts of natural law or metaphysical order and without falling into legal positivism. The institutional structures of society can be interpreted as certain irrevocable, noninterchangeable, and unconditional relationships, structures of human existence in which the static and dynamic elements coincide.[27]

There are mainly three institutions of general importance to be found in the biblical affirmations about man in society, which relate to three basic existential relationships of man: (1) the relation between God and man as man responds to God's call in His covenant—these are the institutions of worship, the *Church;* (2) the relation between man and his fellow man, instituted from the very origin of mankind in the partnership between man and woman—these are the institutions of *marriage* and family; (3) the relation between man and nature, which is handed over to him as his dominion over the world of things—these are institutions of *property* and technical culture. These secular social institutions are to be interpreted as God-given "mandates" for the Christian, to use Dietrich Bonhoeffer's phrase. Their ethical significance is not attached to a "divine origin" but rather to their purpose and meaning in the context of biblical anthropology.

The Bible regards man as that creature who has been elected to exist in the image of God, and with whose history God has identified Himself in the incarnation of Jesus Christ. Man has received a special vocation: to actualize this being as an image of God. Christian anthropology thus depicts man as he encounters God and responds to situations given within history, situations where he stands between crisis and hope, between judgment and mercy, between the opportunities lost and the opportunities restored by God's reconciliation, between self-glory and praise of God, between idolatry and service rendered to Him, between serfdom and freedom, between self-interest and love. For the problem of institutions this means that it is not necessary to describe human existence in terms of supposedly "divine" orders and institutions conceived as static metaphysical entities. Man must rather be understood as being God's child, image, and partner, engaged in social relations—as God manifests Himself by being-in-relation. Instead of compiling a catalogue of divinely given institutions we ought to look for those existential relationships in human life which are visibly embodied in secular social institutions. We ought to consider those institutions as challenges in which man is called to respond to his divine vocation. By stressing this challenge, we can then speak theologically of a personal "status" gained within an institution: God has given men continuity, and man responds by freely accepting this vocation.

This calls attention to the meaning of history in relation to institutions. Man experiences history both as a rigid contingency, a call to an unpredictable future, and as an inherited past which is to be transcended. His attitude toward history is determined both by tradition and revolution.[28] This antithesis is synthesized in God's history with man. It is characteristic of the biblical view of history that we find no clear distinction in it between historical fate and the present call of God.[29] God is at work in the midst of history. History is eschatologically open to something beyond itself, and at the same time God is not working beyond history but transforming it by performing His covenant. For the theological interpretation of institutions this means that historical social institutions cannot be regarded as ethically neutral, for they have their definite place within God's history. Their "autonomy" must be discerned as a "theonomy."

Thus, for example, marriage as an institution is a paradigm of human being-in-relation in which man is called to live not only according to the impulses of his nature but also according to his Christian vocation. His history with his partner in that institution is likewise his history with God. Other social institutions exhibit the same basic institutionality. It would be the task of a fully developed theology of institutions to relate the infinite number of social institutions to that basic fact.

The dialectical relationship between the "vertical" and the "horizontal" dimension of human institutionality, which here has been suggested, comes to particular evidence within the Church. On the one hand, the Church cannot be created anew by the fellowship of its actual believers; it becomes what it is through and by tradition.[30] On the other hand, it is equally true that it must always be actually created anew by the dedication and witness of its believing members. It is becoming what it already is. The Church cannot "go into hibernation." It cannot live without constantly facing the challenge to realize itself as the one Body of Christ.[31] This dialectical tension in which the Church is placed between sacralization and secularization of itself [32] demonstrates once again that the problem of institutionalism within the churches cannot be treated as a purely sociological problem or as a question of "nontheological factors." The "vertical" and the "horizontal" dimension of the Church, that is, her being as a creation of the Holy Spirit and her being as a social institution, can only be understood as essentially interwoven. Moreover, this interwovenness is theologically significant for the understanding of social institutions in general.

These indications must suffice. Our purpose has been to suggest some of the ways in which contemporary Continental thought seeks to understand the relevance of institutions for Christian social ethics in general and for the doctrine of the Church in particular. It interprets institutions as dynamic, yet stable, "ordering factors" in society and in the Church, which challenge the Christian constantly to question his institutional ties by asking what their meaning and purpose is in the history of God with man. "No man, having put his hand to the plow, and looking back, is fit for the kingdom of God" (Luke 9:62).

NOTES FOR ESSAY 2

1. See especially C. H. Dodd, "A Letter Concerning Unavowed Motives in Ecumenical Discussion," *Ecumenical Review* II (1949-1950), pp. 52ff.; and D. Jenkins, *Ecumenical Review* III (1950-1951), pp. 339ff.
2. See the evaluation of these institutional components in culture in W.G. Muelder, *Foundations of the Responsible Society* (New York and Nashville: Abingdon Press, 1959), pp. 53ff.
3. See W. D. Marsch, "Kirche als Institution in der Gesellschaft," *Zeitschrift für evangelische Ethik*, 4 (1960), pp. 73ff., also *The Student World*, 1959, No. 1, pp. 25ff.
4. By this term we mean a society which neither depends upon nor thinks about a "higher," metaphysical or natural order for individual life and for the progress of society, but rather depends upon functional coherence and integration.
5. See P. Tillich, *Biblical Religion and the Search for Ultimate Reality* (Chicago: The University of Chicago Press, 1955).
6. See W. D. Marsch, *op. cit.*, pp. 81f.
7. The problem confronting the sociologist, *i.e.*, to understand the "dilemma of a dual world" is well illustrated by R. Dahrendorf, *Homo Sociologicus* (Cologne-Opladen: Westdeutscher Verlag, 1960), p. 62: "The

consciousness of man as a whole and his right to freedom must be the background of every sentence he speaks or writes; he should always be aware of society not only as a fact but also as a stumbling block; the moral shortcomings of his discipline should be the passionate undertone of all his actions."

8. W. Künneth, *Politik zwischen Dämon und Gott* (Berlin: Lutherisches Verlagshaus, 1954).

9. W. Elert, *Christliche Ethik* (Hamburg: Furche Verlag, 1949); and *Morphologie des Luthertums II* (Munich: C. H. Becksche Verlagsbuchhandlung, 2nd ed., 1953).

10. H. Thielicke, *Ethik des Politischen, Theologische Ethik, II/2* (Tübingen: J. C. B. Mohr, 1958). See also the two preceding volumes. Thielicke uses "model cases" to illustrate "situations of conflict" which confront the Christian in his continuous transition from the "old" to the "coming" *aeon*.

11. This is the characteristic approach of the ethics of Karl Barth. From his very earliest works Barth's crucial question was, How does God's revelation in Jesus Christ penetrate into the immanence of history? In his *Kirchliche Dogmatik* he has developed that specific form of Christian thought which he calls *analogia fidei*. God's absolute truth and at the same time man's ultimate vocation are revealed in Jesus Christ. That they are revealed does not mean that the reality of God has already been transformed into human reality, but rather that man now experiences his own reality as guided by the gracious action of God. In analogy to God's action, man acts in faith as an autonomous self. He shapes his own freedom in analogy to God's freedom: he shows mercy as God shows mercy, he takes God's justice as his example in administering justice. Barth speaks also of an *analogia relationis*. Just as God lives in permanent relationship—Father, Son, and Holy Spirit—man also must be seen in a continuous relationship in which he has the opportunity to create according to God's will. Human reality, therefore, is defined as the process of permanent social relations and self-realization in obedience or disobedience to God's will. This process must not be thought of as chaotic or without *telos* and order. There are certain continuous binding ties in which man perceives very clearly that he belongs to Christ. In the first place marriage must be mentioned as an "example of mutual partnership." Also the Church must be mentioned as the "form of Jesus Christ on earth and in history." Finally the state "represents," despite the fact that it is not a direct manifestation of God's grace, "nevertheless one form of the Kingdom of Grace." See W. D. Marsch, "Christliche Begründung des Rechts," *Evangelische Theologie* 17 (1957), pp. 145ff. and 193ff.

12. For a discussion of the full integration of the Church into society, its absorption into social relationships, and its degradation to a club or to a mere reflection of society, see W. Herberg, *Protestant, Catholic, Jew* (Garden City, New York: Doubleday & Co., Inc., 1955).

13. Characteristic of this approach is G. F. Thomas' *Christian Ethics and Moral Philosophy* (New York: Charles Scribner's Sons, 1955).

14. See Nels Ferré, *Christianity and Society* (New York: Harper & Brothers, 1950). Chapter VI is particularly important.

15. W. G. Muelder, *op. cit.* (p. 66, Note 2). The religious institutions of society, *i.e.*, the churches, as well as a functional sociology of religion, have the special task of providing integration "to the ultimate meanings of society." See also J. M. Yinger, *Religion, Society and the Individual* (New York: The Macmillan Company, 1957), pp. 56f.

16. Especially H. Freyer, *Theorie des gegenwärtigen Zeitalters* (Stuttgart: Deutsche Verlagsanstalt, 1955). See also H. Richard Niebuhr, *Christ and Culture* (New York: Harper & Brothers, 1958), Chapter 1.

17. A. Gehlen, *Urmensch und Spätkultur* (Bonn: Athenäum Verlag, 1956), p. 9. "The same institutions that men create in their common thought and action become an independent power and impose their own laws upon the very hearts of these men." See also Gehlen, *Sozialpsychologische Probleme in der industriellen Gesellschaft* (Tübingen: J. C. Mohr —Paul Siebeck—1949); "Probleme einer soziologischen Handlungslehre," *Soziologie und Leben: Studien für C. Brinkmann* (Tübingen: R. Wunderlich Verlag, 1952), pp. 28ff.; and *Die Seele im technischen Zeitalter* (Hamburg: Rowohlt Verlag, 1957). These positions are based on Gehlen's anthropology, *Der Mensch, seine Natur und seine Stellung in der Welt* (Bonn: Athenäum Verlag, 4th ed., 1950).

18. Gehlen, *Urmensch und Spätkultur*, p. 285.

19. A. Gehlen, "Über die Geburt der Freiheit aus der Entfremdung," *Archiv für Rechts—und Sozialphilosophie*, 40 (1952-1953), p. 352.

20. These phenomena have been observed, *e.g.*, by M. Freedman in respect to the Jewish dispersion: M. Freedman, "Die jüdische Gemeinde in der Diaspora," *Soziologie der Kirchengemeinde*, ed. by D. Goldschmidt, F. Greiner, H. Schelsky (Stuttgart: Verlag F. Enke, 1960).

21. H. Schelsky, "Über die Stabilität von Institutionen, besonders Verfassungen," *Jahrbuch für Sozialwissenschaften* 3, 1952 (Göttingen, 1954), p. 6: "Whereas in the animal world the requirements remain constant within a species and are only changed with the historical evolution of the species, it lies in the nature of man's derived cultural requirements constantly to produce new needs arising from the first, especially institutionalized, concrete needs. This process of continuously creating new needs while already-existing needs are laid down and permanently

satisfied in institutions and other cultural organisms is characteristic of the whole biological and historical development of man."

22. W. D. Marsch, *op. cit.* in Note 3 above, p. 87.

23. This sentence should be understood against the background of P. Tillich's Christology in his *Systematische Theologie,* II (Stuttgart: Evangelisches Verlagswerk, 1958), pp. 109ff., 124ff., and 137ff.

24. H. Dombois, ed., *Weltliche und Kirchliche Eheschliessung* (Glaube und Forschung, VI) (Gladbeck: Schriftenmissions-Verlag, 1953); *Familienrechtsform,* Glaube und Forschung VIII (Witten: Luther Verlag, 1955).

25. See *Kirche und Recht, Ein vom Rat der EKD veranlasstes Gespräch über die christliche Begründung des Rechts* (Göttingen: Verlag Vandenhoeck & Ruprecht, 1950).

26. The results of the first conference have been published in *Recht und Institution,* Glaube und Forschung IX (Witten: Luther Verlag, 1956). See especially the "Thesen," pp. 71ff. See also the chapter by H. Dombois in the present volume. A second volume, containing the results of the Commission's work between 1956 and 1961 will be published before long (probably in 1963 by the same firm).

27. As studies closely related to this Commission's work, the following may be noted: M. Greiffenhagen, "Die Verstehensproblematik im Dialog zwischen Soziologie und Theologie, untersucht am Beispiel der Institution," *Zeitschrift für evangelische Ethik* 5 (1961), pp. 159ff.; E. Wolf, "Eigentum und Existenz," *ibid.* 6 (1962), pp. 65ff.; R. P. Callies, *Eigentum als Institution* (Munich: Verlag Christian Kaiser, 1962); W. D. Marsch, article, "Institution," *Religion in Geschichte und Gegenwart,* 3rd ed., Vol. III (Tübingen: J. C. B. Mohr, 1959), pp. 783ff.

28. See G. Picht, *Die Erfahrung der Geschichte* (Frankfurt/Main: Verlag Vittorio Klostermann, 1958).

29. Both in the procedure of the Covenant in the Old Testament and in the eschatology of the New Testament we find the interwovenness of the maintenance of tradition and the encounter of God in actual event. See J. L. Leuba, *New Testament Pattern* (E. T. London: Lutterworth Press, 1953).

30. It was the tradition of Old Testament's Judaism which made the disciples gather and form the "new people of God." In this way the Church always in her history built upon historical inheritance and traditions from generations to generations. The event of her foundation, Jesus Christ, is not mediated except by tradition. See J. L. Leuba, *op. cit.*

31. This means in the context of this study: the Church cannot exist as an institution without realizing—by her very existence—the ecumenical call.

32. These indications are explained in greater detail in my study mentioned above in Note 3, especially pp. 89ff.

BIBLIOGRAPHY FOR ESSAY 2

Benedict, R., *Patterns of Culture* (Boston and New York: Houghton Mifflin Co., 1934).

Bonhoeffer, D., *Ethik* (Munich: Verlag Christian Kaiser, 5th ed., 1960; E. T. London: SCM Press, 1955).

Dombois, H., ed., *Recht und Institution*, Glaube und Forschung, IX (Witten: Luther Verlag, 1955).

Freyer, H., *Theorie des gegenwärtigen Zeitalters* (Stuttgart: Deutsche Verlagsanstalt, 1955).

Gehlen, H., "Probleme einer soziologischen Handlungslehre," *Soziologie und Leben: Studien für Carl Brinkmann* (Tübingen: R. Wunderlich Verlag, 1952).

———, *Sozialpsychologische Probleme in der industriellen Gesellschaft* (Tübingen: J. C. B. Mohr—Paul Siebeck—1949).

———, *Urmensch und Spätkultur* (Bonn: Athenäum Verlag, 1956).

"Institution," article in Fischer-Lexikon, *Soziologie* (Frankfurt/Main: S. Fischer-Verlag, 1958).

Leuba, J. L., *L'institution et l'événement* (Neuchâtel: Delachaux & Niestlé, 1950); *New Testament Pattern* (E. T. London: Lutterworth Press, 1953).

Malinowski, B., *A Scientific Theory of Culture and Other Essays* (Chapel Hill: The University of North Carolina Press, 1946).

Niebuhr, H. Richard, *Christ and Culture* (New York: Harper & Brothers, 1958).

Schelsky, H., "Über die Stabilität von Institutionen, besonders Verfassungen," *Jahrbuch für Sozialwissenschaften* 3, 1952 (Göttingen: Vandenhoeck & Ruprecht, 1954).

3.

INSTITUTION AND CHURCH IN THE NORTH AMERICAN SITUATION

W ithin the scope of the present essay, several topics receive attention: noteworthy differences between the European and American situations, a sociological consideration of social institutions, the role of religious institutions among other social structures, and a recapitulative statement.

That differences do exist between the European and American situations is already common knowledge. Various scholars have treated the question. However, for the present discussion, let two important references suffice. Robin Williams [1] distinguishes the American situation from the European by means of a protracted account detailing nineteen points. These can be summarized in a way which discloses the cogency of his analysis: no established church; no anticlerical movement; coexistence of diverse religious groupings; strong local autonomy in churches; voluntary financial support; religious aloofness from political struggles; approval of worldly success; perfectionism and optimism; and the existence of religious freedom. To this interesting catalogue, David O. Moberg [2] adds four additional points: the heterogeneity of religious life; the stimulating cultural pluralism; the wide choice of

by FREDERICK A. SHIPPEY

accepted religious expression; and finally the more rapid growth of new cults and sects.

The foregoing observations arise out of a unique context wherein the social sciences have proliferated enormously at the university level and have attracted many competent scholars. In no other region of the world have the social sciences developed so rapidly. As in the case of the proverbial green bay tree, amazing growth has been the pattern. Yet, despite sensational development, distinction in scholarship has been an attractive concomitant. Since the turn of the century, substantive specialization in single disciplines (for example, sociology, psychology, anthropology) has emerged on a grand scale. Such narrow intellectual activity obtains in both teaching and research. In a less strident manner American theology has developed fields of specialization. Unfortunately an unbridged chasm has appeared, separating theology from the social sciences.[3] In America, theology and social science go different ways, rejecting each other's methods and data. A few scholars are concerned about this hiatus which persists as a mocking embarrassment. This concern has manifested itself in the organization of the Religious Research Association and the Society for the Scientific Study of Religion.

No doubt there exists a need for a principle of unity adequate to transcend the disparate cultural situations. Here is the problem. Millions of American Christians regard their life circumstances as normal. Likewise, with equal sincerity, millions of European Christians regard their life circumstances as normal. In view of the self-perpetuating realities, it probably is wise to recognize cultural and religious differences without allowing either the European or the American situation to become normative for the other.

A Sociological Consideration of Social Institutions

Among sociologists no single definition of institution commands wide acceptance at the present time. In the United States, there are at least four ways to approach a definition, depending upon the criteria chosen and the purposes of the investigator. An institution can be defined (a) as a complex of norms which regulate human activity, (b) as a unit of social organization, (c) as a system or complex of roles, and finally (d) as an eclectic combination of diverse referents into a single configuration or system.[4] Though definitions vary greatly, they generally range within the bounds of these categories.

Moreover, the endemic pluralism can be illustrated in yet another manner. Definitions differ in complexity, ranging along a continuum from simply a concept and structure [5] to a sophisticated sevenfold set of attributes [6] (ideation, structure, purpose, relative permanence, authority, social control, and a specialized personnel). Most American definitions fall somewhere along the spectrum between these polar boundaries. What clearly dominate are the culturally patterned behavioral aspects.

In short, a social institution is a significant formal organization which exercises authority and control over its members. It procures a relatively persistent pattern of action or relationship in human society. It fixes the boundaries of the activities of human beings with respect to an important sphere of life. It is a complex in and through which human relationships function toward given ends.[7] Though definitions differ radically from one another, *descriptions* of American phenomena to which the word "institution" may be applied possess a remarkable similarity. The customary referents are family, education, government, economic order, religion, and so on. Descriptions usually contain culturally defined patterns of social structure, norms, and physical objects connected with the institution.

Theories About Institutions

Although various scholars [8] have written perceptively upon the theory of American social institutions, the present discussion will be limited to several pertinent comments. Znaniecki finds at least three categories of theories deriving from (a) the concept of *need*, (b) the concept of *interest*, and (c) a philosophy of *culture*. The widely known need-theory ascribes the presence and persistence of social institutions to universal human needs. A biological emphasis dominates here. Institutions, therefore, come into existence as the products of human will and human experience. They are necessary for the maintenance of society. They satisfy man's sexual, economic, and social needs. Through institutions, people learn to desire what they really need, and then to achieve fulfillment. Despite serious empirical and methodological inadequacies, this theory is widely accepted in America. For many people it forms a suitable basis for an understanding of institutions.

The interest theory explains the rise and development of institutions by the alleged presence and universality of man's basic interests. A psychological emphasis is paramount here. Institutions, therefore, emerge to guarantee satisfaction of interests. Human interests are assumed to be general and permanent. Through human history, they achieved recognition and eventually were institutionalized in society. This outcome is considered organically and psychologically normal. The writings of Lester Ward and William G. Sumner are relevant here. Stress upon interests commends this theory to many Americans caught up in the process of urbanization.

The theory growing out of a philosophy of culture finds the concept of institution an intellectual instrument which conveniently synthesizes data from all the special sciences of culture. Hence integrated clusters or systems of human activities (familial, economic, educational, governmental, religious) are illustrations of the heuristic principles utilized. Here institution is a system in an ideational abstract sense rather than in the concrete sense in which one thinks of the sun and its planets, or a multicellular organism. Znaniecki observes that this theory of institutions is philosophic rather than scientific. Thus, with the steady proliferation of the social sciences, less reliance is likely to be placed upon this theory in the future. The trend is in the direction of emphasis on data and methodology indigenous to the social sciences.

Although one must acknowledge the existence of several theories, it should be noted that the American situation is currently undergoing change. The evident disintegration of the bio-psychological theories has turned scholarly attention in a new direction. It is no longer tenable to regard the social organization of a particular people as consisting merely in the sum of its institutions. Society no longer serves as a center for the conceptual integration of institutions. Rather a new concept of society is emerging. Redefinition is sought with reference to associations or social groups rather than to a society. The concept of the social group is becoming increasingly the main intellectual instrument. The role of the person in the various groups becomes central. The concept of role as the principal theoretical tool is hailed as having great promise here.[9] Across a lifetime or at any period of his life, the individual performs a number of different roles which yield institutional behavior.

Thus institutions come to be thought of as parts of the organization of social groups in general. This means that the collective functions and statuses are partly institutionalized by other social groups and institutions. The individual as role player naturally carries over ideas, attitudes, and action patterns from one institution to another. This concept opens the way to a new approach to institutional phenomena, permitting institutions to be seen as observable phenomena. The newer theory will make more use of empirical data. It will be more thoroughgoingly scientific in the inductive sense. And as such it raises some disturbing questions for the Church and the ecumenical movement.

The Role of Institution in Culture

According to earlier discussion, the institution exists as an imperfect though essential agent of order and of purpose in a developing culture. It confronts the person with both the ideation and the practical implementation requisite to significant achievement in a designated sphere of activities or relationships. Within its domains, each institution sets a pattern of behavior and fixes a zone of tolerance for participation. Always the institution provides the context within which the individual social positions, individual normative patterns, and individual culture traits gain meaning and significance. All these individual efforts and expressions are gathered into a meaningful unit for society. A phase of life is thereby afforded necessary coherence and focus.

Moreover, institutions carry out various primary functions in culture. Taken together, the spheres encompassed cover the range of the fundamental aspects of human life. A preliminary list of functions includes the following: maintenance of social order; utilization of co-operative effort; inculcation of rules and moral education; conservation of the achievements of preceding generations; promotion of group goals, rather than those of the individual; and regulation of ways of meeting recurrent human situations—such as birth, death, marriage, acquisition of material goods, encounter with power relations, and training of the young. Institutions are tied into an operating social system. As such, they become bearers of culture.

With certain dimensions of the sociological structure now before us, attention can be turned fruitfully to an analysis of religious institutions. Consideration will be given to types, relationships, power structure, and church order.

Typologies of Religious Institutions

Far from being a single, undifferentiated social phenomenon, Christianity expresses itself in a variety of authentic forms. In the American situation, at least two well-known typologies of religious institutions have currency: Troeltsch's church, sect, and mysticism; and Becker's *ecclesia*, denomination, sect, and cult. The analyses are essentially heuristic and bear a strong resemblance at several points. Both delineate structured ways in which religion interacts with its milieu.

Troeltsch's typology has attracted the attention of many competent scholars [10] who have sought to relate the concepts of church and sect to the American scene. By common agreement, mysticism is omitted. Simply stated, the church type, recognizing the strength of the secular world, compromises in order to maximize the extent of its influence. In this posture it claims universality. Because the church type tends to be synonymous with society, it stresses mainly individual salvation. Its patterns of control are formal and traditional. Hence the priest is the typical leader rather than the prophet. By way of contrast, the sect type is usually identified with the poorer classes or the outgroup. Asceticism is stressed. The sect is either hostile or indifferent toward the state. It opposes the ecclesiastical order. It rejects compromise and stresses freedom from worldly authority. Troeltsch's sect type, as understood in the American situation,[11] embraces the urban poor as well as the disenfranchised rural resident.

What scholars stress is that the polar types of church and sect tend to flow into each other. The sect migrates along a continuum in the American situation pressing toward the position and outlook of the church type. In the pilgrimage it is likely to alter its theology, change its forms of worship, and modify requirements for membership. This possibility of transition introduces an important element into the American situation, which Muelder refers to as a flexibility in institutional expression. Since there is really no true equivalent of the established church here, more interest can be focused upon the range of institutional forms and its bearing upon the ecumenical movement.

Howard Becker's interpretation [12] of von Wiese for Americans was the occasion for the appearance of a fourfold typology of religious institutions: *ecclesia*, denomination, sect, and cult. *Ecclesia* is approximately equivalent to Troeltsch's church type. It dominates the world and is dominated by it. People do not need to join; they are born into it. It is an inclusive social structure. *Denominations* can be either sects which have migrated upward along the socio-economic continuum into a higher institutional status, or former *ecclesiae* which have been forced to accept a different status as a condition of survival in newer societies such as the United States. Two noteworthy features of the denomination are its adaptability and its willingness to share the field with other religious groups. The denomination stresses practice rather than theological purity and hence has a propensity to embrace practical church co-operation which preserves the pluralistic character of its organizational life. The *sect* is a relatively small plurality pattern which stresses voluntary affiliation, adult membership, rigorous discipline, personal charisma, and withdrawal or aggressiveness respecting the world. The sect bears a noteworthy relationship to troublous times, to social change, and to the upsurge of the lower classes.[13] Becker's *cult* tends to specialize in an interest or a value that is not prominently enough featured in other religious organizations. Modern metropolitan conditions furnish fertile soil in which cults thrive. Leadership can be charismatic, informal, precarious, anonymous, or corrupt. The cult sometimes shades off into a kind of religious underworld.

Additional discussions [14] of church typology emerge from the American Protestant survey movement. Based upon empirical data, these treatments describe rural and urban churches in their community settings.

It is the interaction of the American types of religious expression that engages our interest here. Discussions of typology reveal the pluralistic institutional manifestation of Christianity which is so widely acknowledged among scholars. The migrating *ecclesiae* of Europe become denominations in the United States. Mobile religious groups, indigenous to the American situation, change in form from cult to sect, from sect to denomination. Before, during, and after the period of transition, possibly some kind of relationship exists with co-operative Christianity. What is this relationship? The very existence of a typology of religious institutions raises the important question of differential response to ecumenical conversations and activities. At present, denominations make the most enthusiastic participants. On the other hand, to what extent is the American typology of religious institutions a stumbling block to ecumenical progress?

The Church Among Other Social Institutions

The church is included in every sociologist's list of American institutions. It appears along with the family, state, and education. This grouping is variously referred to as "basic," "primary," and "regulative." Evidently religion is accorded a place of high significance in the culture.

The church is defined both as a social institution and as a spiritual fellowship by many outstanding scholars: H. Paul Douglass, Robin Williams, J. Milton Yinger, H. Richard Niebuhr, David O. Moberg, James M. Gustafson, and others. The two-fold definition must not hinder adequate recognition that the institutionalization of religion is inevitable, necessary, dangerous, and yet manageable. Self-perpetuation involves the means of propaganda, education, and discipline. Yet these very ingredients lead to the formation of an institution. In the American situation, two contrasting viewpoints are in collision: the one accepts the institution with an uncritical naïveté; the other sees in it a kind of pollution.

A solution of the impasse is offered by Robin Williams.[15] In carrying out a comparison of the church with other institutions, he urges that a distinction be made at the outset between religion as a system of ideas and value orientations, on the one hand, and the formal structure of the religious community of participants, on the other. For analytical purposes, this distinction separates intrinsic religion as a cultural fact from the church as a visible institution in society. Systems of religious ideas and values are present in Western civilization. But there are also communities of people who seek to live by these ideas and values. According to Williams, the latter discloses how the church becomes visible and takes the form of an institution in the American situation. It is the formal structure of the community of believers which is observed by the social scientist. However, a caveat is germane here since functionalism has a strong influence upon indigenous sociology of religion.[16]

The church is a social institution in American society. It has a relationship to the family, state, education, and the economic order through the primary function assigned to religion by sociologists. The churches must share people, space, wealth, with other institutions. Williams, Moberg, and others point out that the major institutions of society are affected by religion, although often indirectly. Religion relates to them by means of attack, withdrawal, tolerance, or support. The encounter can take many forms. A particular denomination or sect may change its relationship from time to time, depending uponn the cruciality of current issues.

In considering the relationship of the church with other social institutions in the American situation, it is desirable to hold in mind two important aspects of the church—its rootage in culture [17] and its claim to uniqueness. With reference to cultural indebtedness, it can be pointed out that the church is man-made, thereby inevitably reflecting the cultural values. The church reflects the social system. The church is a human institution with a natural history. The church changes slowly, usually lagging far behind other institutions. It determines individual belief and behavior often arbitrarily. It becomes overorganized. Altogether these sound a caveat respecting culture's grip upon the religious institution. Clearly the church is subject to the play of social forces in its functions and in its operations. This explains in part why certain patterns of behavior which are clearly incompatible with the avowed norms of the church become institutionalized in society. Sometimes the church sanctions mundane interests of classes and special groups. This involvement with culture diverts the church from her true end. Certainly the more completely one understands the European and American cultural environments, the more adequate comprehension he will gain of the dominant features of European and American Christianity.

Finally let consideration be given to the uniqueness of the church in the American situation. The church's own self-interpretation is crucial here. Among other scholars, Muelder [18] proposes the idea of "self-institutionalization" as a means of solving the church's cultural dilemma. Here the church enters willingly into a process of institutionalization, utilizing the values procured therefrom up to a point of necessary efficiency. Thereafter, unless brought under control, institutionalism takes over and eventually the "tail wags the dog." Muelder's mediating proposal recognizes the merits of *limited institutionalization*. The church differs from other institutions. Reliance upon God affects its character and its tasks in society. The church facilitates religious experience, elevates social standards, promotes social solidarity, serves as an agent of social control, influences other institutions, and functions as a therapeutic agent.[19] It plays a unique role in society.

Power Structure in the Church

All institutions, including the church, generate power. Monographic studies [20] by P. M. Harrison, J. M. Gustafson, and other scholars, disclose endemic power struggles and bureaucratic developments within American Christianity. Harrison observes [21] that informal power in the American Free Church tradition often exceeds formal power lodged in episcopal polity. Yinger warns [22] against secular power which remains hidden beneath religious symbols or garb. Moberg [23] contends that the church appropriates power patterns analogous to those utilized by other social institutions. "Vested interests" and "entrenched groups" are phrases which help to delineate religion in the American situation. Power as religious influence wielded over men and their environment becomes inextricably entangled with egocentric secular force competing for personnel, time, funds, and status. Like business, government, and education, the church struggles for survival, position, dominance, and influence.

Bureaucracy is an inevitable concomitant of institutionalization. Evidently the pragmatic orientation and extensive proliferation of activities and subsidiary organizations so characteristic of American Protestantism invest the church with a dangerous vulnerability. Considered positively, bureaucracy performs administrative and promotional miracles in behalf of Christianity, procuring efficiency through the employment of specialists, continuity of leadership (attracted by incremental salaries, tenure, and pensions), and policy stability. Considered negatively, a list of problems which emerge from discussions of power structure in the American situation includes: an overemphasis upon the *de facto* church rather than upon the inner community of faith and belief; the propensity to regard the structure and process of society as normative for religion; the raising up of bureaucratic officials who perpetuate a sterotyped regime; the institutionalized theological justification of a particular form of church polity; the retention of vestigial forms which have lost their religious meaning; and the transformation of the relativities of American history into eternal patterns and principles. Because power is a prominent ingredient here, thoughtful churchmen discern danger in the growing institutionalization of American religion.

The Problem of Church Order

Order is the visible form of human community. The question of church order [24] arises only because the Church on earth is of necessity a visible society. Though the divine rootage of the institution continues to be regarded as significant, visibility and historicity are also integral and essential to the life of the Church. What makes for such complexity in the American situation is the confusion which arises from varying approaches to the problem. Because no single set of terms has won wide acceptance among scholars, one encounters such contrasting expressions as these: primary and secondary; visible and invisible; *esse* and *bene esse;* permanent and temporary; instrumental and essential; function and embodiment; unity and diversity; enduring and transient; and finally, order and organization. All these terms grope in the direction of an adequate statement on church order. Unfortunately some Americans shape their approach in a pejorative mood. Hence, reference to social factors in the church is made as though their very presence furnished a mark of failure and called for a negative evaluation.

At least five approaches [25] to the problem of church order in the American situation have been noted. Though all these answers can be regarded as inadequate, nevertheless the discussion can yield a new understanding of the problem. (1) The Church is a voluntaristic association of individual believers which exists to serve the individual members. God first calls the individuals and then they organize a church. (2) The Church is either a divinization of historical faith, forms, and structure—or the Church is a purely spiritual community. Here is asserted a radical distinction between true Church and institution, strongly depreciating the latter. (3) The Church is visible and invisible: the visible is earthly, partial, and defective; the invisible is transcendent and holy. This yields virtually a dualism or two distinct churches. (4) The Church is hidden from the eyes of the world but visible to the eyes of faith, while being one and the same Church. It possesses an *incognito* aspect. (5) The Church is both the Body of Christ and a religious institution. The inadequacy of these five approaches should suggest the need of a viable blend of both the sociological and the theological perspectives.

A prominent feature of the American situation is ambivalence.[26] On the one hand, institutional expressions of Christianity are viewed as artificial and unhealthy. This low theoretical estimate accorded the visible Church is accompanied by the general opinion that the Church has failed both in proclaiming and living the gospel. Protestants fear institutional mechanics as an obstacle to the Holy Spirit. Hence, adherents criticize the visible institution while pleading for an inner community of faith and belief. On the other hand, despite the widespread willingness to make the institution a Protestant "whipping boy," millions of members attend religious services, subscribe budgets, erect new edifices, support eleemosynary work, and patronize subsidiary church organizations. Many adherents participate in the visible Church, believing it to be the trustee of salvation. Many enter into its life convinced of its spiritual efficacy. The afore-mentioned ambivalence confuses some observers, but it cannot obscure the paradoxical context of hope and reality in which Americans discuss order. Christianity is regarded as much a movement as it is a church. Organization does not appear without order. These ambivalent perspectives comprise in part the thought and life patterns of indigenous churchmen.

In conclusion, several major problems persist in American discussions of church order: (1) the terminological confusion—lack of agreement respecting nomenclature; (2) the pejorative posture—biased assumptions against either *esse* or *bene esse*; (3) the pluralistic context—recognition of inevitable ethnic and cultural differences; and (4) the social and theological "reductionisms" [27]—how to combine the data of disparate disciplines. Thus an unsophisticated approach is neither warranted nor contributory to ecumenical understanding. The forms of the Church are signs pointing to the unrealized fullness of new life in the Kingdom.

Summary

The preceding pages furnish a brief perusal of materials which can yield a preliminary orientation to the North American situation. How it differs from the European setting, as noted by Williams and by Moberg, has been delineated under thirteen salient points. Moreover, definitions of institution which emerge from American cultural pluralism and from the theories of need, interest, and a philosophy of culture were examined also. A new approach, namely that of status-role analysis, was mentioned in order to highlight the context, provided by the institution, within which individual social positions, normative patterns, and culture traits gain significance. Thus individual efforts and expressions are regularized into a meaningful unit of society.

From an examination of religious institutions it was discovered that Christianity expresses itself in a variety of authentic forms. The typologies of Ernst Troeltsch and Howard Becker, as heuristic devices, bear a relevance to the American discussion. Evidently indigenous Protestantism is defined as both a social institution and a spiritual fellowship. Although some churchmen regard the former as a kind of pollution, nevertheless a *limited institutionalization* appears inevitable, necessary, and even desirable. Both the Church's rootage in culture and its claim to spiritual uniqueness are genuine. The power structure embedded in church life bears a strong resemblance to that discerned within secular institutions. Bureaucracy is a constant threat to the inner community of faith and belief. The question of church order arises naturally because the Church is a visible society on earth. Out of the manifold approaches to this issue, a viable blend of sociological and theological perspectives appears to be gaining in favor. The acknowledged ambivalence of the American outlook may yet provoke a sufficiently sophisticated and spiritual approach which can lead ultimately to the unrealized fullness of new life in the Kingdom.

NOTES FOR ESSAY 3

1. Robin Williams, *American Society* (New York: Alfred A. Knopf, Inc., 1951), pp. 315-318.
2. David O. Moberg, *The Church as a Social Institution*, Chapter 4.
3. Possibly psychology is the single exception here.
4. Robert C. Hanson, "Institutions," *Contemporary Sociology*, Joseph S. Roucek, ed. (New York: Philosophical Library, 1958), pp. 64-86.
5. William G. Sumner, *Folkways* (Boston: Ginn and Co., 1906).
6. Lloyd V. Ballard, *Social Institutions*, Chapter 1.
7. Constantine Panunzio, *Major Social Institutions*, Chapter 1.
8. Gurvitch & Moore, eds., *Twentieth Century Sociology* (New York: Philosophical Library, 1945), Chapter VIII, "Social Organization and Institutions," by Florian Znaniecki; Joseph S. Roucek, ed., *op. cit.*
9. Charles P. and Zona K. Loomis, *Modern Social Theories* (Princeton: D. Van Nostrand Co., Inc., 1961), especially Chapter 8; Talcott Parsons, *The Social System* (Glencoe, Ill.: Free Press, 1951).
10. This includes H. Richard Niebuhr, J. Milton Yinger, Russell R. Dynes, Morton Rubin, and others. A critique of these materials is provided in Frederick A. Shippey, "Sociological Forms of Religious Expression in Western Christianity," *Religion in Life*, Spring, 1958; and "Troeltsch and His Critics," an unpublished manuscript, 1960.
11. H. R. Niebuhr, *Social Sources of Denominationalism*, Chapters II and III; L. Pope, *Millhands and Preachers*, Chapter VII; J. M. Yinger, *Religion in the Struggle for Power*, Chapter II; D. O. Moberg, *The Church as a Social Institution*, Chapters IV and V.
12. Howard Becker, *Systematic Sociology* (New York: John Wiley & Sons, Inc., 1932), Chapter XLIV.
13. *Cf.* J. Milton Yinger, "Religion and Social Change" in *Review of Religious Research*, Winter, 1963.

14. Consult the writings of H. Paul Douglass, Samuel C. Kincheloe, Murray H. Leiffer, Ross W. Sanderson, Arthur L. Swift, Jr., Joseph Van Vleck, Jr. Cf. Frederick A. Shippey, "The Variety of City Churches" in *Review of Religious Research*, Summer, 1960, pp. 8-19.

15. *Op. cit.*, pp. 337-338.

16. *Cf.* J. Milton Yinger, *Religion, Society and the Individual;* and Thomas F. Hoult, *The Sociology of Religion* (New York: Dryden Press, 1958).

17. J. O. Hertzler, "Religious Institutions," *The Annals of the American Academy of Political and Social Sciences*, Vol. 256, March, 1948.

18. Walter G. Muelder, "Institutionalism in Relation to Unity and Disunity," *The Nature of the Unity We Seek*, Paul S. Minear, ed. (St. Louis: The Bethany Press, 1958), pp. 90-102.

19. J. O. Hertzler, *op. cit.*

20. Paul M. Harrison, *Authority and Power in the Free Church Tradition;* James M. Gustafson, "A Study in the Problems of Authority in the Congregational Church Order," unpublished paper (Social Ethics Library, Yale Divinity School, New Haven, Conn.).

21. *Op. cit.*, Chapter XII, "Postscript for Baptists."

22. *Religion in the Struggle for Power*, Chapter I.

23. *Op. cit.*, Chapter 19; also Purnell H. Benson, *Religion in Contemporary Culture* (New York: Harper & Brothers, 1960), Chapter 14.

24. James M. Gustafson, *Treasure in Earthen Vessels;* Robert Lee, *The Social Sources of Church Unity;* Paul Minear, ed., *The Nature of the Unity We Seek;* J. Robert Nelson, ed., *Christian Unity in North America;* Claude Welch, *The Reality of the Church.*

25. *Cf.* C. Welch, *The Reality of the Church*, Chapter I.

26. Relevant treatments of the topic include: H. Paul Douglass and Edmund deS. Brunner, *The Protestant Church as a Social Institution;* Winthrop S. Hudson, *The Great Tradition of the American Churches;* Paul M. Harrison, *Authority and Power in the Free Church Tradition;* H. Richard Niebuhr, *The Kingdom of God in America;* Liston Pope, *Millhands and Preachers;* Paul Ramsey, ed., *Faith and Ethics;* J. M. Smith and A. L. Jamison, eds., *The Shaping of American Religion* and *Religious Perspectives in American Culture.*

27. See H. P. Douglass and E. deS. Brunner, *The Protestant Church as a Social Institution;* J. M. Gustafson, *Treasure in Earthen Vessels*, Chapter 8; H. R. Niebuhr, *The Purpose of the Church and Its Ministry;* A. Outler, *The Christian Tradition and the Unity We Seek.*

BIBLIOGRAPHY FOR ESSAY 3

Ballard, Lloyd V., *Social Institutions* (New York: D. Appleton-Century Co., 1936).

Douglass, H. Paul and Brunner, Edmund deS., *The Protestant Church as a Social Institution* (New York: Harper & Brothers, 1935).

Gustafson, James M., *Treasure in Earthen Vessels: The Church as a Human Community* (New York: Harper & Brothers, 1961).

Harrison, Paul M., *Authority and Power in the Free Church Tradition* (Princeton: Princeton University Press, 1959).

Hudson, Winthrop S., *The Great Tradition of the American Churches* (New York: Harper & Brothers, 1953).

Lee, Robert, *The Social Sources of Church Unity* (New York: Abingdon Press, 1960).

Leibrecht, Walter, ed., *Religion and Culture* (New York: Harper & Brothers, 1959).

Lenski, Gerhard, *The Religious Factor* (Garden City, N.Y.: Doubleday & Co., 1961).

Minear, Paul S., ed., *The Nature of the Unity We Seek* (St. Louis: Bethany Press, 1958).

Moberg, David O., *The Church as a Social Institution* (Englewood Cliffs, New Jersey: Prentice-Hall, Inc., 1962).

Nelson, J. Robert, ed., *Christian Unity in North America* (St. Louis: Bethany Press, 1958).

Niebuhr, H. Richard, *The Social Sources of Denominationalism* (New York: Holt & Co., 1929).

———, *The Kingdom of God in America* (Chicago: Willett, Clark & Co., 1937).

———, *Christ and Culture* (New York: Harper & Brothers, 1951).

———, *The Purpose of the Church and Its Ministry* (New York: Harper & Brothers, 1956).

Outler, Albert, *The Christian Tradition and the Unity We Seek* (New York: Oxford University Press, 1957).

Panunzio, Constantine, *Major Social Institutions* (New York: The Macmillan Company, 1946).

Pope, Liston, *Millhands and Preachers* (New Haven: Yale University Press, 1942).

Ramsey, Paul, ed., *Faith and Ethics* (New York: Harper & Brothers, 1957).

Roucek, Joseph S., ed., *Contemporary Sociology* (New York: Philosophical Library, 1958).

Smith, James W., and Jamison, A. Leland, *The Shaping of American Religion* (Princeton: Princeton University Press, 1961).

Smith, James W., and Jamison, A. Leland, *Religious Perspectives in American Culture* (Princeton: Princeton University Press, 1961).

Welch, Claude, *The Reality of the Church* (New York: Charles Scribner's Sons, 1958).

Yinger, J. Milton, *Religion in the Struggle for Power* (Durham: Duke University Press, 1946).

———, *Religion, Society and the Individual* (New York: The Macmillan Company, 1957).

4.

INSTITUTIONS IN THE EARLY CHURCH

Institutions as far as Christianity is concerned must be defined as permanent features in the life of the Christian church whose function is to express and mediate the revelation (the activity of God in Christ, or the Christian gospel, or the Word) which Christianity claims to convey.[1] Institutionalism will in this essay be held to mean a state of affairs, or a tendency toward a state, in which the institutions exist, or are thought of as existing, for their own sake alone, without reference to their function of mediating revelation. It should be noted that by this definition the gospel itself is not regarded as an institution,[2] but as that which may be mediated through institutions. This essay will also accept the distinction made between order and organization in the Interim Report of the World Council of Churches Commission on Institutionalism.[3]

Reinterpretation of Jewish Institutions

Institutionally speaking, Christianity did not begin with a *tabula rasa*. It inherited all the institutions of the Jewish religion which was then in the stage today usually called "late Judaism."

by R. P. C. HANSON

It is worth while enumerating the more important of these institutions: the Temple at Jerusalem with its sacrificial cult and its priesthood; the elaborate observance of the written and oral Torah, as developed by Pharisaic Judaism, including the practice of circumcision, the observance of the major and minor festivals; the Rabbinate; the eldership; the worship of the synagogue; the acceptance of the Hebrew Scriptures of the Old Testament as sacred and inspired. In the earliest days of the Christian church all these institutions were left unmodified,[4] though some of them clearly had less significance for the Church than others. The early Church did not, for instance, dream of denouncing or abandoning the Temple cult, as the activity of the apostles within the precincts of the Temple during the earliest days shows, and the care with which Paul guarded himself against the imputation of being disloyal to the cult (Acts 18:18; 20:16; 21:20-26). But the primitive Church cannot have regarded the Temple cult as possessing great importance, if only because it believed that the Messiah, who in some sense supersedes the cult, had already come once and would soon appear again. This is the meaning of Stephen's speech in Acts, and of many passages in Paul's letters (such as Romans 8:1-4; I Corinthians 5:6-8; Galatians 4:1-5); later it constitutes one of the themes underlying the Passion-narrative of the Fourth Gospel and forms the central subject of the Epistle to the Hebrews. When the apostles were driven by circumstances to lay down a rule of minimal observance for Gentile Christians, they formulated it in terms of Pharisaic Judaism, with no reference at all to the Temple cult (Acts 15:28, 29, whichever version of the text we adopt). Though Jewish priests were among some of the earliest converts to Christianity, there is no evidence at all that they were regarded as having any specifically Christian function as priests. Historically speaking, we must regard Christianity as stemming, not from Sadducean Judaism, but from Pharisaic Judaism, with a peculiar emphasis upon the fulfillment of prophecy to which the tradition of the Qumran Covenanters may have made a contribution. One gains the impression that when Jerusalem fell to the Romans in A.D. 70 and the Temple cult ended forever, Pharisaic Judaism, though it officially mourned, in secret heaved a sigh of relief. This sigh must have been echoed in contemporary Christianity. In the next century among the Apologists it becomes a shout. Again, though Jesus had been called a Rabbi, the Rabbinate cannot have played an important part in primitive Christianity.[5]

Pharisaic Judaism managed to preserve most of the traditional Jewish festivals even when the Temple cult had ceased, but within Christianity they appear to have lapsed into disuse in a comparatively short time, with the important exception of the Passover. But even though Christianity retained the observance of Jewish festivals, it modified and molded them to its peculiar convictions about the Messiahship of Jesus of Nazareth.[6] This is eminently true of the one Jewish festival which it retained permanently, the Passover. To have altered this festival into a Eucharist celebrated weekly, or, if we follow Jeremias, daily, was itself a modification of the first importance. But here the action of Jesus himself at the Last Supper provided the justification. Certainly when Justin Martyr wrote his *Dialogue with Trypho* about a century after the period when Paul was writing his letters, the observance of major and minor festivals was a characteristic which marked off Jews from Christians.[7]

The question of circumcision and of the observance of the *halakah*, the intricate corpus of interpretation of the written Torah devised by Pharisaic Judaism, came to a head early in the history of Christianity. It underlies much of the material in Paul's letters; and Acts gives us an account, probably a simplified and schematized one, of how it was dealt with. Jesus himself had certainly taken a critical attitude toward at least some parts of the *halakah*,[8] though the evidence is not strong that he directly taught that parts of the Torah could be rejected. It can at least be said that the early Church decided that the *halakah* must be modified for the benefit of Gentile Christians, and that circumcision was not insisted upon in their case. Even as late as Justin's day, it was admitted that Jewish Christians could be allowed to follow their own traditions within the fold of the Church.[9] As membership of the Church became more and more predominantly Gentile, the question of circumcision must have faded further and further into the background. No doubt Christians of that early period would have told the inquirer that they were not abandoning the Torah's ordinance of circumcision, but giving it a spiritual (that is, metaphorical or allegorical) interpretation. Alexandrian Judaism, in the persons of such writers as Pseudo-Aristeas and Philo, had already given some encouragement to this course.[10] How far early Christians observed the Sabbath, or rather how quickly the observance of the first day of the week in celebration of the resurrection of Jesus ousted the Sabbath, there is almost no evidence to determine. Two of the later documents of the New Testament, the Fourth Gospel and the Epistle to the Hebrews, spiritualize the Sabbath into the rest which Christ has brought his people.[11] But it would be unwise to conclude that quite vigorous vestiges of Judaism did not linger for some time in the Christian church.[12]

How far the early Church retained Jewish liturgical forms is also a difficult question. The earliest evidence for Christian worship which we possess (I Corinthians 10:14-22; 11:17-34; 14:1-40) does not at all suggest the use of fixed forms, except in so far as the Christian Eucharist's origin in the Passover rite involved it in fixed forms or in a conventional structure. Many scholars hold that at some point between about A.D. 80 and 90 forms of prayer were adopted from the synagogue service and prefixed to the Eucharist, and that this accounts for the origin of the part of the Eucharist called the *synaxis*. Some have detected clear evidence for the use of fixed forms at a very early date.[13] But against this there is strong evidence that from a very early date the celebrant at the Eucharist was at liberty to improvise in the great prayer of the anaphora if he liked, and it is wholly unlikely that this liberty was a second-century development and not an original tradition in the earliest Eucharist.[14] Again, the date of the *Didache* is still an undecided question, and even the *Didache* contains one sentence implying that the celebrant could choose his own words in prayer.[15] We must therefore envisage the early Church as influenced, but not as dominated, by Jewish institutions in its worship.

If we are to count the sacred Scriptures of the Jews as an institution, then they certainly were an institutional heritage taken over permanently by Christianity from Judaism, and one destined to have a lasting, indeed a perennial, influence on the Christian religion. But even here we can mark the freedom and flexibility with which the early Church treated this heritage. It could be said that it was owing to its peculiar interpretation of the Jewish Scriptures that the Church finally broke with Judaism in its determination to see Jesus of Nazareth predicted as Christ in them. And as the Church during the first two centuries moved into a wholly Gentile milieu it found itself engaged in a continual wrestle with the Old Testament, this collection of books which it could not abandon and which yet caused it great embarrassment and great difficulty, both when it faced the Gnostic menace and when it took up the task of reconciling Christian doctrine with Greek philosophy. But whatever we may think of the outcome of this struggle with the Old Testament, we cannot accuse the Church of being either passive or unenterprising in its treatment of it.[16]

We have already concluded that in the sacrament of the Eucharist the early Church held itself free to adapt and mold existing Jewish institutions according to its own convictions and according to the tradition about Jesus of Nazareth which it had inherited. We can safely say the same about the sacrament of baptism. If we search for parallels for Christian baptism we shall indeed encounter an *embarras de richesse*. But most scholars today seem to regard the likeliest source of Christian baptism as being the example of Jesus himself when he allowed himself to be baptized by John.[17] But baptism was for the early Christians, if we are to judge by the letters of Paul, so overwhelmingly a union or contact with the crucified and risen Christ, so uncompromisingly Christocentric a rite, as to leave very little room for influence from pre-Christian rites or institutions.

We have therefore seen reason to conclude that in its attitude to existing institutions the early Church was flexible, creative, and dynamic rather than static and timid. Christianity was not merely a conservative revision of Judaism, but a revolutionary reinterpretation of it. W.D. Davies justly says that Church life in primitive Christianity was spontaneous, creative, and free: "it reveals that live interchange of tradition and freedom which is the genius of great music, art and poetry as of living religion." [18] The spontaneous expansion of Christianity over the whole Roman Empire in a very short time is incompatible with any other character. Such a religion is not at all likely to exhibit dangerous signs of institutionalism. It is important to keep this point in mind when we come to consider the thorny question of the ministry in the early Church.

Many writers have endorsed Streeter's opinion that almost any tradition of Christianity can find *some* support for its ministry in the early Church.[19] But we are bound to add that none can find their form evidenced as the sole or exclusively authoritative one. There is a baffling variety of ministerial functions evident in the early Church, and the surest way of misunderstanding their significance is to plunge into this variety determined to seize one, and one only, as the significant, original, and solely normative one. This is not to say that there is no doctrine of ministry to be found in the New Testament. In three chapters of his recent study, *The Pioneer Ministry*, A.T. Hanson has argued convincingly that we can trace at least Paul's doctrine of ministry and see it as occupying a large place in his thought:

> ... this ministry has a double relationship; it is related to Christ as responsible to him and as being the primary means by which his life is reproduced in the world. And it is related to the Church as serving the Church, and as leading the Church as a whole into the same life which itself is ex-

hibiting. There is no suggestion here of the ministry doing anything which the Church as a whole cannot do; it is rather that the ministry is the pioneer in Christian living for the Church, as Christ was the pioneer for all of us.[20]

The statement of Von Campenhausen that "the doctrine of ministry is not central for early Christian thought" [21] is wide of the mark. The truth is that although the doctrine of ministry is an essential part of the gospel in the New Testament, the subject of who are the particular ministers who carry out this ministry and what are their particular functions is treated by the early Church in a very flexible and almost fluid way.

It is true that the original apostles are permanent and unchanging witnesses to the life, the teaching, and the resurrection of Jesus Christ. But this function does not make them into officials with authority to control an institution. The eleven after the resurrection were not considered as church officers whose places have to be filled, but as witnesses waiting in Jerusalem for the full coming of the Kingdom.[22] Neither for the twelve (once Matthias has been chosen) nor for Paul was the apostolate an office.[23] "What bound together the primitive Church and its apostles in spite of everything was not the unity of the ordered Church but the unity of its witness to Christ and its calling." [24] No apostles have any authority against or over the Word and the Gospel, not even the original apostles.[25] In spite of the immense personal authority wielded by Paul as founder and father of his churches and converts, so that he claims that they encounter Christ in his person for salvation or for ruin (II Corinthians 6:15), he never makes himself into an official possessing official spiritual authority: "not that we have lordship over your faith" (II Corinthians 1:24; see also Galatians 1:4,5; 5:13; I Corinthians 1:13; 3:5,9, 21f; 6:20). This is because the apostle is constituted for and lives by Christ, and only exists so that Christ shall be testified to and reached through him. His personal authority as a man or as an official is nothing.[26] Again, we must recognize the notorious fluidity of the title "apostle" in the New Testament. Its bearers range from Peter himself to the otherwise totally unknown Andronicus and Junias (Romans 16:7), who may well have been the historical founders of the Roman church.[27]

The word "deacon" in the early Church is the title for no less flexible a function. The one point upon which all scholars seem to be agreed is that Luke is misleading when he implies (Acts 6:1-6) that the primary function of deacons was "to serve tables." Deacon in fact simply means minister, and the early Church seems to have regarded its deacons (male and female) as ministers in the most general and varied sense.[28] To say that the early Church borrowed the word from the Gentile environment is irrelevant, because the word was used in so general a sense as to exclude any particular influence from its origin. In the "presbyter" the Church certainly did take over an existing institution, the Jewish elder; a council of elders used to run each synagogue, though not necessarily to conduct the worship there. But it is significant that scholars have found it difficult to determine what were the functions of the elder in the early Church. Paul never mentions elders, though once (Philippians 1:1) he groups together *episkopoi* and deacons in his greeting. Luke represents elders as existing in every church,[29] and once describes Paul and Barnabas as appointing elders in the churches of Lystra, Iconium and (apparently) Antioch (Acts 14:23). He also apparently identifies *episkopoi* with elders,[30] and this identification is certainly found in *I Clement* (whose author knows of no Christian ministers except presbyter-*episkopoi* and deacons), in *Hermas* and probably in the Pastorals.[31] If we are to identify these "presbyters" with the "rulers" in the Church occasionally referred to in the New Testament,[32] then we can find a function for these elders. This certainly is the function of the *episkopos* and/or the elder in the Pastorals, in I Peter and in James. In the "presbyter" we seem once again to find a ministry which the early Church, though it took it over from Judaism, used in an independent way.

The same conclusion holds for the much-discussed title *episkopos*. Conjectures about the origin of this title and the particular function attached to it have been legion. It has been suggested that the *episkopos* was primarily a financial officer (Hatch), the exponent of the self-contained and sovereign local community (Harnack), the understudy for the teacher gifted by God (Sohm), the person chosen according to the old Jewish custom for the honor of leading prayer (Linton), the function peculiar to Gentile Christianity (Von Campenhausen), and the descendant of the "superintendent" *(epitropos* or *epimeletes* in Josephus) found among the members of the Dead Sea Sect (Caster, and with more caution Reicke).[33] There are also those who see in him the direct descendant of the apostles and the sole bearer of their authority.[34] The variety of these conjectures exposes the fluidity of this function. This is a title and a ministry which the Church used for its own purposes. The *episkopoi* with deacons of Philippians, the *episkopoi* of Acts 20 who are also "presbyters," the *episkopos*-presbyter of *I Clement* and *Hermas* and the Pastorals (and perhaps the *Didache)* are none of them quite the same as the monarchical *episkopos* who appears in the Pastorals also. In Ignatius this monarchical *episkopos* emerges as the dynamic center of the organic unity of the Church, representative of Christ but not apparently successor of the apostles,[35] and in Irenaeus as a self-conscious bearer of tradition, standing carefully in succession to the apostles, though not by consecration. Clearly the episcopate was a ministry subject to development.

Though the picture which the earliest sources gives us is not one of anarchy, the exercise of ministerial authority in the early Church seems to suffer the same fluidity as the other ministerial functions. The apostle's authority was evidently considerable, even though it was moral rather than official. As we have seen, there are references to "rulers" in the Church, but there is no evidence that such ministers as prophets, teachers, and exorcists received from others authority to minister; they must, however, have been thought of as conveying in their ministrations the authority of the Word. The exercising of authority or the running of administration is sometimes spoken of as one function delegated by the Holy Spirit among others.[36] Indeed, it is impossible to resist the arguments of those who maintain that originally all ministry in the Christian was charismatic, even the most institutional and authoritative. The early Church saw no antipathy between a ministry which was charismatic and a ministry which wielded authority and ran institutions. "All order is an 'afterwards,' an attempt to follow what God has already designed. It is not because a person has been chosen as prophet or presbyter that he may exercise this or that ministry, but, on the contrary, because God has given him the charism, the possibility is given to him, through the church order, of exercising it." [37]

It is interesting to note that this conception of all ministry as fundamentally charismatic did not die out in the first century. It survived to form what Ellen Flesseman van Leer has called the "Donatism" of the Church of the first three centuries.[38] Irenaeus in a famous passage says that bishops "with the succession of the episcopate have received a certain sacred gift of truth (*charisma veritatis*) according to the Father's goodwill." [39] Flesseman van Leer is no doubt correct in interpreting this to mean that "God makes those men bishops to whom he commits the gift of his *kerygma*." [40] Similarly Clement of Alexandria can speak of the apostle John "intending to ordain somebody among those indicated by the Spirit." [41] Consistent with this idea is the conviction evident in Tertullian and in Origen that bishops who behave immorally thereby cease to exercise any clerical function at all.[42]

In regard to institutions therefore, whether already existing institutions or those which the early Church devised for itself, or received as a tradition from Jesus Christ, we can fairly say that the Church's attitude in the earliest period was characterized by a remarkable independence and flexibility.

Institutional Consolidation in the Second Century

But this period of fluidity could not last long. Flexibility, variety, the wide distribution of authority among a number of people performing different functions, the rule of the Word dissociated from any permanent and inseparable institution, which characterize the early period, were only possible as long as Christianity was conceived of simply as an invasion of history by God in Christ destined very soon to reach its climax, as the arrival of an overwhelming crisis in which the chief concern (almost the only concern) was the proclamation of the gospel. But there had eventually to take place what Charles Williams in *The Descent of the Dove* called "a reconciliation with time." The second century of the Christian era witnesses a process of "setting" in the Church's life, like a jelly solidifying and stiffening into a mold. The life of the Church "sets" into permanent institutions. This is not to say that there had been no institutions before, but it is impossible to regard any of them as permanent up to this point. We can even see the beginning of this process reflected in the New Testament,[43] and its continuation is mirrored in *I Clement*, the *Epistles* of Ignatius, *Hermas*, the *Didache* and the literature of the subapostolic age generally. During the second century there is an increase in rigidity, in stereotyping, in conformity to a few common types rather than the maintenance of a rich variety, in all aspects of the Church's life. The gospel becomes in the Pastoral Epistles "sound doctrine"; faith, which Paul had regarded as the great characteristic of the new order brought in by Christ, becomes "the faith once committed to the saints." [44] We find little mention of prophets, evangelists, and interpreters of tongues; and, instead, the threefold ministry of bishop, presbyter, and deacon becomes dominant. Ecclesiastical organization and church discipline come to the forefront in the minds of Christians. *I Clement* and Ignatius' *Epistles* and the Pastorals are preoccupied with the authority of the ministry, and *Hermas* is engrossed with the subject of penitential discipline. The Eucharist acquires a formal structure, though not yet a fixed liturgy (Justin); the rite of baptism begins its process of accumulating additional ceremonies (Tertullian and Hippolytus). The monarchical bishop is universally installed by the middle of the second century, and he has gained considerable control over the Church. He alone can ordain, though there is some evidence that ordinations by presbyters may have occurred in some places—for example, Alexandria [45] and Gaul.[46] He alone could celebrate the Eucharist; Justin's phrase describing the man who conducts the Eucharist [47] almost certainly means the bishop, though presbyters may have concelebrated; when Clement of Rome wrote his letter, presbyter-*episkopoi* were the only people allowed to celebrate; but Ignatius insists (betraying perhaps by his vehemence that this is an innovation) that no Eucharist can take place without the bishop.[48] By the turn of the third century Tertullian is calling the bishop *sacerdos* and very shortly afterward Hippolytus describes him as *archiereus*, which should probably be translated "chief priest" rather than "high priest." The bishop is peculiarly responsible for teaching. Presbyters also by the middle of the second century are regarded as proper people to teach; one passage in *II Clement* exhorts the people to pay attention to the presbyters' teaching.[49] We can find one example of a bishop, Sarapion of Antioch, about A.D. 200 instructing his flock about what attitude they should take to an apocryphal work, the Gospel of *Peter*.[50] The second century threw up some bishops of powerful character and intellect with a great capacity for leadership, such as Polycarp, Irenaeus, and Alexander of Jerusalem.[51] But it is difficult to determine how much authority was ascribed to their office and how much to their character, or even, as in the case of Polycarp, to their wealth. Late in the second century also the custom of holding synods presided over by bishops began.[52]

Another powerful contribution to this process of "setting" was the formation of the canon of the New Testament. It used to be thought that this formation took place decisively as a response on the part of the Church to Marcion's formation of his own canon about the middle of the second century. But more recent scholarship would place the decisive moment earlier, somewhere between A.D. 100 and 120. It is clear that the *Gospel of Truth*, which most scholars now attribute to Valentinus himself and date to the years A.D. 140-145, already recognizes a canon (though of course it does not use the word *canon*) consisting of the Synoptic Gospels, the Gospel of John, the epistles of Paul, Hebrews, and the Apocalypse.[53] Some confirmation for this may be discovered in some sentences of the Egyptian Gnostic Basilides (flourishing *circa*

A.D. 130), quoted by Hippolytus, which refer to John 1:9 and describe this text as "that which is stated in the Gospels." [54] It might be possible also to discover references to a canon of Paul's letters in II Peter 3:16, assuming that this epistle must be dated between A.D. 120 and 150. Marcion, in short, was probably mutilating an already existing canon. Later in the second century the concept of the "rule of faith" (the teaching of the Church considered as identical in content with the teaching of the Scriptures) is used by Irenaeus, Clement of Alexandria, Tertullian, and by some others as a criterion by which heretical teaching can be judged and rejected. The phrase is found in some third-century writers (such as Origen, Hippolytus, and Novatian), but later fell into disuse, as the canon of the New Testament became more definite and more dominant throughout the Church and as conciliar creeds took the place of the rule of faith.[55] There is no good evidence for the often-repeated assertion that the baptismal, interrogatory creed played any serious part in the stereotyping of doctrine as a safeguard against heresy.[56]

Both the formation of the canon of the New Testament and the stereotyping of the ministry into that of monarchical bishops with presbyters and deacons were a form of appeal to the historical continuity of the Church with the apostles. The emphasis laid upon the rule of faith by Irenaeus and the writers who use this phrase is another way of calling attention to the same appeal. There certainly was much unrealistic schematizing of history involved in this appeal to continuity with the apostles. It was not accurate to maintain that the doctrine of the Church had remained unchanged since the days of the apostles by the time of Irenaeus, Tertullian, Clement, Hippolytus, and Origen. The second-century claim to the "apostolic succession" of monarchical bishops from the time of the apostles as guaranteeing soundness of doctrine, made with greatest confidence by Hegesippus, by Irenaeus, and by Tertullian, reflects and is involved with the same appeal to historical continuity, and is open quite as much to the charge of being an unverifiable schematization of history.

In short, then, the second century witnesses a hardening or solidifying of the hitherto very flexible and fluid life and organization of the Church into permanent institutions, the two most important of which are the canon of the New Testament and the monarchical bishop. The Church becomes conscious of living in history, of having a history, and feels the need to appeal to its historical continuity with the apostles. The process is at the same time the formation of tradition, tradition in doctrine (especially exemplified by the rule of faith), and tradition in practice. Perhaps Montanism sprang up as a protest against this process, but if so the protest was largely ineffective. The formation of tradition in the life of the Christian church was the result of ineluctable forces of history.

Institutional Flexibility and Freedom

But, though we must record the formation of permanent institutions in the Christian church in the second century, we need not conclude that this was the period at which institutionalism gained a decisive hold upon its life. We must not imagine that the second-century Church was a tightly organized, centralized institution, following a single policy with uniform efficiency. On the contrary, it was decentralized and lacking in co-ordinating machinery. Christians from Asia could arrive in Rome about A.D. 160 and find that the Roman Church was celebrating a different day of the week for Easter from theirs without any harsh feelings being aroused.[57] A bishop of Jerusalem could about A.D. 200 wander off to an unknown destination, leaving no address, for an indefinite period (presumably presbyters celebrated in his absence).[58] As late as the period from A.D. 232 to 255 Origen could spend half his career under excommunication by Rome and Alexandria without the bishops of Caesarea or of the rest of Palestine, or indeed of the East generally, troubling.[59]

Again, the authority of the second-century bishop was neither absolute nor without rivals. As late as the middle of the second century when Dionysius, bishop of Corinth, writes to Soter, bishop of Rome, he does not write in his own name but in that of his church.[60] Cyprian is the first bishop to use the episcopal "we," and one suspects that he borrowed it from the Roman magistrate.[61] Von Campenhausen at the end of his work remarks that the early Christian bishop was not a greedy grasper after power; rather, he displayed the opposite weakness of irresolute uncertainty about his use of the power of the keys. The necessity of administering penance or forgiveness drove him *malgré lui* into a position of power.[62] The authority of confessors, also, from time to time challenged that of bishops or other clergy. We can judge the very high authority attributed to confessors not only by the troubles encountered in the middle of the third century by Cornelius at Rome and by Cyprian at Carthage, but also by the strong language used by Tertullian in his *Ad Martyras* and by Origen in his *Exhortation to Martyrdom*.[63] Another rival authority to that of the bishop in the second and third centuries was that of the teacher, who was not necessarily ordained and not necessarily confined to one spot. We can discern a number of men eminent for their gifts in teaching the faith, for learning, and for wisdom—Justin, Tatian, Pantaenus, Clement of Alexandria, and Origen.[64] The Empress Mammaea did not condescend to give an audience to a Christian bishop, but to a Christian philosopher, Origen. It is the Christian teacher, not the Christian bishop, whom we find distorted by legend in the figure of Simon Magus in the Pseudo-Clementine literature (a legend whose origins must go back to the second century), and glorified in fantasy in the *Acts of Paul*, and caricatured in Lucian's figure of Peregrinus.

More perhaps than anything else the attitude of the Church to traditional *praxis* shows that in forming tradition and accepting a "reconciliation with time" the Church had no intention of subordinating the freedom of the gospel to institutions. By the middle of the second century at latest, and perhaps somewhat earlier, it was everywhere unreflectingly assumed throughout the Church that all custom and practice and institutions prevailing in the contemporary Church had existed more or less in the form then known since the time of the apostles. Irenaeus clearly includes more than doctrine in the original heritage of Christianity.[65] An anonymous anti-Montanist author writing about A.D. 192 protests against Montanist devotees prophesying while in a trance; he says that they are acting "against the custom of the Church supported by tradition and long continuance." [66] Clement of Alexandria describes some heretics as using bread and water at the Eucharist "against the rule (canon) of the Church." [67] The assumption that the current institutions and practice and discipline of the Church had always existed in much the same form from the time of the apostles is the very *raison d'être* of Hippolytus' *Apostolic Tradition*.

But even the firmest believer in the primitiveness of inherited *praxis* and institutions in the second century acknowledged that *praxis* and institutions were less important than doctrine, and that it was legitimate for different churches to hold different opinions and to follow different usages about this matter—a concession which was never made about doctrine. The Quarto-Deciman Controversy which broke out at the end of the second century, in the time of Pope Victor, usefully illustrates this point. Irenaeus, though he was firmly convinced that Victor and the Church of Rome were in the right in this debate, reproved Victor for attempting to make the controversy a matter for excommunication, whereas it was one of those unimportant points upon which Christians could agree to differ without breaking their unity.[68] Tertullian was very much interested in the subject of traditional *praxis* and institutions, and discussed the subject with particular fullness in two of his works.[69] From these and from other material in his works we can gain a reliable idea of what was the attitude of the contemporary Church toward this matter. Long-continued custom was allowed as legitimate and as possibly apostolic, as long as it was not obviously in contradiction to Scripture. But each church was allowed to make and to follow its own customs, and, if it liked, to regard them as apostolic. On *praxis* churches could differ, but not on doctrine. Cyprian, even though

FOUNDATIONS

he bitterly opposed Pope Stephen's practice in refraining from rebaptizing heretics who returned to the fold of the Church, still maintained that Stephen's right to do this if he liked must be respected.[70]

We can therefore fairly conclude that by the turn of the second to the third century, in spite of the inevitable growth within the Church of permanent institutions, the fathers of the Church were, according to their lights, alert to the need to preserve the liberty of the gospel. It is not so much by the preservation of such doctrines as Tertullian's hotly championed "priesthood of all believers," which was in the early Church neither characteristic nor widespread, as by its different estimate of tradition meaning doctrine from tradition meaning *praxis* that the second-century Church preserved this liberty.[71] Institutions had not been allowed to stifle doctrine, though doctrine was flowing into a definite mold. Tradition had appeared, as tradition must appear, but the Church knew the proper relation of tradition to gospel. There was of course no conscious examination of institutions as institutions, but there was no conscious imposition of them either. If it was a period during which institutions grew, this was the growth which history brings, not the growth which ecclesiastical power-politics foster.

What Is Normative?

Can we, in the light of this review, identify the original permanent institutions, or the order, of the Christian church founded by Jesus? It is relatively easy to reconstruct early Christian ideas, but extremely difficult to reconstruct early Christian institutions. This is not only because of the nature of the evidence for each, but because early Christianity was genuinely fluid and independent in its attitude toward institutions. We can certainly find plenty of organizations in the earliest period, apostolate, *ecclesia*, presbyter, deacons, baptism, Eucharist, and so on. An account of the early Church which represented it as functioning without organization, without a ministry or without sacraments, would be a travesty. But the organizations seem to have functioned so flexibly and the forms in which the Church's life expressed itself were so fluid that we must pause before we can call them permanent institutions, institutions in the sense in which that word was defined at the beginning of this essay, or order. The *ecclesia*, for instance, no doubt as an institution owed something to the *qahal* of the people of Israel in the wilderness, and something to the contemporary practice of calling a mass meeting to sound public opinion on some question (as described, for instance, in Josephus). But more than anything else it was the society of those who were called together by the Word and in the Spirit. Both baptism and Eucharist certainly had precedents in Jewish institutions, but these are relatively unimportant compared with the significance of both these ordinances as controlled by Jesus Christ believed in as risen and as living in the Spirit. The original eleven apostles were indispensable historical witnesses to the life and the resurrection of Jesus; but they were not officials of an institution, and there is no satisfactory evidence that they instituted a permanent apostolate to succeed to their functions.[72] A permanent form of the ministry did indeed emerge, but only after a period of incoherence and fluidity, during which the thing ministered (the Gospel or the Word) was apparently regarded as more significant than the minister.

There are only two permanent, original elements in Christianity —Jesus Christ and his Church. There are institutional features— baptism, Eucharist, ministry—but they do not control or define the Church, they express it. Jesus did not found a Church as an institution, as Benedict founded his monasteries or Ignatius Loyola founded the Society of Jesus. To see the institutions and doctrine of the primitive Church as flowing directly from Jesus in unbroken continuity is to see them *kata sarka*, to lapse into "reification," [73] into a complacent identification of human institutions and ideas as divine. The Church can be defined only by Christ, not by institutional features nor by doctrinal propositions "left" or "inaugurated" by him. Jesus did not found the Church, he *is* the Church. Its ultimate norm of doctrine can be only his Word; his Church can be recognized only by faith, not by historical demonstration. These conclusions, desirable perhaps in themselves on theological grounds, seem to be supported by our historical inquiry into the earliest state of the Church.

But Jesus was an historical person and his apostles were witnesses in history to his life and his teaching. The Church was a society of people living in history. It was inevitable that sooner or later the Church should achieve a permanent historical expression of itself, of its gospel and of its purpose. It has been shown that this permanent form for the Christian church was achieved in the second century, though it can be seen to be on the way toward the end of the first century. The Church's two chief institutions were the canon of the New Testament and the threefold ministry of monarchical bishop, presbyter, and deacon. This ministry cannot be demonstrated to have derived unchanged from the foundation of Jesus himself or his apostles, any more than the limits of the canon can be shown to have been laid down beforehand by Jesus or his apostles. But both institutions were regarded by Christians of the second century as expressing the Church's historical continuity with the apostles, in doctrine and in structure. The vast majority of Christian communions today recognize the canon of the New Testament as normative. There is no unsurmountable objection to the recognition of this threefold ministry as normative for the structure of the Church, as representing early tradition and as congenial to the gospel. The form of the Church's life in the second century does not represent a fall into institutions from the prelapsarian innocence of the first century, nor a corruption by institutions,[74] but a flowing of the life of the Church into an institutional mold at the irresistible bidding of history. Institutions are not in themselves antipathetic to the life of the Church. Institutions do not necessarily imply institutionalism. They are not allergic to the Spirit and the Word. There have of course been periods and places in which institutionalism has stifled the Church. It may well be that such a period can be discerned fairly soon in the history of the Church, perhaps as early as the fifth century, perhaps in places earlier. The rivalry of great sees and the emergence of ecclesiastical power-politics are suggestive pieces of evidence. But there is no justification for concluding that the institutions which the Church of the second century adopted carried in themselves the seeds of an institutionalism that was inevitably destined to strangle the Church's life.

Institutions therefore were bound in the end to develop not as an obstruction, but as a proper expression of the Church's mission. The "reconciliation with time" had to take place. If it had not done so, the Church would probably have degenerated into a futile millenniarism or illuminism. But the Church's institutions must always be judged by the Word which constitutes the Church itself. It is the business of the Church to see that its institutions express this Word and do not hinder it. We do not even have to conceive of the Church as possessing some original institutions (perhaps to be called the Church's order) which do not need to be judged in this way, and other, later ones, which do. All the Church's institutions are subject to judgment by the Word, even baptism and Eucharist and the ministry. The very *raison d'être* of the Church is the mediation of Christ himself, the proclamation and administration of his Word and Gospel. No institution exists in its own right, but only to serve this end.

The picture which an examination of the Church of the first two centuries discovers is one of a primitive, perhaps an eschatological, flexibility and freedom, followed by a period of settling into fixed order and permanent institutions. Until the twentieth century, scholars almost invariably fell into the temptation of trying to identify in the period of flexibility and freedom the order and the institutions which were evident in later periods, or which commended themselves to them as clearly the right and proper order and institutions. Alternatively scholars attempted to discern with open minds the prominent and significant institutions in this earliest period and either to correct or to condemn the institutions of a later period by them. But suppose—as seems highly likely—there were no permanent institutions in that period? The immediate reaction to this supposition is to conclude that the Church of today should do without institutions. This, however, is an illusion. The Church of the second century found it necessary to have permanent institutions. The Church of the twentieth century has no valid reasons at all to fancy itself dispensed from this necessity. Contemporary sects who have attempted to do without institutional forms have only succeeded in producing a different form of institution from other Christian denominations, but no more. The problem of institutions and of institutionalism is not a problem of historical reconstruction, but a problem which underlies most of the questions which occupy the minds of ecumenical theologians today, the problem of the relation of tradition to Scripture. It is not, for instance, our business to reassemble with archaistic precision the circumstances of the worship of the primitive Church, but it is our business to see that traditional forms of worship express (perhaps in contemporary form) the same significance as the worship of the Church of the earliest period expressed. We shall, again, best serve the Church's ministry, not by identifying in the Old or the New Testament a blueprint for the structure of our ministry, any more than we shall expect to find in the Bible a manual of doctrine or a textbook of ethics. We would do better to consider the traditional pattern of bishop, presbyter, and deacon, and see how they can be integrated fully and effectively into the life of the Church as proper expressions in diverse ways of the ministry in the Church, and by the Church, of the Word of God. We need not assume that the result would be an exact reproduction of the form of ministry of any existing denomination. The evidence provided in the New Testament for the life of the Church in the earliest period will of course be decisive, but as *evidence*, as raw material, not as the finished institutional product. When we have abandoned our habit of using the New Testament (and, less directly, the Old) as what it is not, we shall find it a sure guide in our use of it as what it is.

Perhaps it should be immediately added that the principles here enunciated do not necessarily rule out (any more than they necessarily imply) any of the major forms of existing ministry—congregational, presbyterian, episcopal, or papal.

We cannot now return to that first rapturous period of freedom and flexibility; we cannot walk the roads of Galilee with Jesus nor travel the sea-routes of the Aegean with Paul. But our final impression must not be of a Church crippled with age and stained by compromise with the world, making do as best it can with antiquated but indispensable institutions, every century leaving further behind it its glorious youth when it enjoyed flexibility and freedom. To think this would be to forget the Christian doctrine of the Holy Spirit who both reigns in history and is Lord of history and Quickener of history. The Spirit and the Word are as present as ever to the Church. The Word is, as ever, sharper than any two-edged sword, and the Spirit is no less life-giving than when he was experienced by Peter and Paul, Chloe and Andronicus, and Junias.

NOTES FOR ESSAY 4

1. Compare the sociological definition given in *The Old and the New in the Church* (London: SCM Press, 1961), p. 57.
2. As it is in *The Old and the New in the Church*, p. 79.
3. *Ibid.*, p. 78: Order is "the visible complex of institutions which is held to be essential to the continuous existence and identity of the Church as a community in history." Organization is "the broad range of institutional elements which, under varying historical conditions, express some aspect or other of the community which is structured and sustained by that 'order.'"
4. So E. Schweizer, *Church Order in the New Testament* (E. T. London: SCM Press, 1961), p. 47, Note 3.
5. The arguments, however, of B. Gerhardsson in *Memory and Manuscript* (Uppsala, 1961) must be given due weight.
6. R. Bultmann, *Primitive Christianity in Its Contemporary Setting* (E. T. London: Thames; New York: Hudson, 1956), p. 187.
7. See Justin, *Dialogue* 8.4; "Major and Minor Festivals" is a rendering of Greek words whose literal meaning is "festivals and new moons."

8. Mark 2:15-3:6; 7:1-23; and parallels.
9. *Dialogue* 47.1-4.
10. See R. P. C. Hanson, *Allegory and Event* (London: SCM Press, 1959), Chap. 2.
11. John 5:9-18; 7:14-29; 9:13-41; Heb. 3:7-4:13.
12. *Cf.* Eusebius, *H. E.* 5.1.26; Tertullian, *Apology,* 9.13f.; Minucius Felix, *Octavius* 30.6; Origen, *Hom. on Jeremiah* 12.13.
13. *E.g.,* H. F. Von Campenhausen, *Kirchliches Amt und geistliche Vollmacht* (Tübingen: Mohr, 1953), p. 77. The passages he refers to are Heb. 10:25; Barn. 19.10; *Did.* 4.2; 16:2. We might add *Mart. Polyc.* 14.1-3 and Irenaeus, *Adv. Haer.* 3.6.3.
14. See R. P. C. Hanson, "The Liberty of the Bishop to Improvise Prayer in the Eucharist," *Vigiliae Christianae,* xv.3.
15. *Did.* 10.7.
16. See J. Daniélou, *Sacramentum Futuri* (Paris, 1950), and *Théologie de Judéo-Christianisme* (Paris, 1958); R. M. Grant, *The Letter and the Spirit* (London: SPCK; New York: The Macmillan Company, 1957); R. P. C. Hanson, *Allegory and Event.*
17. See W. F. Flemington, *The New Testament Doctrine of Baptism* (London: SPCK, 1953); G. W. H. Lampe, *The Seal of the Spirit* (London: Longmans, Green and Co., 1951); O. Cullmann, *Baptism in the New Testament* (E. T. London: SCM Press; Chicago: H. Regnery Company, 1950); J. Jeremias, *Infant Baptism in the First Four Centuries* (E. T. London: SCM Press, 1960).
18. W. D. Davies, *A Normative Pattern of Church Life in the New Testament* (London: James Clarke and Company, n.d.), p. 26.
19. B. H. Streeter, *The Primitive Church* (New York and London: The Macmillan Company, 1930; 2nd repr.), Introd. ix, "everyone has won and all shall have prizes." *Cf.* W. D. Davies, *A Normative Pattern,* and B. Reicke, "The Constitution of the Primitive Church" in K. Stendahl, ed., *The Scrolls and the New Testament* (London: SCM Press, 1958; New York: Harper & Brothers, 1957).
20. A. T. Hanson, *The Pioneer Ministry* (London: SCM Press; Philadelphia: Westminster Press, 1961), p. 62; other definitions are on pp. 72, 84, 85, and 88; see also the whole of chaps. 4-6.
21. *Kirchliches Amt,* p. 332.
22. *Ibid.,* p. 17.
23. *Ibid.,* p. 29.
24. *Ibid.,* p. 31.
25. *Ibid.,* pp. 39-41; *cf.* E. Schweizer, p. 73 (5m).
26. Von Campenhausen, pp. 47-57.

27. So A. T. Hanson, p. 98. For an account of the debate conducted by scholarly opinion on this subject, see O. Linton, *Das Problem der Urkirche in der neueren Forschung* (Uppsala, 1932), pp. 69-101 and A. T. Hanson, Chap. 10.

28. See Linton, pp. 31-35; Von Campenhausen, pp. 74, 79, 106-107, 116-117; A. T. Hanson, pp. 98-106.

29. Acts 11:30; 15:2,4,6,22,23; 16:4; 20:17; 21:18.

30. Compare Acts 20:17 with 20:28.

31. Tit. 1:5-7 and perhaps I Tim. 3:2-13. Schweizer and Von Campenhausen strenuously deny that Luke is correct in identifying presbyters with *episkopoi:* Von Campenhausen, pp. 70-72, 87-88, 116-117; Schweizer, pp. 70-71 (5i). One feels that they are protesting too much.

32. *E.g.,* Rom. 12:8; I Cor. 12:28; I Thess. 12:5, 13; Eph. 4:12; Heb. 13:7, 17, 24.

33. A. Harnack, *Constitution and Law of the Church* (E. T. London: William and Norgate; New York: G. P. Putnam's Sons, 1910), pp. 192-193; Linton, pp. 31-35, 36-46, 104-112, 200-203; Von Campenhausen, p. 84; T. H. Gaster, *The Scriptures of the Dead Sea Sect* (London: Secker and Warburg, 1957), pp. 27-28 and 64-66; Reicke, "The Constitution of the Primitive Church," pp. 153-156.

34. *E.g.,* A. M. Ramsay, *The Gospel and the Catholic Church* (new ed., London and New York: Longmans, 1956); K. E. Kirk, ed., *The Apostolic Ministry* (London: The Canterbury Press, 1947).

35. See Von Campenhausen, pp. 106-107, 107-112, 155, 171-172.

36. Rom. 12:8, I Cor. 12:28; Eph. 4:12.

37. E. Schweizer, p. 102 (7m); *cf.* also pp. 49-50 (30), 145 (15f), 184-185 (22e) and Chap. 23 (a-e); Von Campenhausen, pp. 195 and 324; Linton, pp. 206-211.

38. E. Flesseman van Leer, *Tradition and Scripture in the Early Church* (Assen: Van Gorcum, 1954), pp. 119-122.

39. *Adv. Haer.* 4.40.2; *cf.* 4.42.1 and 4.53.2, and Hippolytus, *Elenchos* 1, introd. 6.

40. Flesseman van Leer, p. 119. For other views on this passage, see D. Van den Eynde, *Les normes de l'enseignement chrétien dans la littérature patristique des trois premiers siècles* (Paris, 1933), pp. 181-187; A. Ehrhardt, *The Apostolic Succession* (London: 1953), pp. 113-114; H. E. W. Turner, *The Pattern of Christian Truth* (London: Mowbray, 1954), pp. 327-328; E. Molland, "Irenaeus of Lugdunum and the Apostolic Succession" (*Journ. Ecc. Hist. i,* 1950, 25-26).

41. *Quis Dives* 42.

42. Tertullian, *De Fug. in Pers.* 10.3; Origen, *Comm. on Matt.* 20.14 (see *Allegory and Event,* pp. 330-331.

43. In some late passages in Matthew's Gospel, in the Pastoral Epistles, in Jude, and in II Peter.

44. Sound doctrine: I Tim. 1:10; 6:3; II Tim. 1:13; 4:3; Tit. 1:9, 13; 2:1, 8. Faith once committed: Jude 3; *cf.* Jude 20 and I Tim. 1:19; 4:1; 5:8; 6:10, 21; II Tim. 3:8, 4:7; Tit. 1:13, 2:2.

45. See W. Telfer, "Episcopal Succession in Egypt" (*Journ. Ecc. Hist. iii*, 1952, pp. 1-13); E. W. Brooks, "The Ordination of the Early Bishops of Alexandria" (*Journ. Theol. Stud.* II, 1901, pp. 612-613).

46. E. Molland, "Irenaeus of Lugdunum."

47. *Apology* 1.67,5,6; the phrase is *ho proestos*.

48. Smyrn. 8. 1, 2; *cf. Philad.* 4.

49. 17. 3-5.

50. Eusebius, *H. E.* 6.12.1-6.

51. *Ibid.*, Book 6; 8.6; 11.1-6; 13.3; 14.8,9; 19.17; 20.1; 39; 2.3; 27.

52. *Ibid.*, 5.23.1-4.

53. See F. L. Cross, ed., *The Jung Codex* (London: Mowbray; New York: Morehouse-Gorham Co., 1955), p. 91; Van Unnik, *Newly Discovered Gnostic Writings* (London, 1960), pp. 39 and 64; J. Doresse, *Les Livres Secrets des Gnostiques d'Egypte* (Paris, 1957), p. 57.

54. Hippolytus, *Elenchos* 7.20; *cf.* 22.4; 27.5. See Van Unnik, p. 24; B. F. Westcott, *Canon of the New Testament* (London, 1896, last ed.), p. 301; J. N. Sanders, *Fourth Gospel in the Early Church* (Cambridge, England: The University Press, 1943), pp. 52-53; H. E. W. Turner, p. 185.

55. See R. P. C. Hanson, *Tradition in the Early Church* (London, 1962), Chap. 3.

56. *Ibid.*, Chap. 2.

57. In the time of Pope Anicetus, Eusebius, *H. E.* 5.24.16, 17.

58. *Ibid.*, Book 6:9.6-10.1.

59. It is, however, significant that in Origen's case objections had been made earlier to his teachings as a layman in the presence of bishops. See Eusebius, *H. E.* 6.19.15-18.

60. *Ibid.*, 4.23.10,11.

61. In the *Sententiae Episcoporum* of Cyprian's last Council eight of the bishops used "we" and twenty-five "I."

62. *Kirchliches Amt*, pp. 329-330.

63. For the influence wielded by confessors see also Eusebius, *H. E.* Book 5:3.1; 2; 4.1; 2.

64. Perhaps we may discern another in the old man who succeeded in converting Justin whom he charmingly describes in the early chapters of his *Dialogue*. Was Minucius Felix's Octavius another?

65. *Adv. Haer.* 4.53.2.

66. Eusebius, *H. E.* 5.16.7.

67. *Strom.* 1 (19). 96.1. *Cf. Epistola Clementis* 2.4, "...he will bind what ought to be bound and will loose what ought to be loosed as one who knows the rule (canon) of the Church."

68. Eusebius, *H. E.* 5. 23. 25.

69. *De Corona Militis* and *De Virginibus Velandis;* the latter is written very much under the influence of Montanism and no doubt is not representative of contemporary ecclesiastical opinion. But the former is representative enough; further, we can learn something from the position which Tertullian attacks in his (Montanist) *De Ieiuniis Adversus Psychicos.*

70. Cyprian, *Epistles* 72.3.2; *cf.* 73.26.1; 75.6.1 (the opinion of Firmilian of Cappadocia). On this subject of traditional *praxis* see Van den Eynde, pp. 158ff., 191ff., 241ff., 252ff.; H. E. W. Turner, pp. 310ff.; 334ff.; R. P. C. Hanson, *Tradition in the Early Church*, Chap. 4.

71. Von Campenhausen, pp. 165-167, 190-191, 250-257, justly deprecates the attempt to make much of the doctrine of the "priesthood of all believers," though E. Schweizer devotes a whole chapter to it. See also Linton, pp. 6-7.

72. See Von Campenhausen, pp. 31, 325-326.

73. J. L. Adams, "Rudolf Sohm's Theology of Law and Spirit," in *Religion and Culture*, W. Leibrecht, ed. (London, 1958), pp. 226-227 and 234-235.

74. As, in varying ways, has been claimed by Sohm, Harnack, Bultmann, Werner, E. Schweizer, and all exponents of the precarious theory of an *Abfall* in the infancy of the Church's life.

BIBLIOGRAPHY FOR ESSAY 4

Flesseman van Leer, E., *Scripture and Tradition in the Early Church* (Assen: Van Gorcum, 1954).

Hanson, A. T., *The Pioneer Ministry* (London: SCM Press, 1961; Philadelphia: Westminster Press, 1961).

Hanson, R. P. C., *Tradition in the Early Church* (London: 1962).

Harnack, A., *The Constitution and Law of the Church* (London: William and Norgate, 1910).

Linton, O., *Das Problem der Urkirche in der neueren Forschung* (Uppsala: Almquist und Wiksell, 1932).

Reicke, B., "The Constitution of the Primitive Church" in *The Scrolls and the New Testament*, K. Stendahl, ed. (New York: Harper & Brothers, 1957; London: SCM Press, 1958).

Schweizer, E., *Church Order in the New Testament* (E. T. London: SCM Press; Naperville, Illinois: Alec R. Allenson, Inc., 1961).

Turner, E. W., *The Pattern of Christian Truth* (London: Mowbray, 1954).

Van den Eynde, D., *Les normes de l'enseignement chrétien dans la littérature patristique dans les trois premiers siècles* (Paris: Gabalda et Fils, 1933).

Von Campenhausen, H. F., *Kirchliches Amt und geistliche Vollmacht* (Tübingen: Mohr, 1953).

5.

THE CHURCH AS KOINONIA AND INSTITUTION

A double characteristic of churches constitutes the occasion for our inquiry. In the first place, in all churches there are organizations and administrations which are purely functional. They were not appointed by God: they were created by man, in order to fulfill the tasks of the Church. They can therefore be altered at will, if they no longer perform these tasks. If we alter them, however, we are obliged to replace them with other forms of equal importance. They are therefore indispensable. They spring from a need, a lack, a necessity. Because they are indispensable, these organizations acquire considerable importance of their own, and this may prove an obstacle to the Church's life, its unity, and its vitality; for these institutions combine with the human capacity for conservatism (*vis inertiae*) and self-assertion.

Second, over against these pragmatic, modifiable, but indispensable organizations, all churches also possess forms in which they express some of the essentials of their faith and theology. These forms are derived by the churches from the Bible—for example, the ministry, the synod, the congregation. The Church

by HANS DOMBOIS

(Translated from the German by E. M. Evans)

thinks it cannot renounce these forms without being disloyal to its task.

In accordance with current ecumenical terminology, these two kinds of structural elements may be designated as the "order" and the "organization" of the Church.[1] Both are manifestations of the institutional structure of the Christian community. It will be the task of this essay to examine what these two institutional forms signify for the Church, and how they are related to each other. To do this it will be instructive to analyze in the first place some prevailing usages of the concept of institution, and the involvement of institutions in the changes of social history.

Institution as a Concept

We find the word used in the pedagogical sense in Calvin's "Institutio religionis christianae." In the same sense the manuals of Roman Law are called "Institutions of Roman Law." Here the word "institution" does not denote the object, but the method, the way of introducing people to a field of knowledge. The purpose of this introduction is to ensure that the learner understands the Christian faith or how to apply the law, that he learns how to live in accordance with it (versari in) and so has a basis for his personal action. The object of pedagogical institutions is not merely to impart knowledge, but also to place the learner in the right position, to show him the pattern of relationships within which he has to act. This type of institution is therefore personal and relational.

The concept is used today in sociology with an extraordinarily wide range of meanings. Everything, from the axe of the Stone Age to the United Nations, is described as an "institution." In a lecture entitled "The Church as an Institution and Modern Society" [2] and in an unpublished manuscript, "Zum Begriff der Institution in der Soziologie Arnold Gehlens," Martin Greiffenhagen reveals the main lines of the contemporary doctrine of institutionalism. We may summarize as follows the basic conception of institutions on the part of contemporary sociology:

FOUNDATIONS

Contemporary anthropology agrees about one essential characteristic of man, which it calls his openness to the world (Welt-Offenheit). The difference between human beings and animals, which live by impulse and instinct, is that the nature of human beings is indeterminate. Nietzsche describes man as "an indeterminate being." If one wanted to determine the nature of man, one might go so far as to describe it as openness, possibility, man's search to discover himself. In the sphere of action the spontaneity of his free impulses corresponds to this unfixed nature. Man is a "center of dynamism."

For institutionalism this means that man is the creator of institutions. Out of the "Welt-Offenheit" which is his nature man determines his own nature and fixes it in institutions. Institutions are artificial products of creative man. And from the very outset the social organism is an artificial one; it is not "natural," "instinctive," "an inclination," or anything like that: it is a free, spontaneous creation and "invention."

On the other hand, however, the institutions which he has himself created confront man as objective forces. He is aware of them as supernatural, essential, and finally divine forces, which he can defy only at the cost of infringing a taboo. "Hence the self-same organizations set up by human beings to regulate their intercourse with one another develop into powers which enforce their own laws to the very last iota" (Gehlen).

Without institutionalizing his life, man could not live at all. In the case of animals security of action is assured by instinct; man achieves the same security through institutions. They "meet a deep human need." And "culture" simply means a differentiated but stable group of institutions, which are accepted as an objective order. Institutions cannot be understood in the light of pragmatic thought; in them form and content coincide. Wherever people think they can separate the purpose of an institution from its form, a breach occurs which menaces the institution from within, and finally leads to its collapse.

This means that institutions do not merely cover a deficit, and provide for what is lacking: they also show a marked tendency to extend their original function (*Überbildung*). Man never rests content with just covering his needs, just attaining the level of his natural environment. He always makes a virtue of necessity, a work of art out of his need, a form of life out of his reaction. An order impelled by necessity develops into statesmanship and government. The deeper the need, the stronger is the form of power used to counteract it. "Institutions ... will not and cannot safeguard the inward impetus of the personality, nor the vitality of mind and soul. ... But they guarantee their permanent possibility, by continually providing a minimum of fulfillment for 'the masses,' by stabilizing and repeating the appeal, *the chronic challenge*, to inward control and to a full spiritual life. That is the *appeal from above* which is inherent in all institutions as their norm and guiding principle in *tension* with their trivial stability."

The application of the concept of institution to such varied spheres of technology, culture, law, and social organization is justified by the fact that they are all pre-established for us, so that we do not have to invent and create them; we simply have to accept the existing forms and to use them. We carry on the decision which originally created these institutions, as heirs of a tradition. We can and must make free use of them and change them. But we cannot disown tradition. By accepting tradition I simultaneously accept the spiritual conditions which are pre-established in the organization.

It is important to realize that man takes over institutions in the same way that he adopts language and lives in it. Although there are a great many separate institutions, sociology's main discovery is that *man is himself institutional by nature*. He may modify the existing institutions, but he cannot escape from the confines of his own institutionality.

Also as a legal concept, the term institution denotes a process. For example, a person is "instituted" (appointed) to a certain position. But the position to which he is "instituted" is also called an "institution" because it always stands ready for someone to be appointed to it. "Institution" therefore denotes both the *process*, and the *status* brought about by that process. The temporary process leads to the permanent status. But if this aim is to be attained, the institution must be founded, built up, and instituted as a permanent opportunity of this kind.

When a man and a woman marry it is not they who determine the nature of their relationship, as in the case of a commercial transaction. Their relationship is already pre-established in the institution of marriage—as established by God or by human legislation, or by the nature of the life-relationship which is intended. The institutions therefore have names describing this typical form, for example, "marriage." I am therefore free either to marry or to remain single; but I cannot alter the nature of the marriage-relationship. The *process* of being instituted is therefore the outcome of a free decision; but the *nature* of the institution is predetermined. The two things belong together. As the nature of the institution is predetermined, it is not the consequence of the decision to enter it or to be appointed to it.

Institutional forms of this kind occur in different spheres of law: (a) in family law (such as marriage, adoption); (b) in the law of property; (c) in the laws governing organizations, associations, corporations, and the State.

This third group is of particular interest for the Church. Here there are two main cases: the rules for acceptance into membership (in the case of the State, naturalization); and the rules for appointment to office and other permanent functions.

Here again, free, spontaneous decision is essential; for, as we have seen, this is the process whereby the person concerned is appointed or instituted as a member, a citizen, a judge, an official, or a teacher. Once he is appointed (instituted) to this position (status) he is obliged to carry out the duties involved in that role, as a husband, a guardian, an owner of property, a citizen, if he does not want to give up this position. Institutions therefore are not inventions of man's talent for organization, which have assumed special and ultimately burdensome significance owing to their importance. They are rather part of a general structure which is permanently connected with all human relationships. Institutional forms of this kind therefore occur where the elements of human life are permanent: in the spheres of sex (marriage), property, and politics (the State).

Although the conditions in which such institutional structures occur are very different, and although the obligations involved in the "roles" vary tremendously, nevertheless a comparison may be drawn between the institutions of widely differing epochs and peoples.

But what is really permanent and lasting, if we leave out of account what is changing and transient? There are two things: the first is the institution as a *structure;* that is, the fact that in all permanent relationships one enters a pre-established status through a process, by free decision. Furthermore the "institutional nature" of man, his dependence upon such preconceived and pre-established opportunities, is also permanent.

Second, the *needs* (sexual, economic, political) with which the different institutions are concerned are also permanent. When one asks concerning the precise content of these needs, he receives varying answers. The "functional" view (found especially in American sociology) regards them as "needs" which must be regularly satisfied and explains that the institutions are formed for that purpose. There is a certain amount of truth in this view; namely, that human beings live under the compulsions of sex, of desires for economic stability, and for political self-determination. But the idea is not complete. It leaves out of account all the observations made by sociology itself. For man does far more than merely respond to needs. He allows himself to be challenged to go beyond the point of meeting his own needs and to shape institutional forms suitable for his life. Or, to express it differently, one may say that man has been granted (by Someone, whoever it may be) a talent for organization, and entrusted with that task. Such a statement, of course, does not do justice to the tremendous pressure of primitive needs and brutal necessities.

This brings us again to the point where description ends, and we have to arrive at a philosophical and theological explanation and evaluation. In any case, jurisprudence also contains institutional structures which are very exactly defined, and these structures relate to certain basic relationships in social life—in fact, those very relationships which have the deepest and most permanent influence on people's lives. They are therefore not peripheral phenomena which leave the center of human life unaffected.

Here the question arises whether it is possible to refrain from participating in institutions. One may abstain from the opposite sex, but it is certainly impossible for the great majority of people to do so. Such asceticism is an exception. It is bound to break down if it is laid down as a rule for everyone. And if a person is interested in the opposite sex, then marriage is the only form in which this relationship can find permanence and full development. This is particularly important for the question of the children, so much so that attempts have been made to interpret the purpose of marriage as being essentially to produce children.

If anyone abstains from doing work of economic value, he must do something else of social value; otherwise he will have to go begging—in other words, get other people to provide for him. If someone abstains from voting, he is allowing other people to decide for him. Statelessness is therefore no alternative to citizenship; it is only an unsettled case of citizenship. "World Citizen No. 1" who tried to give up his citizenship was therefore fundamentally mistaken about the conditions governing life in society.

The legal concept of the institutional therefore does not conflict with what sociology and pedagogy understand by it. So far we have been primarily concerned with the general and permanent characteristics of the concept. We must now consider the question of its variability.

Institutions and Historic Change

Institutions are concerned with history in two ways. *First,* a piece of history is enacted within the institutions themselves. It is by forming institutions that man fixes himself in history. Characteristic forms arise. This process cannot be turned back like the hands of a clock, for it is irreversible; yet it can be developed in a forward direction. Every new form of institution, even if it is of the opposite kind, is built on top of the preceding ones. This historical character is particularly clear in the case of marriage. Marriage is a lifelong contract. If it breaks down and the contracting parties have to separate, they do not revert to *single* status as before; their civic status is that of "separated" or "divorced" persons. They both have a broken marriage behind them.

Second, institutions are concerned with history because they themselves undergo change. As we wish to apply the significance of this institutional change to the doctrine of the *Church,* we should not generalize too freely. The changes in marriage and property are less illuminating in this connection than the changes which human associations (from the civic organization to the State) have experienced, and are still experiencing. The concept of the *ecclesia* in the New Testament is itself derived from the gatherings held in the city-state and from the meetings of civic associations. The question, therefore, is whether amid the tremendous variety of forms of human association there exist really important differences which throw light on our present inquiry.

Theological criticism of the organization of the Church has always stressed the fact that the institutional form taken by the Church as an organization does not concern people so much as faith. It has also emphasized the fact that an organization of this kind more or less follows its own laws. The question involved is basically right and important.

The social history of Europe—and probably that of Asia also to a comparable extent—has experienced changes which have a bearing on this very question. Until about A.D. 1500 the European states were based on personal allegiance. Every individual and every social group within the state was bound to the ruler by definite personal obligations, often of a very varied kind. When the king died, the person in whom these rights were invested had gone, and so there was an interregnum until a new king was crowned. This form was later replaced by the modern geographical state, in which everyone who lives in a certain area is subject to a political authority that in principle has nothing to do with a change of persons, or with a definite personal affiliation between the ruler and his subjects. In this way the state has become independent of individual persons and their affiliations, and has become permanent and continuous. The same applies to all the other forms of association, whether economic or political in character.

This may be illustrated by a few examples. In Shakespeare's "Henry IV," Falstaff's comrade Pistol lays a wager with the Judge that he will lose his position, because he has come with the news that the old king is dead. And Pope Clement IX (1667-1669) is praised because, contrary to the custom at that time, when he became Pope he did not appoint new men to all the church offices; he merely changed the most important ones. His action was the expression of a change in the concept of the state and of government, in fact of a changing world view (*Weltbild*). The phrase "The King is dead: long live the King!" does *not* express continuity. It affirms that *in spite of* the short interregnum, the new order will come into force, and it welcomes it. The young king, the heir to the kingdom, is not a functionary within a state which has a continuous existence of its own. He is "the new king" whose coming is awaited as a new possibility of change and renewal. He is not simply identical with the past.

In a state which is based on personal allegiance, which Shakespeare had in mind, there is no continuity apart from the king's own person. In the strict sense his England was not a state but a kingdom, a king's realm, in which the authority was not abstract but personal. In the same way the behavior of the Pope, as a ruling monarch, had also changed as a result of the change in the concept of the state which is now regarded as a causal continuity.

In the U.S.A. not long ago it was customary for all the government employees to be changed if the party in power changed, even if they had no political functions. That, too, is a survival of the older personal form of state.

Consequently our subject "order and organization" cannot arise as a question until those objective, continuous, impersonal social forms have been developed. The result is both a question and a misunderstanding. The question is, What is the relation of a personal institution (order) to a transpersonal institution (organization)? The misunderstanding is due to the assumption that the only type of institution (organization) still existent is impersonal. What we have said above, however, was based on the assumption that today *order* (that is, personal order) and *organization* (namely, transpersonal order) still exist side by side, at any rate in the Church.

Here, however, we must see whether this hypothesis holds true when we examine the facts of social history. We must also inquire whether the Church has possibly developed in a different way from the associations of secular society.

The change in the structure of the state, referred to above, did not completely destroy the personal forms of allegiance. That is clear from marriage and from the laws relating to the family. Today marriage is still a personal institution in which, through the process described above, one becomes the husband or wife of another person. The laws concerning children are based on this fact. In the sphere of the state also some elements of personal institutions are still retained. In spite of the change in the structure of the state as a whole, if one is received into a state association, or appointed to an official position, these are still acts of *personal* institution. We must therefore avoid generalizations and examine the facts separately.

From this point of view, how are we to judge the history of the Church itself? Here those unacquainted with the real facts are misled by the appearance of unity in the legal system of the Roman Catholic Church. In actual fact many different things are combined in the Roman Catholic system, like a house with additional floors built onto it. It tries to cover up the joints and discrepancies as much as possible. It has therefore arranged its functions as far as possible in such a way that they are interchangeable (on the same lines as the modern form of transpersonal organization), although those who carry out these functions are *personally* appointed.

On the other hand, Protestantism did not arise until the old form of state as described above was declining. Only to a very small extent did the Reformation churches build up their institutional forms as "order," as a personal structure; they regarded the church mainly in nonlegal and noninstitutional terms. They took over the transpersonal institution direct from the secular authorities, but it was never respected and was regarded with suspicion. The difficulty in understanding institutional questions in Protestantism is therefore due to their social-historical origin. Many ideas which they claim to be biblical are really only the outcome of their own history.

What do the sociologists think of this historical change? A conservative sociologist like the German scholar Hans Freyer draws a distinction here between primary and secondary institutions. Primary institutions are those with which man is closely involved personally, such as marriage. Secondary institutions are organizations formed to accomplish certain purposes which are independent of the individual. On the other hand, "functionalistic" sociologists are not much interested in such differences; they regard all kinds of institutions as forms which ensure the satisfaction of human needs in different ways.

Neither of the concepts above is entirely satisfactory. The second does not do full justice to its own perceptions. And if one is so radical in attributing the origin of institutions to human "needs," one finds that the *sacramental* functions (food, cleansing, sexuality, and so on) are linked up with them.[3] The first view is justified by the fact that an institution like marriage and an institution like an "authority" are entirely different in rank and significance for human beings as such. But this view is in danger of separating the personal sphere from the technical one, in a way that is no longer possible today. By its assumption that "person" and "institution" are opposed, Protestantism has failed to see the real situation; it has been too romantic, and increased the difficulty of bringing personal and technical institutions into a right relationship. But it is very important to point out that without the form of personal institution as described above it is impossible to understand the transpersonal, technical institution. And if we cannot understand it, we are helpless against the magic "spell" of the powerful institution.

Institutional Elements in the Bible

In order to form an opinion on the question of the sociological mutability of institutions, we have compared the Church and the social institutions (from the civic association to the state), and have not mentioned the other spheres (such as marriage) which are also types of institution. This might expose us to the objection that we have been talking about the Church, but not about what "ultimately concerns" the Christian (Tillich).

In order to describe God's relation to men, the Bible uses institutional concepts drawn from all kinds of spheres. In the Old Testament the Children of Israel are described as God's "special people," His "peculiar treasure." [4] God is described as the Owner of this nation, which He sets aside from the world as a sacred sphere, His personal possession. God makes a Covenant with the people of Israel. By accepting this Covenant the people of Israel belong to God. In this nation there is a tradition of ordained priesthood, and also of kingship, to which the New Testament gives high value.

In the New Testament the Old Covenant comes to an end, but it is not simply destroyed; it is at the same time fulfilled. Let us look first at what is directly related to the individual; the first institutional process is *baptism*. Through baptism, freely accepted in faith, man becomes a member of the Body of Christ. He is incorporated, "instituted" into it. "*Baptismate in ecclesia homo (homo carnalis) constituitur persona (persona coram deo)*," states

Canon 87 of the *Codex iuris canonici*. Here again we see a process which leads to the status of membership.

The relation of God to believers and to the Church is described in concepts of family-law: it is compared with the relation between bridegroom and bride, between father and children, between testator and heirs. They are all reversionary rights bestowed by God on man by His mercy, with immediate effect, and with the promise of fulfillment in the end-time.

Throughout the New Testament it is impossible to separate the faith and the salvation of the individual from the fellowship of the Church. The New Testament establishes a New Covenant, which man accepts through faith and baptism. In this New Covenant God has set up the apostolic ministry, to which the individual is appointed ("instituted") through the process of ordination. Anyone who has left this fellowship is reinstituted by absolution as a member of this body.

The *ecclesia proprie dicta* and its *opus proprium* therefore show institutional characteristics which are directly based upon Scripture and are not the result of development. On the contrary, by promising to be present whenever two or three believers gather in His Name, God made it possible for the congregation to take a special form. However, since these congregations and churches are all parts of the same body, and all have to undertake the same mission, they are all interdependent.

Institutional Elements in the Church

It is already clear that the institutional elements in the Church are not different from those in the Bible. All the processes which help directly to build up the Body of Christ are spiritual institutions. These spiritual institutions are described in the Report of the Commission as follows:

    (i) The Church itself as divinely instituted.
    (ii) The Gospel, the Sacraments, and the Ministry.
    (iii) The community in its responsive functions such as

preaching and teaching, pastoral care, service to the needy, and social action.

(iv) The interdependence of all churches and Christian groups in the Body of Christ, however separated historically.

(v) The gathering of Christians in local congregations and other determinate patterns of common life and activity.[5]

Under a sixth caption, the Report mentions an entirely different group of institutions: "the organizational, administrative, legal, financial and other arrangements and procedures which are needed for the continuous life and mission of the Christian community." We must, however, draw a clear distinction between the first five points and the sixth.

Both groups denote institutional elements; but the two groups deal with different matters and therefore differ in rank and importance for the life of the Church. The institution as *"order"* comprises the spiritual Church and its *opus proprium*. The institution as *"organization"* comprises the Church in its secular legal relationships and its *opus alienum*. The difference may also be expressed as follows: "order" works directly, and "organization" works indirectly. The methods employed by the Church as an "order" are therefore those of a spiritual institution (for example, baptism, ordination); whereas the methods which it employs as an "organization" are secular, and can also be used by non-Christians for comparable purposes (such as raising money, publicity, building projects). The Church-institution as an "order" does what the world does not and cannot do (preaching, baptizing), but the Church as an "organization" does things which the world also does, only for different purposes.

As this concept of the Church as an institution is comparatively new, some serious objections will certainly be made against it. The most important question is, What is the relation of the institutional elements in the Church to God's spontaneous action, and also to His challenge to us here and now?

The first thing that must be said is (to quote Karl Barth), that the Church always has to find a balance between rigidity and confusion. In the present case this means that the Church stands between the doctrine of *opus operatum* and the docetism of a bodiless pseudo-Church, which rejects the *signa externa ecclesiae* (the outward signs of the Church). Or, to express it differently, the Church stands between the belief that a certain institutional act *as such* is essential, on the one hand, and the radical disjunction between spirit and institution, on the other.

The experience of church history shows that errors always occur in pairs. If one violently attacks one error, one usually goes to the opposite extreme. Institutions and freedom are not directly opposed to one another; for the institution includes an act of freedom. One is free to join the institution or not (for instance, one is free to marry or not).

According to Augustine, faith is the *virtus sacramenti*, and this freedom to believe is a gift of the Holy Spirit. Therefore if baptism, for instance, is institutional in character, this is only under the condition of the freedom bestowed by the Spirit. God's commandment is to be fulfilled freely and spontaneously. It may seem as if the act of entering the *koinonia*-institution and this freedom have nothing to do with one another, or are even opposed. But in fact they are closely connected. It is through *koinonia* (fellowship) that we attain freedom. Hence the words "whoever believes *and* is baptized..." Here the difference between freedom and institution-fellowship is overcome. It may be permissible to explain it thus: the God-given freedom to believe leads to *koinonia*, and *koinonia* is the condition for the possibility of being free: "Without me you can do nothing." *Koinonia* is not an aim in itself (an ontological misconception), and freedom cannot exist apart from *koinonia* (an individualistic misconception). The Church can therefore teach that baptism is essential for salvation. In this case salvation is the opportunity of living in a new relationship of fellowship with God.

The second big objection is that an institution has a legal character. There is no cause for misgivings on this score, for three reasons:

- *Exegetical reasons.* The Bible contains many legal statements, both concerning God's relation to men (expressed in legal concepts) and concerning the legal structure of the church. Liberal theology made a great mistake in regarding the Law and the Gospel as opposites. This distorted the interpretation of Paul's theology, especially, and must now be corrected.

- *Hermeneutical reasons.* The Bible uses many legal expressions in order to describe man's relation to God. A closer inquiry shows that the "existential interpretation" of the gospel has always taken this form, and is impossible without it.

- *Legal reasons.* The concept of *Right* and Justice, conceived as being opposed to the gospel, is in itself false. Justice is not "law" (in the sense of Pauline theology); it is not merely a demand which can be fulfilled through our own strength, and which therefore cannot be fulfilled. A right is rather a gift, a commission, an authority.

When God justifies us through grace, He gives us a new right. When the Church baptizes, it does *right*, because it has the commission and authority. This is also the case when it appoints people to offices. When the Church fulfills the commandment to evangelize, it proclaims God's claim and His offer of grace, and thus its action is *right*. This "*right*," which the Church derives from the commission and authority of Jesus Christ, is different, it is true, from the legal rights of bourgeois society, such as the right to acquire property; but the word "right" retains both connotations.

These two misgivings and objections are really misunderstandings and prejudices. It is only after they have been overcome that a more essential idea can be considered, which is often confused with them. The spiritual action in the whole history of salvation (*Heilsgeschichte*) has two sides: one, the institution; the other, the event. In his book *New Testament Pattern* [6] Jean-Louis Leuba has drawn attention to this. There is an institutional tradition which extends from the making of the Old Covenant up to

Pentecost, and this can be clearly shown from the titles given to Jesus Christ. There is also a tradition of events, where the prophets of every epoch have broken into this continuity in the history of salvation. Neither event nor institution can be derived from the other, nor attributed to the other. It is only when we accept them both together that we accept the whole of the gospel. It is therefore impossible to establish an antithesis between institution and the spirit.

Therefore the "organization" can serve the Church only if we understand and accept the "order" as a spiritual form of institution. Institution in the spiritual sense can be understood rightly only if we understand both things, event and institution, as two aspects of the same fact.

NOTES FOR ESSAY 5

1. See, *e.g.*, *The Nature of the Unity We Seek: Official Report of the North American Conference on Faith and Order*, Paul S. Minear, ed. (St. Louis: Bethany Press, 1958), pp. 229-236.
2. Published in the *Zeitschrift für evangelische Ethik*, Vol. 3, 1960, pp. 159ff.
3. *Cf.* G.v.d. Leeuw, *Sakramentales Denken.*
4. Exodus 19:5; Deuteronomy, 7:6, 14:2; Psalm 135:4.
5. *The Old and the New in the Church* (London: SCM Press, 1960), pp. 78f.
6. E. T. London: Lutterworth Press, 1953.

BIBLIOGRAPHY FOR ESSAY 5

Dombois, Hans, *Naturrecht und christliche Existenz* (Kassel: Johannes Stauda Verlag 1952).

——, *Das Recht der Gnade*—Ökumenisches Kirchenrecht I (Witten: Luther Verlag, 1961).

——, *Recht und Institution*, Eine Fortsetzung des Göttinger Gesprächs von 1949 über die christliche Begründung des Rechts mit Beiträgen von E. Wolf, U. Scheuner (Witten: Luther Verlag, 1956).

Ellul, Jacques, *Die theologische Begründung des Rechts* (München: Chr. Kaiser Verlag, 1948).

——, *Kirche und Recht*, Ein vom Rat der evangelischen Kirche in

Deutschland veranlasstes Gespräch über die christliche Begründung des Rechts (Göttingen: Vandenhoeck & Ruprecht, 1950).

———, *Die Treysa-Konferenz 1950* über das Thema "Gerechtigkeit in biblischer Sicht" herausgegeben von der Studienabteilung des Ökumenischen Rates der Kirchen (Genf: 1950).

Gehlen, Arnold, *Urmensch und Spätkultur* (Bonn: Athenäum Verlag, 1956).

Heckel, Johannes, *Lex charitatis*, Eine juristische Untersuchung über das Recht in der Theologie Martin Luthers (München: Verlag der Bayerischen Akademie der Wissenschaften (C. H. Beck), 1953).

6.
TYPES OF RELIGIOUS INSTITUTIONALIZATION

Firmly established role systems and institutions have always existed in the history of the Church. Though some liberal theologians in the beginning of the twentieth century assumed that at least in the primitive church, continuing even into the beginning of the second century, some sort of charismatic anarchy prevailed, more recent research has shown that the episcopal office and a cohesive ecclesiastical order originated within the Church.

Institutionalization of the Church

There is always an institutional aspect in a church; only the mystic and the liberal, who are found outside the Christian parochial fellowship of divine service and communion, live religious lives without any marked institutional characteristics. Though religious individualism essentially denies the institutional, at the same time the representatives of this individualism are dependent upon traditions and a heritage of ideas.

It is, however, apparent that the institutional characteristics within the life of the churches vary radically, not only from

by BERNDT GUSTAFSSON

church to church, relative to the differences between episcopal, presbyterian, and congregational forms of government,[1] but also from time to time. These historical variations are intimately connected with the changing sizes of the churches; they are connected also, and even more significantly, with the extent of interaction between the church and the community setting.

We may here take our starting-point in the changing firmness of the institutional pattern. An institutionalism that regulates everything in detail, from the seating in the church to the knowledge required for entering into marriage, involves an all-inclusive interaction with the community setting, an interaction that will keep its inclusive character only in so far as it does not conflict with the social setting of any social subgroup.

When the interaction with the social context becomes more rigid, the general social structure will influence the churches as institutions. A developing class structure will in great degree influence, and often disturb, church life and create disunity. This happened to several Lutheran churches in northern Europe toward the end of the nineteenth century.[2] The disturbing effect of the developing class structure in a growing industrial society was dependent upon the fact that the churches were institutions of all social classes, institutions that were influenced by the nations in their entirety and by the general social development. We are here concerned with national churches, which were woven together with the whole social context and strongly impressed by the older cultures.

The institutional patterns of common moral sentiments and definitions of statuses and roles [3] are apparently connected with the types and extent of groups and social configurations that influence the institutional roles. Of greatest importance, therefore, is research into *what it is that institutionalizes*. The schema with four different types of religious organization—church, denomination, sect, and cult [4]—is very illuminating as it relates to the question of adaptation to social change, but this schema seems to be too formal to get hold of the dynamic element within the religious organizations as institutions. This element is what pulls the individual into certain patterns of behavior and gives him his institutional roles. Elsewhere I have developed my reasons for this statement, [5] starting from the social behaviorism of George H. Mead, who uses the concept of role as key unit. An institution is, according to this theory, a relatively rigid series of common responses to certain situations on the part of all in the society or the subgroup. These responses are always roles, and the situations are expectations derived from the generalized other, "what he wants me to do."

The differences between church, sect, denomination, and cult are connected to the differences in these expectations. If the society that defines the roles is a voluntary association of individuals within a multigroup society, we have a denomination. If the group which defines the roles is a voluntary organization of adults with rigid and strongly deviating norms, we have a sect. If the roles are defined by all the organizations which penetrate and control the society, we have churches.

When we distinguish between different religious institutions, the essential point is the difference in roles, and these roles have different sources. These sources are partly to be sought outside the institutions; but the primary religious institution defines roles that are accessible to all, whereas the secondary religious institution defines roles that are accessible only to some persons and, therefore, their voluntary character is stressed. We can get hold of the role sources if we approach the question of religious institutions from the point of view of *what it is that institutionalizes the roles*. Why are the role systems sometimes very exclusive (especially in the case of the sect), sometimes more differentiated and open (the church type)?

It is necessary to stress that religious institutions are not institutionalized solely from outside, even though influences may come from either a local community or a national social setting. The religious roles and functions are in a very high degree settled by tradition, theology, and preaching. There is always a great measure of self-institutionalization within the religious organizations which have traditions to keep and to hand on. The socializing effects of one period in the life of the church affect the socialization of later periods, though in a less degree in epochs of rapid change. But in this heritage we also meet an older social context, where behavior and definitions of roles are dependent upon the type of cultural and general social institutionalization that occurred in the past. The continuing self-institutionalization of the religious institutions, however, always takes place *within* a social context, and the occasion that is dangerous to the unity of the churches, as regards the process of institutionalization, is often to be sought in the dependence upon this social context.

The importance of this search for the different role-sources will be quite evident, if we try to define the concept of institutionalization more precisely. That the roles become institutionalized means that they achieve *stability* and *uniformity*. Stability means here that the roles become *regular* and are performed repeatedly whenever the same situation arises. The individual behaves in the given situations in a certain manner; the mode of behavior becomes firmer and firmer. But the roles also get *something of a life of their own* and offer themselves to individuals as ready-made behavior patterns. Therefore they can be performed by the individuals without any need of choosing in each instance what to do. One by one, firmly fixed patterns of roles are built up. They get modified in single cases, but always remain self-evident to the individuals who perform them. This stability renders every attempt to change the roles and the attitudes more difficult.

By uniformity we mean that *the same role is performed in the same way by several individuals.* If religious life did not display this uniformity, it would make no sense to speak about religious institutions. Institutionalized roles are thus roles that are common to a great number of people. One also can point to an inner uniformity, an inner correspondence, that is, the way in which roles correspond with each other and get the character of a more or less closed wholeness, in which each single trait contributes to the totality. Such uniformity can in a higher or lower degree be coterminous with other social boundaries, and thus coincide with the cultural uniformity of a whole nation, a particular region, or a neighborhood. It can also correspond to the role systems of a certain social stratum, for example, a social class, or a marginal group such as rural people who have migrated to a city. *To the degree that such a correspondence between the religious role system and the role system of a group or a nation is discernible,* we must assume that not only has the religious role system become institutionalized by this latter role system, but also that there may have been processes of interaction between the two systems. Both the stability and the uniformity of the roles are to be traced back to some common role sources.

Different Kinds of Institutionalizing Agents

We may start with the agents of a *geographical* type. In most countries there are striking differences between different *regions.* In Sweden, for example, the different denominations are concentrated in different regions. These regional differences can be traced not only to a common religious heritage within the region and a common regional historical development, but also to the socio-cultural characteristics of the region, for instance, common dialect and common cultural attitudes.[6] Both the dialects and the ethno-cultural attitudes show in many cases the same geographical distribution as certain denominations and religious activities. Then we must assume an institutionalization of the religious life within the region by characteristics within the region itself.

The same can often be said about the differences between rural and urban regions, though in some instances neighboring rural and urban regions have the same religious geography. Different kinds of communities can be examined: for example, those of urban type in small cities, cities of middle size, metropolitan areas. There are also great differences in institutionalization in downtown areas, apartment areas, and suburban areas.[7] Clearly, the institutionalization by a region or a community may be a factor that causes disunity between churches and denominations.

Institutionalization by a *nation* can disturb the relations between churches even more. The Protestant churches in northern

Europe have to an especially high degree become institutionalized by national cultures. By mission or emigration, these national religious role systems have spread to other parts of the world. In America, in India, and elsewhere, ecumenical efforts have been obstructed by this type of institutionalization.

Races and racial heritages must also be mentioned as examples of institutionalizing agents. Also social classes can to a high degree institutionalize the roles within a religious organization. Some churches are more institutionalized by the upper classes in their patterns of attitudes and roles, others by the lower classes. Conflicts between different churches are sometimes also conflicts between class attitudes and class manners.

Of special interest are marginal groups of different kinds: groups which are isolated, socially, culturally, or geographically; groups which are maladjusted in a changing society; and immigrants. There exists a great number of institutionalizing agents, sometimes operating independently, sometimes interacting. Christian divisions are dependent in part upon this fact.

The process of institutionalization and its social mechanisms need to be described. Of this process the individual is unconscious, at least to a very high degree. The institutionalization and continuing control of behavior, as exercised by various groups and especially by the family, partly function on the conscious level. But this conscious part of the institutionalization and of social control is relatively small.

Of course, there are direct methods of influencing human behavior. But these, as Mannheim stresses, are always based on personal influence and work from near at hand.[8] Most behavior is natural and self-evident. Role carriers use many social norms without ever thinking about which social roles and values they are trying to enforce.[9] Therefore, the sociologist can help the ecumenical movement by unmasking the institutionalizing agents, of which individuals themselves are unaware. In modern society the old, closed milieus which earlier institutionalized the roles are disrupted to a marked degree, and the complicated nature of modern groups has caused great difficulties in the process of institutionalization. The effects of different role sources cross each other, and these opposite effects cause trouble and inner difficulties for the individual. This new situation should be favorable for ecumenical efforts, but it can not be exploited unless we know which role sources are in conflict.

Three Types of Cultural Institutionalization

We can distinguish three main types of cultural institutionalization of a church: those where institutionalization is accomplished by an inclusive culture, by exclusive dominant cultures, and finally by marginal cultures. These types are not always mutually exclusive. Sometimes they co-operate, but usually they lead to schisms and disturbances.

Institutionalization by an inclusive culture is usually applied to the church type of religious organization. Several combinations can be found, but most important is institutionalization by the state and by the whole nation, or by groups which more or less identify themselves with the whole nation and are firmly rooted in the cultural and social heritage and thinking of the nation.

Not until the fourth century A.D. was the Christian church institutionalized by the state; however, the Church was institutionalized even earlier by an inclusive culture, that is, by groups who regarded themselves as a nation, the new Israel, the new kingdom. The definition of roles was wide and inclusive, and though the faith in Jesus Christ was considered very exclusive, it had a universal meaning, transcending all boundaries. In the primitive church this "boundary-transcending" inclusiveness was manifest in the fact that the Church regarded itself as the rightful heir of the whole Jewish tradition: the Old Testament, the temple, and the synagogue. The Christians did not live within a small sector of Judaism, but rather identified themselves with the whole Israel, and thus the Jewish heritage left its traces in the divine service and in the general behavior.

The oldest Jewish-Christian church gradually was isolated and capsulated. Conquering instead was the Pauline Christianity, whose inclusiveness extended to Greek culture (Acts 17:22-31) in certain important respects. Pauline preaching was freed from an exclusively Jewish background. In the early church the boundaries of other cultures were transcended. Inclusive forms and roles were created continually, although local and regional differentiation remained for a long time—or was ever growing—in the history of the ancient church. In Augustine's time, he could still write that when the local parishes had different customs one ought to accept the customs of the parish where one was staying.[10]

The universal Mediterranean culture began, however, to disintegrate more and more, and this involved the Church in great and difficult adjustments. The Roman culture became more exclusive, and the Church became, through its dominant status as the church of Rome, something like a national church institutionalized by a more or less exclusive culture. Schismatic movements appeared, and in their background was this disintegration of the older inclusive culture into one dominant exclusive culture with certain marginal subcultures. The different national and sectarian trends in the fourth and fifth centuries were characteristically institutionalized by small marginal groups.[11]

By the outset of the Middle Ages the situation was greatly changed. The Western church was firmly tied to Latin culture, but already the invasions of the Goths and later the increased international contacts, not least through increased international commerce, enlarged the opportunities for a new inclusiveness to develop. By one stage after another the Church gained ground and became an integrating part of the medieval societies. The Church institutionalized, on her part, the various daughter churches, but in its entirety it was institutionalized by a culture that was already inclusive and creating inclusiveness through its international character. The basis of this universal thinking had been laid by Augustine, whose ideas about *Civitas Dei* became the medieval equivalent of the older idea of the Church as the new Israel.

This inclusive medieval culture was finally broken down. The breakdown was intimately connected with the appearance of national subcultures which, together with the low status of the laity and an increasing institutionalization by a hierarchical top, threatened the inclusiveness of the Church. Again it is noteworthy that disunity within the Church took place during the breakdown of an inclusive culture. A rigid, hierarchical form of institutionalization has its weakness in the difficulty with which it meets changes within the socio-cultural setting. With the new social structure and the new cultural upheaval, the medieval culture was no longer inclusive. Only in the northern parts of Europe were the emerging national cultures inclusive.

Within early Protestantism the national organization of the Church was kept, except by the Baptist movements. Among them, the cultures that institutionalized roles and behavior were marginal though often on a high cultural level. For the rest, the Reformation signified that the institutionalization by an inclusive culture was renewed, and that the unity of the Church was kept within the framework of national culture. This was possible because the medieval society survived in several countries. The state replaced the ecclesiastical hierarchy as an institutionalizing agent; but the state was often balanced by the laity which had been made free. The roles and behavior within the churches were settled by an inclusive religious culture, with a certain delegating of the responsibility downward to the laity in the local parishes.

In the seventeenth century, congregationalism demonstrated quite another trend of institutionalization by an inclusive culture. The rising congregationalism was a protest against the growing power of the bishops. Some of the Independents in Cromwell's England, facing the threat of a growing ecclesiastical hierarchy, regarded institutionalization by the state as a safeguard against disunity in church affairs.[12] When the government administration of the nation was extended, the control of the bishops over the parishes increased; and the bishops demanded uniformity in church customs, in liturgy and ethics. These demands for uniformity, typical of hierarchic tendencies, threatened unity, and the mass of nonconformists grew rapidly. The Independents looked to the state as a safeguard against this strengthened episcopal control, but the state could be such a safeguard only on one condition: if the institutionalization of cult and doctrine were handed to the local parishes.

History teaches us that the Church itself must often create the inclusive culture—that which can unify Christendom; and it is possible for the Church to do this. Preaching and ethics must include and embrace all social situations. Out of the disintegration of modern culture the Church must seek to create integration and common basic values. This necessity is a tremendous challenge to the ecumenical movement as a whole.

But the problem here is not only one of the general disintegration of culture, but also a question of the local substratum. An inclusive culture can not be spread from an organizational top, but must grow from below. And it appears that churches with more rigid confessional attitudes, but without any lively local substrata, are strong factors of disunity in rapidly changing and disintegrating cultures. Also with local substrata sagging, the basis of an inclusive culture is snatched away. In such a new situation, the Church, in its role systems and behavior patterns, is no longer institutionalized by an inclusive culture but by an exclusive culture. Then faith in Jesus Christ loses its uniqueness and becomes easily identified with the religious experiences of a particular group.

Churches institutionalized in this manner have always had difficulties, for their thinking and role system often develop a closed character when confronting new cultures, including local and national subcultures. The effect has often been a disintegration of church life. On the other hand, churches that have made a healthy adjustment to such new situations have, with attitudes characterized by openness and inclusiveness, transcended the cultural boundaries.

Such difficulties of institutionalization are very well illustrated in material from missionary areas. The difficulties of the younger churches in their efforts to achieve cultural autonomy are rooted in the crisis in Western Christianity during the nineteenth century. This crisis is related to the lack of inclusiveness, and a narrowing of the process of institutionalization. In several of the

European Lutheran churches the development of the new industrial society with its impersonal relationships between employers and employees was considered an event outside of God's creation.

Not until the twentieth century did Christian people in these churches begin to recognize God's creative activity behind the new society that had emerged, and to give it a positive ethical interpretation. But already large groups, especially among the workers and the new middle classes, had joined new churches in their search for an interpretation of their situation, for the agrarian Lutheran churches had only left them baffled.

It was not simply by chance that the missionary enterprise first received its strongly Western character during this period of radical social change. The lack of universality caused many missionaries to preach a message that was highly exclusive in relation to the social situation and the cultural heritage of the native people. Nineteenth-century missionary Christianity was seldom socially and culturally conquering and inclusive.

Excessive dependence upon older Western cultural traditions in the shaping of a Christian milieu is surely also today a great hindrance to ecumenical fellowship beyond nation and race. In this connection the statement made by the International Missionary Council at Willingen in 1952 is important:

> While the Church of Christ in any place and at any time must exhibit the marks without which it will not be a church, it has the responsibility to exhibit them in a distinctive way, *incorporating into the service of Christ whatever heritage of cultural values it may have been given by God's grace* [italics added]. This is not being "rooted in the soil" but *related* to the soil. The Church can only be rooted in Christ. But the eternal Gospel must be so presented to men and women that its contemporary and compelling relevance is recognized. It cannot be so recognized as long as it appears in a foreign guise, imitating and reproducing the characteristics of a church in some remote and alien land.

Foreign in one sense the Church must always be; its citizenship is in heaven, and it is an agent of transformation. Despite the dangers of identification with this world, we urge that foreignness in the more earthly sense of the word is something to be outgrown with all possible speed. Churches should take a positive yet critical attitude to the national cultures.[13]

Every critic of the involvement of the churches in disturbing subcultures must greet this statement with satisfaction as a step toward overcoming the cultural and social isolation of the Church.

Institutionalization by Marginal Cultures

The institutionalization of churches by exclusive cultures, which is currently so common, of necessity compels certain marginal groups to break with the older religious institutions. Each time an older inclusive culture breaks down, the same risks that operated in the breakdown of the Old Mediterranean culture appear again in an acute form.

Marginal cultures always presuppose conflict between dominant cultures, on the one hand, and deviant value-systems, on the other. The marginal group is antagonistic to the culture of the dominant society. The difference between institutionalization by an exclusive culture and institutionalization by a marginal culture thus is that in the latter case particular roles are overemphasized and shaped by a *conscious opposition to all other culture patterns and value-systems* in the society. The marginal culture is a negative reflection of the dominant culture.

Problems are thus presented that are most difficult to solve, for they will tend to create sects. Sects are often institutionalized by marginal groups who retain norms and values from older cultural strata. John B. Holt's hypothesis, that in these cases there is some sort of cultural shock,[14] is of great interest in this connection though it is not yet sufficiently verified. According to this hypothesis, religious movements that strive for a more holy behavior are dependent upon the migration from rural to urban communities, and upon the difficulties the migrants have in adjusting to the urban cultural milieu. The migrants are frequently firmly rooted in a revivalistic religious tradition, and when they confront the urban culture some sort of shock is created. The adjustment to the new cultural milieu tends to be a totally negative reaction. Thus the marginal groups take their concepts, norms, and habits, from the cultural background they just have left, namely, a rural tradition that is breaking down. From an ecumenical point of view, therefore, religious organizations with such a cultural background are of special concern. These movements, and above all the Pentecostal movements, are institutionalized, at least in part, by cultures that are marginal to modern urban society. The consequence may be a strong anti-ecumenical bias.

Thus an enormous difficulty is presented for the work of Christian unity. The failure of traditional forms of religious organization is a *failure to adapt to dynamic social change without disturbances*, that is, a failure to adapt and at the same time give freedom to marginal groups to keep the old values and cultural attitudes that the mother organization is abandoning as it adjusts to a new situation. These problems appear in large measure to be unsolvable at the present time.

The Emergence of Administrative Strata

Studies of marginal religious groups would be very illuminating for our purpose. Above all, research is needed on marginal groups that are the result of centralizing tendencies within institutional patterns. For example, in the 1930's a crisis erupted in the Swedish Baptist Union over the issue of local self-government. Those who wanted no centralization went their own way, and finally a new organization grew up. According to my studies of Swedish church life, the marginal religious groups increase in number and power when contacts between the administrative top and the popular base of religious institutions weaken. Also for this reason, an orientation of the ecumenical movement toward the local substratum would therefore appear to be highly desirable.

Such an orientation is even more desirable because a new trend in the institutionalization of religious institutions is under way which deeply conditions this involvement in middle-class cultures. This is the emergence of administrative "tops," which, in the institutionalization of religious organizations, become so isolated from the membership that they do not even come into conflict with these subcultures. Through the growth of administrative strata, and often with a change in the status of the clergy, the importance of the local substratum has decreased and the old local variations in church life have begun to be blurred. Institutionalization from below has decreased.

We have already observed that hierarchical strata and hierarchical tops are dangerous to the unity of a church in a changing society as, for example, in Europe at the end of the Middle Ages and in England at the beginning of the seventeenth century. In modern society these risks are increased in many ways, and the authority pattern tends to become more and more administrative.

These tendencies reflect the impact of modern society. The breakdown of the old primary groups, not least the neighborhood, demands an adjustment to larger units as substitutes. The local parish or congregation becomes less important both as a basis for activities, and as a religious home milieu. More than before, religious institutions rely on large administrative units. Territorial boundaries are to a certain extent blurred, and the local communities are regarded more as areas to be institutionalized than as institutionalizing agents.

This change has required an administrative top and has created an administrative stratum more and more independent from the local substratum. It is not even elected by this substratum, but often appointed by the already existing administrative top itself. As a consequence institutionalization by an inclusive culture has decreased in accelerating tempo.

In a marked top administration of the bureaucratic type, the behavior pattern of the leaders is to a certain extent independent of the local substratum, and stamped more by the institutionalization that takes place within the administrative stratum itself. The leaders institutionalize each other. The dynamics of the administrative apparatus itself creates new personal influences, "those of the administrators themselves seeking their own ends and engaging, as newly powerful participants, in power relationships." [15] The behavior patterns, in the informal organization of the institutions, are centered "primarily around the ties of influence among the functionaries" and "tend to concentrate the locus of power in the hands of the officials." [16] In an institution with the modern type of top administration a cleft easily develops between the administrators and the common people, for the administrators have immediate purposes to fulfill that are not those of the common people.

Such a development is also reflected in a tendency toward managerial thinking among denominational delegates engaged in ecumenical activities. Bureaucrats certainly are inclined to present formalized responses to outside presentations, and it is very difficult for such bureaucratic personalities to enter into serious ecumenical conversation without hesitation.[17] The most striking point to note is that these formalized responses are institutionalized by the interaction within the administrative top and not also with the local substratum. What is often needed in ecumenical conferences are the frankly expressed responses that are institutionalized from below. Ecumenical delegates are not private persons, nor administrators, but delegates of certain religious organizations, and, if they do not have lively contacts with the common people in their organizations, their responses will be formalized and, above all, ineffective because they do not have any broader social meaning. Thus an integration of the ecumenical movement with local congregations is as necessary as a breakdown of the existing managerial thinking within the denominational institutions.

Administrators and officials run, above all, the following risks: those of superficiality, expertism, and bureaucratic escapism. In each of these the ecumenical problem is real. All the risks are linked up with the fact that the roles of the administrators tend to be institutionalized only by the leadership stratum and by its way of thinking.

A risk of *superficiality* is always prevalent when successful organization and statistical results are the things that the administrators basically strive for. Activity and high percentages are then easily confused with the growth of faith and conviction. The number of Sunday schools, the statistics of church attendance, and the collection figures are assumed to be indices of religious life, and high numbers become the primary end of all endeavors. Such thinking may already infect the ecumenical climate. In such cases, religious statistics have become the administrators' masters, not their servants and critics.

The competition between different churches and denominations which always prevails in modern society is greatly increased through such administrative superficiality. "Right or wrong—our denomination." This temptation is the chief temptation of the administrative top. This top aims to organize the church or the denomination more adequately, and then applies this superficial way of thinking. Whereas in the local substratum of common people the fact of belonging to a particular denomination often does not exclude open-mindedness in the relations to other denominations, the administrators frequently fall victim to the temptation of trying to close the doors. It is not unusual in certain regions for the common people to visit churches belonging to other denominations, and to let their children attend a Sunday school of another denomination where their own church has no established congregation. Administrators sometimes judge this open-mindedness to be a serious threat to one's own denomination.

The second risk is *expertism*. Of course, the need for experts cannot be denied in a modern complicated society, even in religious life. The tasks are so manifold that the need for specialists is constantly growing. With expertism we mean, however, that state of affairs in which the distribution of roles has become so rigid that the experts do not want to do any other job than their specialized job, and so rigid that the experts tend to act *autonomously* without any inspection from the local substratum. There may be inspection from the top, but seldom from below. Expertism may evidently be a hindrance to the ecumenical movement, since the openness that is fundamental to all ecumenical endeavor disappears and is substituted by an attitude of self-sufficiency.

Bureaucratic escapism also is a factor which may cause division and disunity. This escapism is found where each administrator tries to define his own job, and does not wish to work in teams. The result is to cut off all possibilities of genuine co-operation with other people both from their own church and from other churches, and to make even more tenuous the contacts with the local substratum.

Communication as the Crucial Test

The relationships between the managerial top and the common people within a church has not yet been the subject of any thorough sociological research. Here we shall only suggest some problems that need to be explored.

We may start with *the problem of communication*. Experts in the art of administration also have stressed that organization must be coupled with communication.[18] As social scientists have pointed out, informal organization and communication has obtained greater importance with increasing bureaucratic efficiency.[19] The impersonal character of administration is softened by informal communication.

The problem of communication within a denomination gets its importance from the fact that open communication between top and bottom prevents an institutionalization of administrative roles solely by the leadership stratum. It is evident that several schisms have their roots in deficient communication.

An inquiry into this problem should first aim at examining the general conditions for communication. Necessary to all social communication of a more informal and personal type is that the people use the same language. One gets the impression that the cleft between managerial thinking and the lay points of view is often one of a purely linguistic type. The administrators speak one language, the common people another. This is applicable also to religion: the emergence of a special lay theology has in certain cases been one of the factors behind divisions. Already in the early Eastern schisms in the fifth and sixth centuries, language as a social medium had an extraordinary importance. In the Western church, where there was only one ecclesiastical language, Latin, there never was the same kind of conflict as occurred in the Eastern church where the national churches were institutionalized by national cultures, and where each people had its own ecclesiastical language. Thus, to the degree that an administrative upper stratum of a denomination speaks another language than the common laymen do, there are risks of disunity.

Further, such an inquiry would have to explore *the ways of communication:* in what degree they are of the formal and the informal types. Are they used only in one direction—for example, from the top to the laity, or in both directions? Personal contacts are most decisive; these evidently must be considered to be the most important form of communication. Where the personal informal contacts are poor and sporadic, the bases of communication are weak. It was no mere contingency that the ecclesiastical divisions both in England in the seventeenth century and in Sweden in the nineteenth century were related to a revival of a more formal system of episcopal oversight.

The fact that these administrative risks are also connected with differences in status and class position between the top and the rank and file must not be overlooked. This is valid especially in churches where the middle classes are not dominant in the congregations.

Finally, differences in the *definition of ends* need to be examined. The communication must to a certain extent be concerned with the end and purpose of the activities, and often this end is defined differently by the administrators and by the laity. The managerial top runs the risk of overstressing organization and statistical figures as ends in themselves, whereas lay people are more interested in personal problems of a moral and religious nature.

The definitions of the ends of the different denominations in our time tend to conflict more often at the level of the administrators than at the level of the rank and file. Both the differences in language and the differences in definitions of ends cause serious trouble between denominations; this is even more so in modern church life where the administrative top is the only effective institutionalizing agent. Sometimes the communication between administrative strata of different churches may be poor, but the communications are not always open and free between the administrative stratum of one church and the common people of other churches. Informal, personal contacts with persons from other churches may often create better and more immediate ecumenical contacts than high level conferences. The administrators also often run greater risks than the men in the pew do in disrupting the bonds of Christian fellowship with other churches over definitions of purpose. These risks must be underscored because the administrators tend to try to institutionalize the roles and the habits of men in the pew.

It is evident that the ecumenical thinking of the churches is correlated with the degree of inclusiveness of the culture that institutionalizes the churches. Where a church looks upon itself as a member of a universal Church and is open to the common Christian heritage, ecumenical attitudes are quite natural. International contacts and acquaintance with other churches at home and abroad thus ought to be very helpful when we try to break down the walls of exclusiveness and national-marginal thinking. But a broad international interest and a universal outlook in social and cultural affairs are also of highest importance. A narrow ecclesiastical outlook may impede the growth of an international orientation of a nation as a whole.

The cultivating and deepening of international communication must not be restricted to an élite of experts, nor must the experts alone work on a universal interpretation of the gospel. The broader the communications are between the churches, the more important will become the idea of the unity of the Church. If ordinary people do not become engaged in the ecumenical work, a managerial ecumenism may take over.

Finally, it is more necessary than ever to develop an ecumenical theology in the full sense. Significant efforts have been made in this respect. But more than hitherto such a theology must seek to bridge also the chasm between ecclesiastical cultures and non-Christian cultures. It ought to aim not only at the unity of the Christian churches but also at the unity of mankind, furnishing an inclusive interpretation of the gospel for the whole world.

NOTES FOR ESSAY 6

1. W. G. Muelder, "Institutional Factors Affecting Unity and Disunity," *The Ecumenical Review*, January, 1956, p. 123.
2. See my book *Kyrkoliv och samhällsklass i Sverige omkring 1880* (Church Life and Social Class in Sweden Around 1880), with a summary in English (Stockholm: Svenska Kyrkans Diakonistyrelses Bokförlag, 1950).
3. Cf. T. Parsons, *Essays in Sociological Theory* (Glencoe, Ill.: The Free Press, 1949).
4. Muelder, *op. cit.*, pp. 116-118.
5. "Sociologien och kyrkan (Sociology and the Church)," *Svensk Teologisk Kvartalskrift*, 1953, pp. 93-107.
6. See my *Svensk kyrkogeografi* (Lund: Gleerups Förlag, 1957), pp. 167ff.
7. See, for example, F. A. Shippey, *Church Work in the City* (New York: Abingdon-Cokesbury Press, 1952).
8. K. Mannheim, *Man and Society in an Age of Reconstruction* (London: Routledge and Kegan Paul Ltd., 1940), pp. 274-275.
9. Cf. T. T. Segerstedt, *Social Control as Sociological Concept* (Uppsala Universitets Årsskrift, 1948:5, Uppsala, 1948), p. 43.
10. Augustinus, Ianuario, I:ii:2. *Bibliotek der Kirchenväter*, 29, pp. 209-210.
11. W. H. C. Frend, *The Donatist Church* (Oxford: Oxford University Press, 1952).
12. See my *The Five Dissenting Brethren* (Lunds Universitets Årsskrift NF: Avd. 1: Bd 51:nr 5), Lund 1955.
13. Cf. E. A. Asamoa, "The Christian Church and African Heritage," *The International Review of Missions*, 1955, pp. 292-301.
14. J. B. Holt, "Holiness Religion: Cultural Shock and Social Reorganization," *American Sociological Review*, 1940, pp. 740-747.
15. P. Selznick, "An Approach to a Theory of Bureaucracy," *American Sociological Review*, 1943, p. 50.

16. Selznick, *op. cit.*, p. 50.
17. Muelder, *op. cit.*, p. 121.
18. O. Tead, *The Art of Administration* (New York: McGraw-Hill Book Co., Inc., 1951).
19. P. M. Blau, *Bureaucracy in Modern Society* (New York: Random House, Inc., 1956).

BIBLIOGRAPHY FOR ESSAY 6

Blau, P. M., *Bureaucracy in Modern Society* (New York: Random House, Inc., 1956).

Mannheim, K., *Man and Society in an Age of Reconstruction* (London: Routledge and Kegan Paul Ltd., 1940).

Niebuhr, H. Richard, *The Social Sources of Denominationalism* (New York: Henry Holt & Co., 1929).

Parsons, T., *Essays in Sociological Theory* (Glencoe, Ill.: The Free Press, 1949).

Segerstedt, T. T., *Social Control as Sociological Concept* (Uppsala Universitets Årsskrift 1948:5). Uppsala, 1948.

Znaniecki, F., "Social Organization," *Twentieth Century Sociology*. G. D. Gurvitch and W. E. Moore, eds. (New York: The Philosophical Library, 1945).

7.

PROBLEMS OF
CHURCH BUREAUCRACY

Bureaucracy in church organization and institutional life has many of the same characteristics as bureaucracy in the political or economic order. Generally speaking, bureaucracy refers to the concentration of power in administrative bureaus or to a body of officials administering government bureaus. Government in this broad sense is, of course, not confined to political orders but is an aspect of all group life. In a pejorative sense bureaucracy implies excessive formalism, red tape, legalistic impersonality, jurisdictional rigidity, or pretentious officialdom. So expressed bureaucracy exhibits the vices of its virtues. In this essay both positive and negative traits are recognized. Throughout the discussion bureaucratic government is understood as a phenomenon common to such otherwise widely different institutions as modern business management, trade union organization, the military, educational enterprises, and the churches. Each of these develops a distinctive profile of organizational structure as the administrative patterns are shaped to serve the goals of these respective institutions. As the goals and values of a denomination tend to determine its administration, so the technical know-how required for its management tends to shape the contrived bureaus

by WALTER G. MUELDER

and the roles of its bureaucrats. When the churches become involved in the institutions of the ecumenical movement, they take the ambiguities and ambivalences of bureaucracy with them.

Characteristics of Bureaucracy

Most modern church bodies have well-developed bureaucratic agencies controlling such functions as publications, mission, pensions, education, social service, benevolences, investments, women's work, men's work, personnel, evangelism, church extension, and the like. It is the purpose of this essay to note some of the relationships which these administrative bureaus have to questions of unity and disunity. In so doing we must note the authority, power, and freedom of the agencies under review.

When we define the characteristics of bureaucracy we are able to note its similarities to, and differences from, such other characteristics of historic and current church life as hierarchy, patriarchalism, charismatic authority, sacerdotalism, collegial control, and polity. Since the Church is not only a theological institution having a dominical order but also a social institution, there are bound to be ambiguous and overlapping relationships between these theological characteristics and those sociologically described as bureaucracy. It will be apparent that bureaucratic structures sometimes assist and sometimes resist church mergers and other forms of church unity. Whatever their function a few common traits may be noted.

The rational character of bureaucracy is one of its notable traits. This trait stands in sharp contrast to what is often called charismatic control. As an "ideal type," charismatic power knows only inner determination and inner restraint, whereas bureaucratic organization of offices requires a rational form, including an ordered procedure of appointment and dismissal of leaders, a regulated career with graded advancement and income, expert training, functional and impersonal jurisdiction. The modern bureaucratic agency follows the principle of fixed areas of jurisdiction, the ordering of rules and administrative regulations, the formulation of official duties and functions, a prescribed procedure for arriving at decisions, and the establishment of standards for personnel and program. In addition there is generally a recognized hierarchy of graded authority, with a clearly defined system of super- and subordination, so that there can be, when needed, an appeal from a lower office to a higher authority. Max Weber observes that "the principle of hierarchical office authority is found in all bureaucratic structures; in state and ecclesiastical structures as well as in large party organizations and private enterprises. It does not matter for the character of bureaucracy whether its authority is called 'private' or 'public.' " [1] In addition to the traits above we may note the use of files and written documents, with the tendency to appeal to the written regulations and notations governing the use of the files. Office administration requires delimitation of responsibility and expert training for achieving the prescribed functions. The functionary is generally a full-time office holder. The office holder is devoted not so much to a person in his organization as to impersonal rules, functional roles, and defined tasks.

In describing an organization like a denomination or a council of churches an "outside" view may be very different from the "inside" view. From the "outside" view, if not from the "inside," a bishop, priest, and preacher today are no longer, as in the earliest Christian times, holders primarily of personal charisma. From the "inside" view the old theory of charismatic and divine authority is often asserted, but most religious leaders, especially those placed in charge of offices and agencies, serve a functionalized purpose. The church hallows the office which expresses a routinized charismatic grace or gift. Usually a bureaucrat is appointed, but sometimes he is elected, a procedure which modifies the way in which the office or the work of the administrator is legitimated. Tenure is extended, often for life, the incumbent having thereby a constant income.

There are obvious advantages in devising a bureaucracy. The most decisive reason for its development are its technical (rational) superiority over other forms of complex institutional organization. Max Weber's classical study of bureaucracy summarizes the advantages as follows: "precision, speed, unambiguity, knowledge of the files, continuity, discretion, unity, strict subordination, reduction of friction and of material and personal costs—these are raised to the optimum point in the strictly bureaucratic administration, and especially in its monocratic form." [2]

The pure type of bureaucracy is seldom found in a church. It is likely to be modified by elective rather than appointive processes, by collegial organization at several levels, and by the interposition of authority resting on a distinctively personal or theological basis, as for example, a bishop. Modifications of bureaucracy may be found both in the horizontal and the vertical relationships of offices and systems of control. Collegial bodies composed of specialized experts tend to modify the decision-making processes of the strict super- and subordination of ideal-type professional bureaucrats. In various churches there are colleges of cardinals, colleges of bishops, or councils of board secretaries with analogous collegial relationship to each other.

Bureaucracy and Hierarchy

Bureaucratic structure is generally related to a hierarchical order of social organizations. Hierarchy refers to a regular system of subordination and rank within the organization. However, bureaucracy and hierarchy are by no means identical, for hierarchy is not necessarily bureaucratic. Hierarchy may be monarchical, patriarchal, or sacerdotal without the well-developed bureaucratic traits described above. On the other hand, the two sometimes interpenetrate.

Modern organizations which may be both hierarchical and bureaucratic include the military, business, political government, and the Church. In military hierarchies there are ranks such as generals, major generals, colonels, and the like. In business there may be a president, vice-president, general manager, supervisor, and so on. In a church there may be pope, cardinal, archbishop, bishop, priest, and so forth. Bureaus help to serve their respective hierarchies and in so doing reflect deep organizational needs relating to goals, efficiency, and communication. They involve, of course, problems of basic relationship between the administrative peak and the people at the base of the institutional pyramid. Sometimes efforts are made to effect a circular hierarchical structure by requiring the election of the executives at the top by the people whom they will control. In all cases the role of the bureaus and bureaucrats in a hierarchical organization raises the question of authority and legitimation. As we shall see, this question is also raised by modern developments in churches whose polity is ostensibly nonhierarchical.

Before proceeding, a further word about hierarchy in the church should be added for clarification. There are several theories and forms of hierarchy among the churches and they are reflected in the administrative function and bureaucracies. We may note first that form in which hierarchy is classically sacerdotal as in the Roman Catholic Church. By sacerdotal is here meant "the existence in the Christian Church of a ministry consisting of certain persons set apart or ordained by authority of the Church to minister the things of God to their fellowmen, and to be the exclusive instruments in the divine covenant of sacramental graces." [3] A modified form of sacerdotalism is held in the Church of England. On the whole, the Reformation was against sacerdotalism in the sense of an assumption of authority on the part of the priesthood to undertake the whole charge and responsibility of the souls of the people. In the Roman Catholic Church the "sacred government" is usually referred to simply as the Hierarchy. The vertical hierarchical order is modified in practice and fact by the vestigial conciliar aspect of the Roman Catholic Church. The term vestigial is employed here because the conciliar conceptions and tendencies, though not wholly lost, have not exhibited in recent centuries any marked modification of papal power.

Hierarchy and bureaucracy have somewhat different relationships in an organization like The Methodist Church (U.S.A.). Here the constitution of the church is federal in form, the Annual

Conferences and the General Conference being composed of an equal number of laymen and ministers, and the authority being divided among Annual Conferences, Jurisdictional Conferences, and the General Conference. The bishops are organized into a Council at the top and into colleges at the Jurisdictional level. They are presbyters with considerable administrative authority and power, set apart as bishops for administrative purposes.

The most impressive bureaucratic structure of American Methodism is seen, however, in the general boards of the Church and in their counterparts in the Annual Conferences. Administration is exercised through boards and commissions in a highly involuted complexity. The General Boards are created by the General Conference. Their functions and basic control patterns are defined by the *Discipline*. Their executive secretaries tend to have long terms of office, though elected by the boards; and in these boards many of the program and the legislative proposals on basic policies in the denomination emerge. Ordained clergy are in most instances the executive secretaries of general boards, though their functions as bureaucrats have little directly to do with ordination into the ministry of Word and Sacrament.

Thus far we have noted the distinction between bureaucracy and hierarchy and also some of their interrelationships. We have also noted different forms of hierarchy, its sacerdotal form in the Roman Catholic Church, and its complete absence at the episcopal level in The Methodist Church, despite the effective administrative power of bishops. In either case no one is surprised to find a great and complex bureaucratic structure in a connectionally organized church body. But a question arises more often when bureaucratic organization is well developed in a denomination with a congregational polity as in the Baptist churches and in the United Church of Christ.

The organized Church as an institution is for Baptists not primary but secondary, that is, functional and instrumental. Ideally each local congregation concretely and socially embodies the universal spiritual Church as the Body of Christ in each community. "It is the declarative agency of that power but has no direct saving authority or power. It proclaims salvation and offers it to man in the name of the Redeemer; it does not definitively administer or withhold salvation." [4] Baptists thus find no place in or place for any hierarchy and no saving value in any sacrament, since the ministry is functional rather than organic. "We provide pastors ('elders,' including teachers and administrators) and deacons in each congregation under the lead of the Holy Spirit; and set them apart for these functions by prayer and quite generally by the laying-on of hands." [5]

Sociologically speaking we may note that strict congregational organization limited to a local community is ineffective for communicating the gospel in the modern world. Baptists have found it so and have worked out co-operation among the single units in associations, conventions, or councils. Theoretically Baptists have no "church courts" and no superior organization that has any authority or control over the "local Church" except in an advisory capacity, as an agency for voluntary co-operation.

Owing to modern social conditions, these functional and practical agencies have created an impressive bureaucratic structure. Effective power and authority of some kind is operative. It is one of the most interesting aspects of church bureaucracy to see how power and authority do function in such a free church tradition. The fact and necessity of bureaucracy raises some interesting dilemmas in the strong national conventions of Baptist churches.[6]

From the foregoing analysis it is evident that bureaucracy is bound to play an important role in questions of unity and disunity. Visible institutionalized organizations have to find a way to unite whether at the level of co-operation or at the level of organic merger. In either case the power, authority, relative autonomy, and mode of organization are significant factors. James Gustafson in his study of the union that has led to the United Church of Christ (described elsewhere in this volume) notes that as much planning, provision, and time must be envisaged for bureaucratic integration as for questions of doctrine, ministry, and polity. We have already noted that these groups of questions are not entirely separable.

At this point we must return to the distinction between an "outside" and an "inside" view of the Church and its related organizations. The "outside" view may be that of a public official or a sociologist, for example. Roswell P. Barnes notes that "outside" views may regard the churches as voluntary institutions organized for religious purposes, and recognized by the state as having a right to exist, to be incorporated to hold property and enter into contracts, like many other voluntary associations not organized for making financial profit. From this "outside" point of view the state may regulate some of the organizational features of churches without seeking to interfere in its internal life.[7]

From the "inside" a church has its basic nature predetermined for it as a creation of God in Christ. Here its theological self-understanding is essential. This self-definition conditions how it conceives its external organization and its bureaucratic agencies. They are seldom purely adjunct organizations uninfluenced as to power, authority, and freedom by the church's "inside" view.

But we must note that the "outside" view is not only that of a secular politician or scientist. A Baptist may take an "outside" view of what the Roman Catholic approvingly calls the Hierarchy. The Baptist's "inside" view of the Church predetermines his "outside" view of Roman Catholic sacerdotalism. From a Baptist point of view all sacerdotal developments in the history of the Church would be differently described than by a Roman Catholic scholar. What is theological and what is sociological receives not only a different interpretation but also a different definition.

Church Bureaucracy from the Perspective of Sociology

Students of bureaucracy have found that the problems of authority and legitimation offer a particular challenge. Two typological approaches, those by Max Weber and Joachim Wach, have proved fruitful. Weber's typological classification divided authority among three forms: charismatic, traditional, and rational-legalistic. Wach's typology of ecclesiastic bureaucracies embraces the maximum and the minimum type. We shall examine each of these in turn and note certain adaptations currently in vogue.

Charismatic authority roots in "charisma" understood as an *extra-ordinary* quality of a person, regardless of whether this quality is actual, alleged, or presumed. Hence charismatic authority refers to a rule over men, either external or internal, to which the governed submit because of their belief in the extraordinary quality of the specific person.[8] Traditionalism refers to the psychic attitude set for the habitual workaday life and to the belief in the everyday routine as an inviolable norm of conduct. Here domination rests upon piety for what actually, allegedly, or presumably has always existed.[9] Such traditionalist authority is evident in patriarchalism. In early religious history, including both the Old Testament and the New Testament, charismatic authority and traditionalist authority have divided dominant authoritative relationships between them. The bearers of charisma could occasionally integrate "new" laws and principles or oracles into the pattern of traditional sanctions.

With the development of religious institutions there has emerged a third type of authority, rational-legalistic. In the Occident this rational, juristic, formal or legal authority appeared at the side of the transmitted types. In legal authority, submission does not rest upon devotion to charismatically gifted persons nor upon tradition, but upon an impersonal bond to the generally defined and functional "duty of office." The official duty (together with jurisdictional competency) is fixed by "rationally established norms, by enactments, decrees, and regulations, in such a manner that the legitimacy of the authority becomes the legality of the general rule, which is purposely thought out, enacted, and announced with formal correctness." [10]

A church body may actually appeal concurrently to all three of these types of authority. Bureaucratic administration tends, however, to rest more typically on the rational-legalistic foundation of constituted authority than on the other bases. The various forms of hierarchy noted above reflect the mixture of these types. In the corporate authority of church bodies their hierocratic patterns of power are supported by their presumed or alleged monopoly in the bestowal of sacred values. As we shall note, these merge with the polar typologies of maximal or minimal constitutions.

Weber's fruitful typology has not been systematically used in studying voluntary associations. The types are primarily applicable to three forms of social system: an army, a business enterprise, and a totalitarian bureaucracy. Weber held that it applied explicitly to the Roman Catholic Church of modern times. Paul M. Harrison has attempted to show that Weber's categories can be fruitfully applied to a voluntary association like the American Baptist Convention if certain subcategories are added and developed. To the charismatic he would add quasi-charismatic; to traditional, mimetic-traditional; and to rational-legalistic, rational-pragmatic.[11]

Bureaucratic control has an important relationship to the way administration is legitimated. The nature of the claim to legitimacy determines, Weber held, the type of authority as well as the mode of social organization of the group. Conversely, we may add, the requirements of social organization may influence the type of authority and its legitimation, the later stages of an organization modifying in due course the operating system of bureaucratic authority, whether theoretically acknowledged or not. Bureaucracy and the theory of leadership thus have a close correlation.[12] A variety of factors bind staff members to their administrative superiors: affectual ties, custom, material interests, ideal motives, and the like. In addition, the element of legitimacy of authority is highly effective.

Summarizing then the Weber typology, we note that in the *charismatic* type of authority validation, the leader "is set apart from ordinary men and treated as endowed with supernatural, superhuman, or at least specifically exceptional powers or qualities." [13] In the traditional type of legitimacy the authority is based on the belief in "the sanctity of the order and the attendant powers of control as they have been handed down from the past, 'have always existed.' " [14] In the *rational-legal* legitimated bureaucracy there is a continuous organization of official functions bound by rules. The member lowest in the organizational structure accepts the statutory authority of the leader. Moreover, within the bureaucracy there is a specified area of competence related to functions delineated in a systematic division of labor; there is provision of necessary authority to carry these out; and there are appropriate compulsions and definite conditions for applying sanctions.

Weber's typology may be fruitfully supplemented by that of Joachim Wach who has observed the significance of *minimum* and *maximum* types of ecclesiastical organization. In passing we may note that these types bear some resemblance to the classical distinction made by Ernst Troeltsch between sect-type and church-type, a nomenclature hardly suited for classifying member denominations of the World Council of Churches. The *minimum* type, according to Wach, "is represented by a highly spiritual conception of fellowship with partial or total rejection of organization, law, and discipline within the body, insistence upon the principle of equality, and periodic returns to the ideals of its inception." The charismatic factor is obviously strong in such a body. Such bureaucracies as may develop in such bodies raise distinctive problems both internally between the administrators and the members, and externally in relationships to other bodies of Christians. We shall note below the usefulness of the categories "quasi-charismatic" and "mimetic-traditional" in analyzing such bodies.

At the polar extremity from the minimum type is the maximum type. It is "characterized in the first place by a more or less unqualified acceptance of tradition." This attitude is justified by the church both on historical grounds and as a matter of principle. A second characteristic "is the active encouragement of the development, standardization, and codification of expressions of religious experiences, which are deemed adequate." [15] Bureaucracies developed in the maximum type raise fewer internal problems of authority than those of the minimum type, but they present formidable obstacles in efforts at church mergers.

Among the Christian *minimum* groups Wach would place dissenting Protestant bodies like the Anabaptists, Baptists, Quakers, Mennonites, Disciples, spiritualists, mystics, and rationalists, including Unitarians and Universalists. Among the *maximum* groups he would place Eastern Orthodoxy, Roman and Oriental Catholicism, Anglicanism, and to a lesser degree Presbyterianism, Lutheranism, and Methodism.

In Roman Catholicism the administrative structure is highly authoritarian, but in Eastern Orthodoxy and Anglicanism the hierarchical authority tradition takes on a markedly conciliarist form. The administrative posture of the authoritarian monarchistic hierarch together with the bureaucratic substructure of cardinals and congregations, or national organizations, and of diocesan organizations is quite in contrast with the over-all posture of councils and diocesan structures among Orthodoxy and Anglicans. Among the minimalist groups the tendency is to stress the authority of the local congregation in opposition to a hierarchy or to any centralized or collective authority. In congregationalism today the rejection of hierarchy does not preclude a recognition of regional associations or a well-developed board structure to carry on associational, benevolent, educational, pension, and mission activities.

In bringing this section of our analysis to a close we must anticipate some of the problems which ecclesiastical bureaucracy poses for unity and disunity of the churches. We must always keep in mind the organic relationship between the church as *koinonia* and as a social organization. Taken as organized wholes many churches are incongruent with respect to each other. Though bureaucratic procedures and patterns have, as we shall note, their own autonomous tendencies, their own reality and stubborn givenness, they are influenced significantly by the parent body's historical development and its "inside view" of the church, its nature and mission. A.V.G. Allen emphasizes this point in saying that "the form which the government of the church assumes in any given age is not an accident, but must be regarded as an outward expression of a spirit working from within—the embodiment of an intelligible purpose. Just as a deep significance attaches to the variations of Christian doctrine, so also there is a meaning in the changes which have taken place in ecclesiastical organization." [16] The other side of the issue is, of course, that churches are socialized by the varying forces of their historical and social environments.

Problems Endemic to Bureaucratic Administration

Some bureaucrats have used the platform, power, status, or prestige of their office to promote ecumenical unity. The Stated Clerk of a General Assembly, the Secretary of a Council of Bishops, the President of a Convention can throw into the ecumenical conversation a great deal of energy and can involve others in processes toward mergers and church co-operation. Bureaucracies are often sufficiently removed from the day-by-day problems of local churches and diocesan units of denominational life that they can strike out in new directions. Denominational leaders who know each other well and who have learned trust and confidence through co-operative action are often far in advance of rank-and-file officials and church members in thinking through the theological and organizational problems of united church life. In this way bureaucrats can anticipate further benefits in efficiency, expertness, economy, and effectiveness when division is overcome and the walls of separation have toppled.

On the other hand, there are some problems which are endemic to bureaucratic administration and which must be confronted if they are to be overcome. The problems listed here are taken not only from studies of church life but from analyses of bureaucracy in a wide range of social institutions. For this very reason they are instructive. They cut across the typologies of Weber, Wach, and Harrison and reflect issues which are, in a sense, the vices which are the other side of organizational virtues, the dysfunctional aspects of otherwise functional attributes. Function and dysfunction are always, of course, relative to particular social contexts in concrete historical situations.

• Bureaus and bureaucrats have a tendency to protect the interests assigned to them in their terms of reference. In their representative capacities church bureaucrats are often in conflict with each other. This roots in the drive for institutional self-preservation. The protective tendency may be partial, that is, by one bureau or office, or total, by a denomination as a whole. Max Weber observes: "Once it is fully established, bureaucracy is among those social structures which are hardest to destroy." [17]

• Bureaucracies tend not to take a whole view of problems but only of a limited set of interests and goals. Their efficiency often resides in the specificity of the tasks assigned. The official is entrusted with specialized tasks and normally the mechanism cannot be put in motion or arrested by him, but only from the very top. Though bureaucracy generates and commands great power, subordinate units may lack freedom of motion and experience general impotence. Sometimes power is so organized that few in an organization have any responsible comprehensive overview. Yet, commitment to church unity requires this. Operational agency roles may overrule inclusive Christian vocation. Missions may thwart mission and the unit may block unity.

• Bureaus tend toward rigid structures and attitudes because of the rules and regulations which legitimate them and which are used for rational effectiveness. They are subject to "the iron law of oligarchy," rule by the powerful few. Bureaucratic organization is technically a highly developed means of power in the hands of the man or men who control it or its units.

Organizational success tends to become the criterion of institutional life, and this success is then emulated. Often the criteria of measuring success become quantitative. Quantitative administrative development makes for quantitative standards of success. The impersonal element in bureaucracy in contrast to charismatic leadership makes for objective and calculable rules and for the calculability of results.

• Bureaus encourage introversion and complete self-absorption in institutional life. Administrators tend to promote and cultivate support for their own unit in the division of labor. Thus, means become ends in themselves.

• Bureaus have a tendency toward "empire building," that is, developing their agencies to include activities not originally or necessarily assigned to them. Thus, they tend to become the expanding centers of power rather than remaining the servants among other servants with diverse tasks.

• Bureaus are inclined to resist piecemeal attrition by other bureaus or by more general authorities in an organization. Jurisdictional lines are carefully guarded. Jurisdictional or agency conflict is frequent.

• Bureaucrats tend not to communicate significantly with bureaucrats in other offices or aspects of an organization. As bureaucracy perfects communication in one dimension, it inhibits it in other dimensions. Church leaders may use the limitations of authorization as an excuse for noncommunication across denominational lines. For example, they may hold that churches should not do those things together which they are able to do separately. On the other hand, they may not know how to behave apart from specific authorization.

• Various bureaus tend to develop ideologies appropriate to their own limited goals and thus to splinter the philosophy of the organization as a whole into competing fragments of truth. Sometimes these are ideologies of loyalty to the group within which one is at work.

• The group processes of large bureaucracies encourage the personality traits of the "organization man." Committee decisions protect personal indecision, and they conceal and inhibit the emergence of vigorous personal dissent and independence of judgment. Individuals tend to hide behind board actions. In the words of William H. Whyte, Jr., "Ideas come from the group, not from the individual." When the organization develops in this way the processes of control may vary considerably from that envisaged in strict vertical control or in an oligarchy.

General Bureaucratic Problems in Church Union Processes

As part of the "organizational revolution" of modern times church bureaucracies develop two distinct sides, one which they present to their constituencies and one which they present to outsiders. From the foregoing analyses we can appreciate more fully the "two-sidedness of organizations," especially in the case of the churches as they relate to church union processes. Every organization is an expression of solidarity within the organized group and an expression of lesser solidarity (or complete lack of it) with those outside the group. Bureaucracy by definition is the administration of a complex organization for the enhancement of its values and the achievement of its goals. Many of the problems which confront church unity arise from the two-sidedness of organizations. How can the churches manifest their inclusive unity in Christ? How can the churches command the effective loyalty, devotion, and fellowship of their members, without violating the inclusive unity of Christ? What are the problems which bureaucracy poses with respect to processes of exclusion and inclusion in the ecumenical movement? Seven of these can be isolated for further analysis and study:

- Administrative church bodies with long histories, procedures laden with custom, and incongruent with respect to each other in range of goals and responsibilities, offer formidable problems in negotiating mergers.[18] There is often a blindness to needed change, a trained incapacity to sense new needs, inadequate flexibility in the adaptation of skills to changing conditions, occupational psychoses whereby personnel develop special preferences, antipathies, discriminations, and emphases not adapted to social reality, a fixation on goals and objectives however obsolescent, an excessive conformity to prescribed patterns which have become routinized, and a transference of sentiments and motivations from the aims of the organization to the particular details of behavior required by rules and rubrics.[19]

- When churches are to be integrated the primary question is likely to be not what the mind of Christ means for the structure of administration, nor what pattern of administration immediately corresponds to the theoretical political organization of the church, but how to allocate effectively the available personnel and resources in order to expedite certain tasks to which the churches are committed. Since they have ongoing programs, the churches are reluctant to change the machinery which these programs have required for implementation. There is likely to be absence of any euphoria or enthusiasm about a projected church union, because the staffs of the respective denominations are always deeply involved in their given commitments. The process of unification may therefore be quite bothersome to these staffs.

- The two typical clusters of problems indicated in the paragraphs above have led some organizations to attempt loose federal types of mergers rather than to create completely new institutions. The National Council of Churches of Christ in the U.S.A. became a kind of loose ecclesiastical cartel for the member councils that entered into it; there was relatively little organic fusion. The federal and conciliar solutions are not so potent when denominations merge or otherwise unite, but compromises in agency structure and control are likely to be pragmatically arrived at rather than based on a redefinition of basic polity growing out of theological reappraisal.

- Bureaucratic organization intensifies the contrasting differences among denominations with respect to the sense of mission, the style of life, and the focus of program. Moreover, class status is reflected in the operations of an administrative staff. Churches differ greatly in all these factors. The amount of energy and concern which denominations devote to the world mission of the Church varies considerably and is reflected in the size and scope of mission board activity. In some cases the boards are relatively autonomous; in other cases they are controlled directly by the denomination. Analogous problems arise with respect to education, social action, pensions, and so on.

- There is always an acute problem of what to do with the

excess personnel in specified areas of competence and status during the period after the merger. The key personalities in a staff are focal points for the resolution of difficulties in effecting union or greater unity. Because of these problems of handling key personnel, a transitional period may be employed for balancing the representation and perhaps for assigning quotas among the varying interests. The problem of reducing key personnel may be complicated by the fact that different types of hierarchical authority have been dominant in the negotiating churches.

• Administrative staffs vary widely in the amount of freedom that they have as professionals and the manner in which their authority is validated. Where bureaucratic processes are set by denominational rules and where these procedures affect the fundamental goals of the respective bodies, major difficulties are bound to be experienced. Whatever the best arrangements of polity may be, it is evident that the practical problems of integrating bureaucracies accentuate the more basic issues of freedom and authority.

• The concluding problem is the need to allow adequate time and planning not only for the resolution of questions of faith and order in the dimension of doctrine and polity, but also for other institutional processes. Many of the details of administration and polity are subject to processes and procedures as characteristic of politics and the market place as they are of the Church and they are governed not only by theological convictions and traditions but by cultural factors which are deeply intertwined with them.

Church Bureaucracy and Councils of Churches

There are some significant interrelationships between the bureaucratic (including other administrative) structures in denominations and the conciliar movement in church co-operation. Where there are many different types of denominations in a given area (local, state, national, global), the practical step toward unity is generally to form a council of churches. The council provides for the maximum autonomy of the various church bureaucracies and for the least risk to denominational life while patterns of co-operation and ecumenicity are being explored and formed. Obvious practical areas of co-operation can be developed on a piecemeal basis, while denominational bureaucracies are left largely intact. In their early stages councils of churches are, of course, weaker than their constituent members. Council officials have sometimes been little more than errand boys for denominational executives. Under these circumstances a great deal of strain may exist between denominational bureaucrats and strong council executives.

As a council of churches grows it develops its own specializations and bureaucratic structure. The churches participating in the new conciliar patterns begin to modify their practices. Just as the pluralistic bureaus of the churches shape the institutional growth of the councils in the first instances, so the conciliar process in time modifies the bureaucratic structure and shape of the churches.

Comity committees, for example, develop professional standards of surveying community needs which influence the procedures of research and strategy in the participating denominations. Departments of institutional chaplaincy tend to standardize, along with hospital chaplaincy associations and theological seminaries, the way clinical training is conducted for most churches. Other forms of pioneering or specialized ministries tend to be basically patterned by conciliar institutions. Radio, television, journalism, the preparation of church school materials, approaches to government, church lobbying, strategies of social work, policies on church-state questions in education and welfare—these are a few of the areas in which bureaucratic development in ecumenical bodies tends to modify and make more uniform the corresponding boards and commissions of the denominations. All this can be and is done without radically challenging the doctrinal distinctiveness or the theological foundations of the polity of churches.[20]

These observations do not ignore the fact that the several bureaus of a church may vary a great deal from each other in theological emphasis. They may even fail doctrinally to communicate with each other. Departments in church evangelism both in denominations and in councils of churches may differ a great deal in theological orientation from those developed to handle chaplaincies, social work, or legislative action in the political and economic field. The Bible Society leaders both denominationally and interdenominationally may have different theological emphases from the religious education personnel. In the U.S.A., at least, it must be recognized that the specialized ministries in a number of churches and their counterparts in councils of churches tend to socialize theological and ethical emphases in distinctive ways. There is, therefore, often a different theological climate in the various bureaus of a large complex denomination or an interdenominational body. Such distinctiveness does not rule out a great deal of difference from one denomination to another as well. Sub-bureaucracies form in-group patterns of thought and action which shape and determine conflict within the power struggles of denominations and across denominational lines.

These tendencies stand in contrast to a force which has been called a "lay doctrine of equivalence." This means that the laity who migrate a great deal from one denomination to another look upon the functional or practical side of church life more than they do upon the theological uniqueness of a local church. Functional effectiveness is what they favor. They are impatient with competition on "nonessentials." "Success" or "practical efficiency" is what seems important to them.

Bureaucratic successes of co-operative bodies may tend to produce an indifference toward advanced ecumenical unity, since laymen are often satisfied with the practical level of unity in its external manifestations which co-operation has expressed. The resistance to self-criticism and radical revision which any denominational bureaucracy exhibits is likely to have its analogue in all levels of conciliar ecumenism as well. If the goal is evangelism, seen simply as establishing churches for the unchurched, an inter-denominational board may respond to the growing interchange-ability of church membership with an indifference to denomina-tional claims. The erosion of allegiances and the modification of loyalties found in extensive interdenominational migration pro-vides fertile soil for the growth of interdenominational approaches to membership evangelism.

Several additional tendencies should also be noted in the rela-tionships of bureaucracy to church unity. Professor Lee has shown how certain drives toward institutional strength in church mergers parallel those which we have already recognized above. He says: "In view of the organizational revolution characterizing present-day society, and in order to exercise significant power, the pressure toward centralization and organizational co-ordination operates as a contributing source of organic merger. As with organized bureaucracies in other areas of life, so churches are caught up in the inherent logic of established boards and agencies to expand in outreach, to solidify their gains, to multiply their functions, and to perpetuate themselves. In addition, the increas-ing demand for technical services calls for specialized and tech-nically trained personnel, for which the supply is hardly adequate. Such organizational pressures often function covertly, but remain a reality underlying many mergers." [21] Bureaucracy obviously persists under ecumenical auspices.

Bureaucracy presents problems to the ecumenical movement through the tendency of the various denominational adminis-trators to predominate numerically at ecumenical assemblies. The *Christian Century* has observed: "The procedure now being fol-lowed is not propitious for the World Council of Churches, which cannot maintain its leadership unless it can find a way to summon to its assemblies the best minds of Christendom. Not all of these are found in the ranks of denominational administrators, who tend to outnumber all other categories among the delegates who have been chosen to date. As usual, lay men and women, pastors of local churches, college, university and seminary teachers, are conspicuous by their absence. As usual too, the delegations are hoary with age." [22]

A chief purpose of studies of institutional factors is to help churches and church leaders to be more self-aware of the relationship between doctrinal and nondoctrinal aspects of church unity and disunity. Such awareness should help to release critical thought and creative response in dialogues and negotiations within the ecumenical movement. This essay on bureaucracy, as part of an analysis of institutionalism, should function, therefore, as a counterfactor to some of the main tendencies of bureaucracy especially as they affect leadership. Bureaucracy's virtues in organizational devices readily become its vices in the personality traits it develops in its leaders. At the very moments when flexibility, originality, and creativity are most needed to meet the challenges of a new ecumenical situation, the highly disciplined bureaucrat may exhibit what Veblen called a "trained incapacity" to see what needs most to be seen and to do what needs most to be done. As one writer puts it, "people may be unfitted by being fit in an unfit fitness." In an age when the ecumenical movement has made all the participating agencies and institutions obsolescent, self-awareness about bureaucracy may help to overcome some of the "unfit fitness" of the churches' organizational life and the bureaucratic professional deformation of its leadership. Denominational fitness may mean ecumenical unfitness, and denominational efficiency may mean ecumenical inefficiency. But it must also be noted that the organizational instruments contrived to serve the unity and mission of the churches up to the present may also have developed characteristics which inhibit the fullest possible manifestation of the unity, witness, and service of the Church.

NOTES FOR ESSAY 7

1. Max Weber, *Wirtschaft und Gesellschaft*, Teil III, Kap. 6, in *From Max Weber* (New York: Oxford University Press, 1946), p. 197.

2. *Ibid.*, p. 214.
3. R. M. Woolley, article, "Sacerdotalism," *Encyclopaedia of Religion and Ethics.*
4. W. O. Carver, "Baptist Churches," in R. N. Flew, ed., *The Nature of the Church* (London: SCM Press; New York: Harper & Brothers, 1952), p. 289.
5. *Ibid.*, p. 290.
6. See Paul M. Harrison, *Authority and Power in the Free Church Tradition* (Princeton: Princeton University Press, 1959).
7. Roswell P. Barnes, *Under Orders* (Garden City: Doubleday & Co., Inc., 1961), pp. 15-16.
8. Max Weber, "The Social Psychology of the World Religions," in Gerth and Mills, *From Max Weber*, p. 295.
9. *Ibid.*, p. 296.
10. *Ibid.*, p. 299.
11. Paul M. Harrison, "Weber's Categories of Authority and Voluntary Associations," *American Sociological Review*, 25 (April, 1950), p. 233.
12. Max Weber, *The Theory of Social and Economic Organization*, tr. by A. M. Henderson and Talcott Parsons (New York: Oxford University Press, 1947), pp. 324-385.
13. *Op. cit.*, pp. 330, 333.
14. *Ibid.*, p. 341.
15. Joachim Wach, *Sociology of Religion*, pp. 145-146.
16. A. V. G. Allen, *Christian Institutions* (Edinburgh: T. & T. Clark; New York: Charles Scribner's Sons, International Theological Library, 1897), p. 5.
17. Max Weber, *op. cit.*, p. 228.
18. The following paragraphs emphasize and partly draw on, occasionally verbatim, James M. Gustafson's essay in the present volume. See also World Council of Churches Commission on Faith and Order, *The Old and the New in the Church* (1961). W. G. Muelder, "Institutional Factors Affecting Unity and Disunity," *Ecumenical Review* (January, 1956), p. 110. The work by Robert K. Merton, *Social Theory and Social Research* (Glencoe, Ill.: The Free Press, 1949) is instructive here. See also the studies by K. Mannheim, C. Kluckhohn, O. H. Mowrer, and Burleigh Gardner.
19. Robert K. Merton, "Bureaucratic Structure and Personality," in C. Kluckhohn and Henry A. Murray, eds., *Personality in Nature, Society, and Culture* (New York: Alfred A. Knopf, Inc., 1956), pp. 376-385.
20. See Robert Lee, *The Social Sources of Church Unity*, p. 82.
21. *Op. cit.*, p. 105.
22. Editorial, *The Christian Century* (July 13, 1960).

BIBLIOGRAPHY FOR ESSAY 7

Gerth, H. H., and Mills, C. Wright, *From Max Weber* (New York: Oxford University Press, 1946; London: Routledge and Kegan Paul Ltd., 1948).

Harrison, Paul M., *Authority and Power in the Free Church Tradition* (Princeton: Princeton University Press, 1959).

Kluckhohn, C., and Murray, Henry A., eds., "Bureaucratic Structure and Personality," in *Personality in Nature, Society, and Culture* (New York: Alfred A. Knopf, Inc., 1956).

Lee, Robert, *The Social Sources of Church Unity* (New York: Abingdon Press, 1960).

Merton, Robert K., *Social Theory and Social Structure* (Glencoe, Ill.: The Free Press, 1957).

Wach, Joachim, *Sociology of Religion* (Chicago: University of Chicago Press, 1944).

Weber, Max, *The Theory of Social and Economic Organization*, tr. by A. M. Henderson and Talcott Parsons (New York: Oxford University Press, 1947).

Whyte, William H., *The Organization Man* (New York: Simon and Schuster, Inc., 1956).

PART II
Case Studies

8.
THE CANADIAN CHURCH
UNION, 1925

On June 10, 1925, twenty-one years after the first official joint meeting to discuss organic union, the Methodists, many Presbyterians, and the Congregationalists came together to form the United Church of Canada. By this union was established the largest Protestant denomination in Canada, numbering in the 1931 census, 2,017,375 followers, and in 1951, 2,867,271 or 20.5 per cent of the population.

Early Glimpses of Nontheological Factors

Even the most sketchy history of the union movement provides hints of significant nontheological factors, beginning as early as 1899 when the General Assembly of the Presbyterian Church, recognizing the vast problems of ministering to sparse populations, officially stated its approval of co-operation with other churches in *new* fields. Again when official union proposals were launched in 1902, at the quadrennial gathering of The Methodist Church held in Winnipeg, a local editor commented that "the Methodists would discover that their future in Canada was linked up with their future in the western provinces." [1] Also Dr. Car-

by W. E. MANN

men, the General Superintendent, in the opening address stressed the lack of men for new fields and the need to find more effective and economical ways of placing ministers on mission fields. And Dr. Bryce, a Presbyterian fraternal delegate to the conference, emphasized the many things the two churches had in common, among them a common form of church government, the common experience of opposition to the Anglican Clergy Reserves in Ontario, and a somewhat similar stand on the prohibition of alcoholic beverages. Dr. Patrick, Principal of (the Presbyterian) Manitoba College, after noting that "the history of the Canadian Church had been a history of unions and consolidations," and spontaneously appealing for organic unity, concluded by asking, "Has not the time come for further advance into a great national church?" A day or two later, the Conference passed a memorable declaration in favor of church union among the Protestant Churches in Canada, and then proceeded to invite the Congregational and Presbyterian Churches to begin negotiations." [2] The following resolution was passed unanimously:

> While the conference declares itself in favor of a measure of organic unity wide enough to embrace all the evangelical denominations in Canada, and regrets that hitherto all efforts and negotiations have failed to result in the formulation of such a comprehensive scheme, so that the outlook for it at present does not seem practicable; yet inasmuch as the problem of the unification of several of these denominations appears to present much less serious obstacles, since *their relations are already marked by a great degree of spiritual unity*, and they have already become closely assimilated in standards and ideals of church life, forms of worship and ecclesiastical polity;
>
> And since further, the present conditions of our country and those in the immediate prospect, demand the most careful economy of the resources of the leading and aggressive evangelical denominations both in ministers and money, in order to overtake the religious needs of the people pouring

into our new settlements, which economy seems impossible without further organic unity or its equivalent;

This general Conference is of the opinion that the time is opportune for a ... movement ... aiming at the practical organic unity of these denominations already led by Providence into such close fraternal relations.[3]

Thus as early as 1902 some significant institutional influences were being noted.

The Negotiations Period, 1904-1925

Subsequent developments clarified both the difficulties of union and the sociological forces active in the general ecclesiastical situation. In 1904 both the Congregationalists and Presbyterians appointed Committees to study a Basis of Union and meetings were held annually with the Methodists in a Joint Committee. Although they were invited in a general way, two churches—the Baptists and Anglicans—never took part in the negotiations. Whereas "The Regular and Free Baptists in the Maritimes had been united in a Convention in 1906 and the new body expressed a willingness to confer on a federal union," [4] the Baptist Convention of Ontario and Quebec after appointing a committee which met briefly with the Joint Committee drew up a statement denying "that organic union of all Christians is an essential condition of Christian unity." They rejected the essential value of forms, rites, and ceremonies—infant baptism, in particular—and declared their belief in their special mission within Christendom. This response discouraged negotiations with the Maritime convention and ended matters. In 1908 the Anglicans took up the question at their General Synod, and there authorized the appointment of a committee, but demanded that it adhere to the requirements of the Lambeth Quadrilateral. The Joint Committee for their part found the necessity of accepting episcopacy a barrier to serious negotiations, but said the door was open if ever this stipulation were made less rigorous. After 1921, when the Anglican General Synod accepted the modified version of the 1920 Lambeth statement on the ministry, with certain reservations regarding preaching and the episcopacy, the Primate invited the Methodists and Presbyterians to a conference, but formal negotiations never materialized before 1925.

Nontheological factors doubtless played an important role in depressing Anglican and Baptist interest in early union proposals. For instance, Anglican congregations were often separated from Methodists by a higher social standing, especially in central Canada. Their congregational life was also strongly tradition bound and their clergy largely recruited at this time from the Old Country. Many nonconformist ministers were both Canadian born and trained, and thus shared a much different viewpoint upon their church and ministry. Such social factors thus served to cut the Anglican church, still rigorously divided into over twenty dioceses and preserving a strong link with Britain, from serious negotiations with the Methodists and to a lesser extent with the Presbyterians. The Baptists, on the other hand, were more "working-class" in their following and also much less bureaucratic in their institutional arrangements than either the Methodists or the Presbyterians.

At an early stage a Presbyterian minority showed reluctance to go beyond increased co-operation on Home Mission Fields, but Methodist enthusiasm for union proposals grew quickly, resulting in 1911 in an overwhelmingly favorable vote. (Among members over 18 years of age, 150,941 voted for union and 25,357 against it.) At the same time Presbyterian opposition in the General Assembly gradually grew and hardened. In 1910, a vote of the Assembly was taken which strongly favored the Basis of Union, and a resolution was then passed designed to seek initially a vote of the presbyteries rather than of the whole membership. This move aroused certain feelings of injustice and led to organized opposition, especially since it repudiated various earlier statements by "unionist" leaders that no action would be taken without full support. Then, the whole membership was polled, late in 1911, and the results showed 113,000 members and 37,175 adherents in favor, and 50,753 members besides 14,174 adherents opposed to union. In 1913, undeterred by the large dissenting vote, "the majority of the Assembly, urged on by 'unionist' leaders, resolved to press forward." [5] In reaction, a group of delegates formed "The General Committee of the Organization for the Preservation and Continuation of the Presbyterian Church in Canada," which shortly numbered 170 ministers and more than five hundred leading laymen.[6] A Women's League was soon organized and eventually became very influential. At the 1914 Assembly the "continuing Presbyterian group" met separately between the regular sessions, and the split became formally organized. A new vote of the membership was taken in 1915, and though the ayes made slight gains, the nays increased by 23,000 member and almost 6,000 adherent votes.

In 1916 by a large majority the General Assembly decided to proceed to union. This decision aroused further resentment and the continuing group held "a nationwide convocation and reorganized their defence as 'The Presbyterian Church Association.'" [7] Controversy was intense for a year until a truce in negotiations was called for the duration of the war. When in 1921 the Assembly again voted for union by an 80 per cent majority, the Presbyterian Association was revived and in 1923 became fully institutionalized, hiring an executive secretary, a general organizer, and four "lieutenants." The Association began a fiery pamphlet war, organized its supporters in every synod, presbytery, and congregation and even placed large advertisements in newspapers. Women supporters made house-to-house canvasses, and a card-signing campaign won 114,000 signatures. In reaction, the "unionists" appointed a bureau of publicity; and in 1923 this became "merged in a bureau of literature, information and public meetings of the Joint Committee, and the literature was issued not alone in the name of the Presbyterian Church but of all three churches." [8] Controversy became intense and bitter, and split congregation after congregation. A final vote of the Presbyterians was taken in 1923, but "because of the disputes, later settled or never settled ... it is difficult to offer an adequate summary." [9]

According to Silcox, "if one were to add together the total votes by ballot, it would result in 122,966 (52 per cent) to 114,298 (48 per cent) in favor of Union." [10] Dr. E. Scott, a Presbyterian writer, asserts the vote was 113,000 for and 114,000 against.[11] Other ways of calculating the results including congregations voting by resolution, or entering union by default, give the "unionist" 178,630.[12] In terms of congregations, "one-fourth of all those in self-sustaining charges did not enter the Union ... while more than nine-tenths of all aid-receiving churches [did]." [13] The final step was the passage of legislation in both Canada's Federal House of Commons and in provincial legislatures to set up the new church. This also involved a fierce struggle and left its own legacy of bitterness.

Historical Influences Prior to 1902

Certain ecclesiastical developments prior to 1902 played a significant part in readying the ground for union discussions. For instance, a series of unions within the Methodist and Presbyterian churches in both the Maritimes and Ontario throughout the nineteenth century established the practicality of union efforts and gave the term "Church Union" much popularity. "A widely read pamphlet by Dr. W. T. Gunn showed that the Presbyterian Church was itself the result of nine, the Methodist Church the result of eight, and the Congregational of four [unions]." [14] It seems clear, as Silcox says, that "every successful consolidation of religious groups in the same denominational family stimulated interest in, and hope for, a larger union of all Protestantism.... If nothing succeeds like success, nothing promoted church union in Canada like the actual achievement of various unions of churches." [15] Thus a tradition of successful union which undercut the more rigid claims of denominationalism and demonstrated to the lay public the effectiveness of union was a not insignificant factor in paving the way for the merger in 1925.

The popularity of church union before 1902 is further attested by the existence of a somewhat amorphous church union movement. Thus, in 1901, "there were already 267 union churches in Canada and 554 union Sunday Schools. Most of these were ... in Ontario. These union enterprises had nothing whatever to do with the local union churches ... afterward developed especially in the West." [16] Also a number of societies and associations formed in the nineteenth century fostered co-operative endeavors between Protestants and developed institutionalized relationships of trust and mutual co-operation; among these were the Bible and Tract Societies, Sabbath and Sunday School Associations, numerous temperance movements as well as Christian Endeavor and the Evangelical Alliance. The last, active after 1874, attracted some of the best minds in the evangelical churches and "had hearty support from the evangelical or low church element in the Church of England, as well as from the Presbyterian, Methodist, Baptist, and Congregational denominations." [17] After 1902, as church union took the limelight, this movement languished.

Protestant churches also were early united on issues of moral and social reform. Thus, for Sunday observance, there was formed in 1888, the Lord's Day Alliance, which appointed its own field secretary in 1899. In the university field, the federation of denominational colleges in 1887 in the University of Toronto was a signal step in co-operative intellectual activity. "This had not a little to do with preparing the way for church union, and it is not without significance that one of the recognized leaders in the church union Movement, among the Presbyterians, was Sir Robert Falconer, the president of the university." [18]

Several other ecclesiastical developments in the pre-1902 period are worthy of mention. Beginning in the late 1860's the main Protestant denominations began the practice of sending fraternal delegates to the annual meetings of the other churches. These clergy habitually stressed points of agreement and occasionally made actual suggestions regarding church union. "Their visits dramatized the get together movement; their impact ... over a period of years [was] considerable." [19] They may be credited with leading to unofficial Presbyterian-Congregational discussions in 1893 and to the appointment of standing committees on union.

These beginnings were abortive, as were discussions in 1886 on co-operation between Presbyterians and Methodists in sparsely settled areas, and a resolution passed in the same year by the Anglican House of Bishops appointing a committee to conduct union discussions with other denominations. Nonetheless, such procedures and official expressions of interest doubtless helped to ease the way for serious deliberations later. It is also significant that in 1898 and again in 1902, two specific Church Union societies were founded in Eastern Canada, uniting clergy and laity from most of the Protestant communions.

Consideration of the self-images brought by the three denominations to the union discussion in 1902 will help to focus certain historical forces already referred to and their interaction with pertinent theological concepts. The Congregationalist self-image was dominated by a democratic, individualistic, and liberal orientation, a concern for lay opinion and for Congregational smallness *vis-à-vis* other Canadian Protestant groups and especially for its proportionately numerical decline within the Canadian population. (In 1871, they represented .63 per cent of the total population, in 1921 only .35 per cent.) Few clergy could see it contributing much by itself to the Canadian scene, but many saw union as providing an opportunity to belong to a big influential church as well as a way out of pressing financial problems.[20]

In the Methodist self-image a vigorous concern for the world's salvation, an emphasis upon practical adjustment to the needs of the missionary situation, and a certain flexibility of approach, figured prominently. Historical tradition and rigid theological or ceremonial formulations had little weight. Among the clergy, such ideas as denominational and missionary advance, adjustment to local needs, sensitivity to public and world opinion were prominent in the self-image. Finally, an acceptance of congregational and ministerial obedience under the district superintendent along with the four-year clergy rotation system is perhaps worthy of mention.

Certain elements in the Presbyterian self-image doubtless contributed to their split over union. Among these are a history of schismatic hold-outs exemplified by the Church of Scotland and the Free Church, a pride in resistance to Erastian pressures as well as in traditions of democratic liberty and opposition to officialdom. In addition, a certain accent upon creeds and theological dogma institutionalized in the Westminster Confession and upon legal and procedural order formalized in church courts was important. An emphasis upon individualistic thinking and a relatively high social status within the Canadian community, especially in central Canada, were also not insignificant. In sum, Presbyterianism constituted perhaps the most influential Protestant denomination in the Dominion—influential in scholarship, in general culture, in numbers, in the wealth and success of the members ... "such was their assured position and they faced the future hopefully." [21] Finally among the clergy, theological erudition and rigidity, respect for order and established precedent, and pride in Presbyterian tradition loomed large.

In addition to various elements in Presbyterian history and self-image which have already been noted, there were other ethnic, social, and economic factors which contributed to opposition to union. The great majority of Presbyterians were of Scottish origin. Social or class alignments in local communities often went along with jealousies or rivalries between Presbyterians and Methodists. Distrust of the English who dominated Methodism in Canada, and love for Scottish independence were sentiments which doubtless played a significant role in the anti-union decisions of many Presbyterians. A certain apprehension of clerical hierarchy among the clergy, specifically the powers of the district superintendent, may be noted. Coincident with growing Presbyterian votes against union was an increasing regionalism in the Canadian economy. "By 1913, the open frontier had disappeared" [22] and the postwar period saw a "decline in the unifying influence of national policies and growing diversity of regional interest." [23] This economic trend was not unrelated to the fact that opposition to union was slight on the prairies, fairly weak in the Maritimes, and strongest in Central Canada. The Ontario situation was doubtless associated with the high social status of many Presbyterian congregations in Central Canada. Also of significance was the Presbyterian democratic, antihierarchical ethos. It was the disregard of this tendency by the General Assembly in 1913, after the substantial anti-union vote of 1911, which led to the beginnings of the continuing Presbyterian movement. Subsequent actions of the General Assembly, indicating a similar insensitivity, led to the institutionalization of the protest group, the demand for a final vote (1923) and the eventual split in 1925.[24]

Unitive Factors Within the Churches, 1902-1925

We may now proceed to examine the dynamic institutional forces which, in spite of substantial Presbyterian opposition, swept the church union movement to its consummation. These consisted in the main of two developments, originally distinctive, which converged and produced, before 1925, over 3,000 "union" congregations in 1245 charges in both Western Canada and Ontario. Beginning in 1908, and significantly in Saskatchewan, there emerged independent union churches, founding themselves upon the Basis of Union worked out by the Joint Committee in that same year. In 1912, when the Presbyterian General Assembly decided to postpone action "with a view to securing greater unanimity, a strong impetus was given to the formation of additional independent unions." [25] Concerned about the rapid growth of this spontaneous movement, the negotiating churches made representations in 1913 with the result that "representatives of the Local Union Churches agreed not to have an organizing secretary nor to go into any community for the purpose of stimulating the formation of a Union Church, nor to meet together at intervals for the purpose of discussing matters of mutual interest to themselves." [26] This attempt to forestall expansion subsequently failed, for provincial gatherings of union church representatives began in 1916, three presbyteries were formed, and three organizers appointed. These actions led, after considerable debate, to the appointment of an Advisory Council from the negotiating churches,

180

which advised on tenure of property, status of ministers, and the like. The unofficial function of this Council was to delay the growth and independent institutionalization of these union congregations, pending union. "There was apparently some talk of an independent church in the West, and this was apparently what the denominational leaders . . . really feared." [27] In 1919, the General Council of these independent unions hired a salaried field secretary. By 1921, there were fifty to seventy [28] of these independent congregations, and in this year, their General Council secured official representation on the Joint Union Committee.

The second development began in 1911 when the Home Mission Committees of the two main churches reached an agreement not to compete in new territory, nor to plant new congregations within six miles of each other. "From that date, Presbyterians in some places became Methodists and Methodists in some places became Presbyterians." [29] This was an autocratic type of plan which meant, in effect, that the religious affiliation of many Westerners was decided according to the railway stations. As one church historian points out, "Such a plan was made possible and endurable only by the hope of Church Union." [30]

Following the decision of the 1917 Presbyterian Assembly to consummate union "sometime"—while calling a truce as to dates—the Joint Committee approved a suggested plan for local church unions. This plan envisaged the affiliation of local union congregations with one or another of the negotiating churches. This proposal failed to win support, and numerous congregations began to apply for double affiliations, that is, with each church. "In 1921 the national bodies formally approved the method of single or *double* affiliation." [31] By 1925 the number of double affiliated congregations came to considerably outnumber the independent ones. Silcox points out that "the progress of these [independent] churches had been definitely checked by the promotion of the double and triple affiliation scheme on the part of the denominational leaders." [32] By 1923 there were about 170 of these affiliated congregations (140 of them in the West) and over a thousand "co-operative arrangement congregations" based on delimitation of territory (824 of which were west of Ontario).[33] These latter included frontier fields where Home Mission co-operation had designated particular areas Presbyterian or Methodist in advance of any congregational organization, and older communities where, by mutual agreement, the first of the two to establish a congregation was left in undisputed control.

The implication of these co-operative arrangements, namely, that theological, administrative, or canonical differences between the two denominations were negligible, must have been widely influential in the popular drift toward union. In addition, the experience of so many churchgoers that they could get along in the same congregation satisfactorily with members of the other denomination must have been psychologically very significant. As Archbishop Temple writes of John R. Mott, "it was in the conferences of . . . the World Student Christian Federation, that he first experienced the *reality* of ecumenical Christianity and became converted to its possibility." [34] Doubtless in much the same way thousands of Methodists and Presbyterians became converted to the value of church union by the experience of belonging to forced amalgamation or spontaneous union congregations.

Some attention should be paid to nontheological factors of a permissive character which contributed indirectly to the union of 1925. First is the fact that the accepted form of church government in the three denominations, though not exactly the same, was such as to raise no great barrier to merging. Also this common form of church government, with its absence of rigid clerical hierarchy, permitted all three denominations to be quite sensitive to lay opinion and initiative. Moreover, when lay concern was expressed and mobilized, no clerical institution such as a House of Bishops existed to block execution of popular demands.

A second facilitating factor was the common Protestant ethos. This included a similar outlook in respect to the sacraments and the role of the ministry. Related here, too, is their general similarity in social standing in the Canadian community and also in educational requirements for the clergy. Each denomination had reached the status of a national church. Contrariwise, the Baptists, though sharing a Protestant ethos, had yet to achieve this national status. Their common self-image, too, as that of a "denomination" rather than an historical church, undoubtedly facilitated co-operative and unitive activity.

Factors of organizational structure and outlook also played a part. None of the denominations by 1925 had yet developed an extensive bureaucracy whose officials were liable to personal loss from the economies of unification. The smallness of the bureaucracy is related to Canada's geography, which strung out congregations along a 3,000 mile line, making the overhead costs of a centralized bureaucratic apparatus largely prohibitive at this stage. At the same time the anticipated expansion of the country and its churches seemed to guarantee career openings for most if not all of the professional leaders whose positions might be threatened at union's consummation. All three churches had, by the turn of the century, broken their legal ties with their mother churches in the U. S. or in England. Confederation in 1867 and succeeding national developments, as well as the Great War, had upgraded indigenous values and institutions and weakened sentimental links with Europe, thus allowing independence to these ecclesiastic institutions. Also, by 1925, these churches had to a large extent achieved a Canadian-born ministry, so that important decisions were now in the hands of a predominantly indigenous clergy.

Influential Socio-economic Forces

From a socio-economic standpoint, union may be viewed as an attempt to meet the insistent demands of geography and economics on the prairies, where in 1925, "outside the cities there were comparatively few places in any of the four provinces where Presbyterians and Methodists maintained competitive churches." [35] In effect the geography of the West as well as its economic development led to social conditions which greatly hampered the expansion of denominational-based ministries. Although settlers poured into the prairies after the turn of the century, the density of population in the prairies was only 1.87

persons to the square mile. For the most part these people lived very isolated lives, each family squatting on its quarter-section of 160 acres. Roads were very poor and the long, severe winters were especially isolating. The isolation was increased by great diversity of language and culture. The early towns were originally only small groups of frame buildings near railway lines and grain elevators. The work of ministers under these circumstances posed problems unknown in eastern congregations familiar with compact settlements, better communications, and an easier climate.

The planlessness of the early settlement period meant that many immigrants settled on poor land, and soon had to move further west. One-third of the three million settlers who came to Canada between 1895 and 1914 returned home or migrated to the U. S. This mobility of population made for social instability and hindered the building up of well-organized communities. The introduction of mechanized farming after the Great War also contributed to population movement, and increased social isolation by making larger farm holdings common. One writer has described the typical situation on the prairies with which the denominations had to deal as follows:

> The pioneer . . . must be satisfied with a glorified packing-box for a church, and he is fortunate to get that; for in many pastoral charges . . . there are few, if any, church buildings, and most of the services are conducted in the one-room school houses provided by the government. If one could foresee where a permanent community would rise, an investment in church buildings and equipment would be safer. But when the lumber is cut down or a mine exhausted, a village may be abandoned and only the shell remains. . . . A church to keep up with this (frontier) situation, must depend less on equipment and more on personnel, and must develop a ministry capable of carrying on its work over a vast area and satisfied to hold services at many preaching points, where perhaps at the best, not more than a handful of people may constitute the congregation.[36]

A crucial problem was securing enough clergy to man the many new congregations. Before 1900 this was serious but with the flood of new immigration up to 1914, the demands for new clergy became quite unmanageable. In this period the annual reports of all the major religions, including the Roman Catholics, speak of serious shortages of clergy.

The small and scattered nature of the settlements also meant that few rural congregations attained self-support. Financial help from Eastern Canada and from abroad was needed in ever-increasing amounts. Periodic crop failures after 1910 often made it impossible for even well-organized congregations to pay their minister's salary, and additional burdens were placed on Home Mission funds. The financial shortage was felt most acutely during World War I, at a time when the ranks of the clergy were further depleted by enlistment in the chaplaincy service.

In the face of this situation, competition for supporters among churches of similar ethos appeared to many lay people both a scandal and an economic waste. Among the idealistic the cry was for more effective use of resources, for "good stewardship" of men and money, to facilitate opening up "new works." One writer notes, "Communities blessed with favorable locations were the scenes of disgraceful rivalries between several competing churches, all struggling for their existence among an inadequate population, while outside these places there were hundreds of settlements which never saw a church, and in which a new generation was growing up, sometimes at no far remove from paganism." [37] Denominational rivalry was charged with wasting both funds and men. Thus, the peculiar geography and settlement pattern of the West resulted in elevating matters of economy and efficiency to a place of central importance.[38] Economically, it was a matter of overhead costs; as Canada's outstanding economic historian, H. A. Innes, observes: "The peculiar character of the Canadian economy with its emphasis upon overhead costs has been largely responsible for a persistent trend toward unity." [39]

Two institutional trends in the field of business were probably not without their influence. First, in the opening decade of the twentieth century the merger movement swept Canada. "Large primary and secondary producers ... endeavored to integrate vertically with complementary concerns in order to extend their control over sources of raw materials." [40] This development was virtually completed by 1929 or even earlier. "The influence of overhead costs on the merging enterprises in the early years ... is quite apparent where causes can be isolated." [41] To what extent church leaders, especially those in business, were influenced by this successful economic pattern is impossible to gauge, but intelligent observers see a connection. A second and corollary development was the rise of the trade association.

> In Canada these combinations commenced following the introduction of the Combines Investigation Act of 1910 and represented the attempt of industry to achieve in an orderly fashion, short of corporate merger and amalgamation, the market control formerly resulting from mergers. This phenomenon reached its zenith in the early twenties; ... the Great War and the necessity for the orderly use of raw materials and the equitable distribution of the finished products, gave impetus to these intercompany relationships within industries. [42]

One writer points to an interesting coincidence between this economic institution and "the presentation of 'Federalism' as a substitute for organic union by Presbyterians opposed to Church Union." Here again, economic institutional patterns may be credited with some suggestive influence. [43]

Concern for economy spurred on the cause of union, but specific social developments within many prairie communities combined to undermine denominational loyalties. The uprooting of Westerners from settled communities in the U. S., Eastern Canada, or Europe, often weakened their allegiance to early religious ties, all the more when they settled in districts seldom or never served by a Christian minister. After years of inability to attend any church service, only those most devoted to their beliefs refused to attend services offered by Protestant ministers

186

of other denominations than their own. Meantime, in the larger or less remote centers where several churches coexisted, the highly independent, tradition-free frontier social climate, combined with the great mixture of creeds and nationalities, provided a social atmosphere more favorable to exploring new churches than to strict adherence to childhood allegiances. The continuing social mobility of Westerners, incessantly moving westward in the search for economic security, weakened old social ties while the need to secure status in one's new community fostered participation in secular activities and community-creating associations. In this situation strict denominationalism often appeared as a barrier both to social organizations or community "progress," especially to the laity. And in frontier society where clerical status was weak, the objectives of lay opinion were often more influential than theological considerations. S. D. Clark, one of Canada's leading sociologists, writes, "Union of the Methodist, Presbyterian and Congregationalist churches in 1925 was a reflection of the growing dominance of secular values associated with Politics and Big Business." [44]

Social and Cultural Climate

A major characteristic of the newly developing communities in the West were institutions stressing co-operation and mutual aid. Such institutions developed more or less spontaneously to meet conditions of desperate economic need or social organization posed by problems of climate, marketing, or settlement. They reflected a deep concern for aids to material security in the face of great threats and instabilities.

In the period 1900-1925, western farmers created a whole series of co-operative enterprises and in so doing developed both a philosophy and value system in which co-operation and mutual aid ranked high. Among literally dozens of organizations, the following may serve as examples: The Territorial Grain Growers, a producers' co-operative, formed in 1901; the United Farmers of Alberta, an organization for political action, founded in 1909;

and the Saskatchewan Co-operative Elevator Company, set up to aid sellers of grain, established in 1911.

The magnitude and effectiveness of these farmers' co-operative enterprises seemed to point a finger at the pettiness and weakness of the poor and divided churches. Whether this judgment was right or wrong, it sprang from an experience of success in the secular world. Joint co-operative activity brought together people of diverse ethnic and religious backgrounds and led many (of the men especially) to believe that their religious divisions were archaic and alien to prairie life. Out of convictions like these came the rapid development of local union churches.

Frontier devaluation of intellectual disciplines and distinctions was also a significant element in the prevailing social climate. History shows that the maintenance of a clear-cut denominational tradition requires adequate interest in facilities for education. This is true whether it be formulated doctrine or ignorant prejudice that is to be perpetuated. Frontier life provided neither the time nor the facilities for education in doctrinal subtleties. Moreover, in the early decades settlers were very largely of the aggressive, adventurous, nonconformist type. Faced with the necessity of winning a livelihood against great odds, and living in considerable isolation, there was little or no environmental stimulus to intellectual pursuits. Schools were few, teachers hard to secure, and the curriculum confined to an elementary level. In addition, the scarcity of ministers meant that Sunday schools, which had never been adequate, were often closed for long periods. Under such conditions, many young people received little indoctrination in denominational differences. In these ways, educational deficiencies played a part in weakening intellectual obstacles to union.

The social mood of the West between 1900 and 1925 was largely optimistic and liberal, and was fired by boom developments in wheat, oil, and natural gas. In theology, this optimistic spirit found expression in the emerging liberalism of the twenties. Liberal professors teaching in Saskatoon, Winnipeg, and Toronto, in both the Methodist and Presbyterian churches, tended to share a common world view and a common optimistic ethos. They saw church union as a progressive movement and came out strongly for it.

While extremely powerful nontheological forces fostered the church union movement on the prairies, somewhat similar influences emerged in the East. Many people in Ontario, little removed from the frontier stage in 1910, were hardly less concerned than Westerners with practical results and economy. Economic arguments weighed heavily although counterbalancing forces of tradition, conservatism, and entrenched denominationalism were vigorous. The success of previous church unions was also impressive.

In the period 1900-1925 Eastern Canada was exhibiting a growing sense of nationalism. With the Laurier government of 1896 had come the British preferences, the stimulus of East-West trade, the wheat boom; gradually the idea that the twentieth century belonged to Canada took root. The great burst of new immigration after 1900, the unifying common tasks and problems of settling the frontier and the Great War served to strengthen the impulse to nationalism. Dr. Pidgeon, one of the great leaders of the Presbyterian Church wrote, "A Church with community spirit suggested a Church which would express the national spirit religiously. Canada is just rising to a new national consciousness and the desire is for a Church in which this shall be embodied." [45] A number of Protestant leaders shared the same view, so that more than one observer has maintained that this growing national spirit was a factor making church union an urgent necessity.

Protestant interest in a national church was partly a reaction to the steady expansion of Roman Catholicism, especially that of French Canada. Eastern Protestants were very sensitive to Roman Catholic political power, and had organized before 1902 several specifically Anti-Roman organizations which vigilantly scrutinized Roman Catholic actions and expansion. As each census since 1911 showed a rising percentage of Roman Catholics in the population, many people looked on a united church as the way to save the West and Canada for Protestantism.[46] World War I tended to clarify the country's basic cleavage along ethnic and religious lines and strengthened both the French and English varieties of nationalist sentiment.

Conclusion

Major ecclesiastical developments since 1925 underline the influence of nontheological factors. For instance, protests against theological vagueness and liberalism in United Church doctrine constituted a prominent rallying cry in the expansion of evangelical sects in the depression and thereafter. Some of these, such as the Nazarenes and Pentecostal Assemblies, notably emphasized certain Methodist teachings and practices and made an impact especially in the prairies. The Pentecostal Assemblies, begun in 1918, numbered over 100,000 by the late fifties. The continuing Presbyterians after slowly recovering from the bitterness and setback of 1925 began to grow again in the forties, and steadily increased—with the exception of certain prairie areas—in the fifties, reporting 198,023 communicant members in 1960.[47] The Anglicans though losing a number of supporters to the uniting church, particularly in the West where clergy were shorthanded and denominational loyalties weak, have largely held their own in central Canada. Their proportion of the Canadian population was 16.1 per cent in 1921, and 14.7 per cent in 1951. Though engaging from time to time in discussion of union, many of its members, especially among the clergy, remained for a long while unimpressed by the theological results of 1925. Quite recently this communion has again entered into reunion conversations, this time with perhaps a little more general enthusiasm than earlier.

Certain emphases in the United Church structure stand out suggestively: a tendency to pragmatic as opposed to theological concerns; a flexibility of adjustment to new social developments exceeding that of other non-Roman denominations, not unrelated to the predominance of ex-Methodists in key posts; a deep strain of moralism, associated with a widening range of social concern particularly at headquarters' level; a continuing zeal for union with non-Roman bodies, which may soon bring inclusion of the

190   CASE STUDIES

small Ontario-based (German) Evangelical United Church; a fast developing and large Toronto-based bureaucracy, not unassociated with higher professional and academic standards among the clergy; notable successes in money raising, building of new churches, particularly in suburbia, and the utilization of mass media; some strengthening of self-appraisal as the national Protestant church; attempts to clarify uncertainties regarding basic doctrines by periodic theological "White Papers," combined with a new interest in theology on the part of many clergy; a firm alliance with the respectable Anglo-Saxon middle classes along with some success, especially in the prairies, in assimilating European immigrants.

These trends underline the rather influential role of pragmatic and sociological considerations in union, their consequences for building up a "national" church, and something of the price exacted by accommodation to such forces in order to meet the challenge of the social needs of the Western Provinces.

NOTES FOR ESSAY 8

1. Silcox, p. 120.
2. Morrow, p. 15.
3. *Ibid.*, p. 16.
4. Silcox, p. 131.
5. Scott, p. 52.
6. *Ibid.*, p. 53.
7. *Ibid.*, p. 56.
8. Silcox, p. 195.
9. *Ibid.*, p. 281.
10. *Ibid.*, p. 281.
11. "These figures are based upon returns received at the offices of the Presbyterian Church in Canada." Scott, p. 60.
12. Silcox, p. 281.
13. *Ibid.*, p. 282.
14. *Ibid.*, p. 25.
15. *Ibid.*, p. 103.
16. *Ibid.*, p. 74.
17. *Ibid.*, p. 87.
18. *Ibid.*, p. 100.

19. *Ibid.*, p. 105.
20. *Ibid.*, p. 181.
21. *Ibid.*, pp. 69-70.
22. *Report of Canadian Royal Commission, 1938* (Ottawa: Queen's Printer, 1938), Book 1, Chapter 3, p. 87.
23. *Ibid.*, p. 97.
24. *Cf.* Scott, p. 113. Some writers maintain that having gone so far toward union, the leaders felt that they could not go back.
25. E. H. Oliver, *His Dominion of Canada* (Toronto: The United Church Publishing House, 1932), p. 140.
26. *Ibid.*, p. 80.
27. Silcox, p. 224.
28. Silcox says 70 on page 224 and 54 on page 227.
29. E. M. House, "Century Plant in Canada," *The Christian Century*, LXII, May 16, 1945.
30. Oliver, *op. cit.*, p. 138.
31. Silcox, p. 224.
32. *Ibid.*, p. 224.
33. *Ibid.*, p. 227.
34. H. P. Van Dusen, *World Christianity* (New York and Nashville: Abingdon-Cokesbury Press, 1947), p. 84.
35. Silcox, p. 295.
36. *Ibid.*, p. 9.
37. Excerpt from "Century Plant in Canada" by Ernest Marshall Howse in May 16, 1945 issue of *The Christian Century*. Copyright 1945 Christian Century Foundation. Reprinted by permission.
38. Slosser, p. 309.
39. H. A. Innes's Introduction in H. A. Innes and A. F. M. Plumptree, *The Canadian Economy and Its Problems* (Toronto: University of Toronto Press, 1934), p. 21.
40. O. J. McDiarmid, *Commercial Policy in the Canadian Economy* (Cambridge: Harvard University Press, 1946), p. 243.
41. G. M. Morrison, "The United Church of Canada—Ecumenical or Economical Necessity?" (unpublished B.D. Thesis, Emmanuel College, Toronto, 1956), p. 62.
42. *Ibid.*, pp. 66-67.
43. *Ibid.*, p. 67.
44. Clark, p. 431.
45. G. Pidgeon's Documents in Morrison, *op. cit.*, p. 100.
46. For all Canada the Catholic percentage rose from 39.4 per cent in 1911 to 46.1 per cent in 1951. It shows a steady growth in every decade, after 1941, if we remember to combine the Roman Catholic and Greek Catholic figures from the census. Lumping of Greek Orthodox and Greek

Catholic adherents in the early decades of the century serves to hide the total Catholic strength from the unobservant. (Later censuses show that well over 60 per cent of the combined Greek Catholic and Greek Orthodox total represents Greek Catholic strength.)

47. The census records a decline in 1941 and 1951, but this count of nominal and actual supporters cannot be taken as definitive. In actual communicant membership there was an increase of almost 20,000 from 1930 to 1960; from 179,530 to 198,023. However, it is significant that this gradual comeback since 1930 in no way kept pace with Canada's increase in population, which grew by roughly 80 per cent in this period.

BIBLIOGRAPHY FOR ESSAY 8

Chalmers, Randolph Carleton, *See the Christ Stand!* A study in Doctrine in the United Church of Canada (Toronto: Ryerson Press, 1945).

Clark, Samuel Delbert, *Church and Sect in Canada* (Toronto: University of Toronto Press, 1948).

Mann, William Edward, *Sect, Cult, and Church in Alberta* (Toronto: University of Toronto Press, 1955).

Morrison, George M., "The United Church of Canada: Ecumenical or Economic Necessity?" (Unpublished B.D. Thesis, Emmanuel College, University of Toronto, 1956).

Morrow, E. Lloyd, *Church Union in Canada: Its History, Motives, Doctrines and Government* (Toronto: Thomas Allen, 1923).

Riddell, John Henry, *Methodism in the West* (Toronto: Ryerson Press, 1946).

Scott, Ephraim, *Church Union and The Presbyterian Church in Canada* (Montreal: John Lovell, 1928).

Silcox, Claris Edwin, *Church Union in Canada: Its Causes and Consequences* (New York: Institute of Social and Religious Research, 1933).

Slosser, Gaius Jackson, *Christian Unity: Its History and Challenge in All Communions, in All Lands* (London and New York: E. P. Dutton, 1929).

Walsh, Henry Horace, *The Christian Church in Canada* (Toronto: Ryerson Press, 1956).

9.
THE METHODIST UNION IN ENGLAND, 1932

This paper is concerned with the reunion of the three major branches of British Methodism in 1932. After a brief account of how Methodism became divided, there follows a description of the reunion movement; this involves a discussion of why, toward the close of the nineteenth century, changes in attitude made union a practical possibility. The next sections describe some of the objections raised to union, and the compromise which was finally accepted. The remainder of the paper contains a discussion of the interplay of doctrinal and institutional factors in the negotiations, and some tentative conclusions.

The uniting churches were the *Wesleyan Methodist Church*, whose tradition ran back to John Wesley (membership 500,000); the *Primitive Methodist Church*, which had grown steadily since 1807, and was largely rural or mining in background (membership 225,000); and the *United Methodist Church* (membership 140,-000). This last body, set up in 1907, contained three older groups, the *Methodist New Connexion*, a small but significant secession from Wesleyan Methodism in 1797; the *Bible Christians*, another small body, limited to the southwest of England, where it began

by JOHN H. S. KENT

about 1815; and the *United Methodist Free Church,* which was founded in 1857 by various groups of seceders from the Wesleyan Methodists.

The Background

Methodist Union in England goes back to the day in 1878 when lay representatives became part of the Wesleyan Conference, the governing body of the Old Connexion. This step removed the biggest single constitutional difference between the English Methodist denominations, and involved a definite break with the traditional Wesleyan view of the ministry. According to this view, the ministry was charged with the *episcopé,* or oversight, of the Connexion, and must therefore have the authority to carry out its pastoral responsibilities. This view was slowly replaced by a vaguer "representative" theory of the pastoral office, according to which the minister, though still thought of as "called of God," was chiefly regarded as "representative" of the laity, with no kind of authority which the laity did not already possess. It is difficult to link this change in attitude to any identifiable change of theological opinion; but it brought Wesleyan Methodism into line with the other Methodist churches, in which the idea of pastoral "oversight" had been largely replaced by the ideal of the minister as a "leader" and the idea of a specific call to the ministry often took second place to that of the minister as a kind of full-time layman, a professional executant of the priesthood of all believers. Once the Wesleyan ministry had adopted this view, it was possible to admit laymen to the Wesleyan Conference, and for many Wesleyan ministers after 1849 the admission of lay representatives took priority over everything else. The practical price in division and secession of upholding the original Wesleyan constitution had become unendurable. Memories of the older Wesleyan view of the ministry lingered on, however, to complicate the negotiations about reunion.

Several other factors help to explain why Methodist Union became practical politics toward the end of World War I. (Wes-

196

leyan Methodism had set up a committee to explore the situation as far back as 1913, but it was not until 1918 that a united committee, Wesleyan, Primitive, and United Methodist, was given powers to draw up a draft scheme.) Perhaps the most important of these factors was the transient idealism which affected so much English thought and action for a few years after 1918. Advocates of reunion emphasized the need to have a new church to face an allegedly new era and they took for granted that a united Methodism would have an increased moral influence on the nation. This prophecy was not fulfilled. The attempt to advocate Methodist union as "progressive," however, only half-veiled the sense in which the movement was a consolidated retreat; what the leaders hoped to recover was the power and influence which the English Free Churches had briefly possessed in the later nineteenth century, and social changes had made that impossible.

Doctrinally the postwar period was also propitious. The negotiations were taking place in the trough of the wave of liberal theology which in 1920 still had enormous prestige as the "progressive" point of view. There was a general feeling that biblical criticism had freed men (and especially ministers) from the dead hand of creeds, official doctrinal statements, and the past as a whole. This attitude was so strong that A. S. Peake, the distinguished Primitive Methodist scholar who did so much to persuade his generation to accept biblical criticism, said quite openly at an early stage that he would have preferred to omit any reference to John Wesley's writings from the doctrinal statement of the united church. Though the Wesleyan Methodists saw such a reference as a necessary act of piety, the non-Wesleyan representatives saw it as suggesting that Methodism was a sect. The negotiating committee never acted on the suggestion that they should draw up a list of specific doctrines, but pointed instead to vague but respectable terms like "evangelical" or "the Reformation."

Other more purely Methodist factors were involved at the institutional level. There was, for example, a general hope that unity might help to stem the declining membership. In 1921, for example, Aldom French, the secretary of the Wesleyan section of the Union Committee, made a public statement along these lines. He said that in the previous fourteen years the Wesleyan Church had suffered a loss of thirty-five thousand members; that the Primitive Methodists had lost ten thousand members in the same period; and that the United Methodists had lost nine thousand members in the previous twelve years. Moreover, the decline was more serious than the figures suggested, for there was no longer the margin of uncommitted hearers which had been a fruitful field of evangelism in the past. Aldom French suggested that union would help to solve this problem by making Methodism as a whole more efficient. He quoted the example of the United Methodist Free Church, which since its formation twelve years before had been able to dispense with 150 ordained and 93 unordained ministers, at a financial saving which he put at £50,000 a year.

Another internal factor which made Methodist union feasible was that the social pattern of England was changing steadily and that the social differences between the Wesleyans and the other two bodies had largely disappeared.

A third internal institutional factor underlines the similarity between the three denominations at the local level of organization. In 1924 nearly half the circuits of Methodism were what is called "single minister stations"; that is, groups of churches to which only one minister was appointed. Thus for the whole of Methodism in 1924 almost every second circuit was a single-minister station, and almost every town of any size had at least one minister who worked in virtual isolation from his brethren. This showed how deeply local particularism had bitten into Methodism since the disruption of 1849-1857. There was something very non-Methodist about a situation in which so many ministers worked largely by themselves, almost independent of any hierarchy. One of the greatest blessings of Methodist Union was that it led to the abolition of a large majority of these single stations and a return to a more Methodist way of working. On the other hand, the existence of so many of these single stations

198

helps to explain the stubborn resistance to circuit amalgamation and to effective union at the local level which was one of the features of the generation after 1932.

Such were some of the factors which made Methodist union practical politics by about 1918. The Wesleyan acceptance of the principle of lay representation mattered most, because it vastly simplified the institutional side of the negotiations. But this lay in the background. The catalyst which brought popular opinion into the issue on the side of union was the aftermath of World War I. A. W. Harrison, the Wesleyan leader, describing this postwar mood to the Ecumenical Methodist Conference of 1931, said:

> There was a phase of violent emotional disturbance, unrest dangerously near to revolution, with a deep sense of exasperation at the disappointments of peace. These were days when there was much talk of reconstruction, with little to satisfy the dreams of idealists. If we could sum it up again in one expression, it would be in the aspiration of the younger generation, "Let us tear the whole rotten structure down and begin again." [1]

The negotiations went ahead quickly in response to such an atmosphere immediately after the war; they bogged down as the mood changed to one of depression. At this stage the absence of strong social or doctrinal differences between the three churches helped to sustain the work.

Methodist Union ran into very few snags of an institutional nature; what held up the scheme from 1920 to 1932 was the opposition of a powerful Wesleyan minority deeply concerned about the doctrines of the Church, Ministry and Sacraments. Institutional differences presented so little difficulty that the compromise proposed in 1920 was hardly altered in succeeding years. This was not entirely what was expected at the time. Despite the changes indicated at the beginning of this essay, the Ministry still had more authority in the Wesleyan than in other Methodist constitutions. Thus in the case of Wesleyan Methodism the Annual Conference, the real source of authority in all forms of Methodism, was divided into two sessions, the second of which, known as the Pastoral Session, consisted only of ministers; in Primitive Methodism and United Methodism there was no such division, and the Conference was in each case made up of representatives of the ministry and laity. In an itinerant system like Methodism, the committee which stations ministers plays a vital role; in Wesleyan Methodism, final decisions about the stationing of ministers had been in the hands of the Pastoral Session, whereas in the other two churches laymen had shared the responsibility. Another unique feature of the Wesleyan Conference was the Legal Hundred. This was a body of one hundred ministers, elected by their brethren according to rules which were constantly being reviewed, who were permanent members of the Conference and therefore provided an element of continuity theoretically independent of both the departmental officers and the constantly changing elected representatives. This was regarded by the Primitive and United Methodists as highly undemocratic—and "democracy" was a word to conjure with in 1920—although there were very small permanent groups in the other conferences. Finally, in the non-Wesleyan churches the highest offices in the connection, such as the presidency and the secretaryship of Conference, had been regarded as open to laymen, although laymen were not often elected to them; in Wesleyan Methodism such appointments had always been purely ministerial.

The Reunion Compromise

Out of this rather unpromising material a rough compromise emerged quickly, probably because most Wesleyan leaders no longer held the view of the pastoral office which was still implied by parts of the Wesleyan constitution. The president, for example, was always to be a minister, but there was also to be a vice-president, who was always a layman. The non-Wesleyans regarded this introduction of a lay vice-president as an important concession on the part of the Wesleyans; they felt that the vice-presidency was a guarantee that the rights of the laity would be respected in the new church. It can hardly be said that the office has been as important as some of the supporters of the idea expected, but in 1920 the change played a big part in the institutional compromise.

The negotiators also quickly agreed that there ought to be a Pastoral Session. For a short time this was a lively issue, especially as the first draft scheme suggested that the Pastoral should follow the Representative Session, as was the Wesleyan practice. When the Primitive Methodist District Meetings considered the scheme in 1921, fourteen out of twenty-five voted that the Pastoral Sessions should come first, in order to make sure that the Representative Session should have the last word. This alarmed many Wesleyans, who thought that what mattered was that the Representative Session should have the first word. The point attracted so much discussion that in June, 1921, Sir Robert Perks, perhaps the best-known Wesleyan layman at the time, actually wrote an article along these lines for the Primitive Methodist denominational newspaper, *The Leader*. He said that when the Representative Session was first introduced in 1878 it had followed the Pastoral Session, just as the Primitive Methodists were now suggesting, but by 1887 the Wesleyan laity were already asking that the Representative Session should have priority. J. M. Rigg, almost the last convinced exponent of the old Wesleylan doctrine of the ruling ministry, had opposed this, saying that it would deprive the Pastoral Session of its initiative. Rigg had said: "I ask who are the prime guardians appointed by the Master. That sacred interest ought to come first." (This, whether Sir Robert Perks liked it or not—and he did not—was the authentic voice of Wesleyan tradition.) Dr. Rigg was defeated in the Representative Session but from 1889 the experiment was tried of sandwiching the Representative Session between two meetings of the Pastoral Session. This lasted for ten years, but in 1889 the Representative Session once again requested priority, and this time the Pastoral Session accepted the change by 172 votes to 154. Perks concluded: "There can be no doubt that by this great change the initiation of legislation, and also the more effective control of the administrative work of the Wesleyan Methodist Church, passed from the hands of a purely clerical body and became vested where it ought to be, in a Representative Assembly of ministers and laymen chosen by the Church." Since his conclusion was precisely what the non-Wesleyan critics had in mind, this letter really settled the issue. I have dealt with it at length for two reasons: in the first place it illustrates once more how the development of Wesleyan Methodism facilitated Methodist Union, and it also shows how much in common Wesleyan and non-Wesleyan laymen might have in their attitude to church polity.

The Primitive and United Methodists had conceded a point in accepting the idea of a Pastoral Session. They did so on various conditions. The most important was the disappearance of the Legal Hundred, whose origins went back to John Wesley himself. The non-Wesleyan negotiators were anxious to make the new Conference as "democratic" as possible, and regarded anything like permanent membership as improper. The Hundred was rather a glaring example of permanency, and ministerial permanency at that. At union, the whole system was abolished, which may not have been the wisest solution. An attempt was made to provide some continuity in Conference membership. In the 1920 scheme it was suggested that Conference itself should elect thirty ministers and thirty laymen to serve for terms of six years, five of each group retiring every year. But the idea was unpopular, even with the addition of laymen. In the 1922 scheme, the length of term was reduced to three years, ten of each group retiring every year. In the present Standing Orders of the Methodist Church the process has gone a stage further. Twenty-one ministers and twenty-one laymen are elected for three years, seven of each group retiring every year. The intention of the original negotiators was to spread the membership as widely as possible, and the Primitive and United Methodist advocates of union claimed that the proposed constitution was even more democratic than what already existed. Not all Primitive Methodists were convinced; in their Conference the laymen outnumbered the ministers by two to one, which seemed to them very democratic indeed.

From these examples it should be obvious enough what was the basis of the institutional compromise. The non-Wesleyan churches were prepared to accept certain features of the Wesleyan constitution (such as the Pastoral Session and District Chairmen), as long as the Wesleyans in their turn agreed to such modifications of Wesleyan practice as would make it quite clear that they accepted a "representative" theory of the ministry. The last traces of what early nineteenth-century Wesleyans approvingly called "pastoral supremacy" disappeared; ministerial leadership and connectional democracy were the watchwords. This was true in the case of the Stationing Committee, which was "democratized" as far as possible in make-up and methods of work, and also in the case of the administration of the Holy Communion. From the start the negotiators assumed that the administration of the Holy Communion by laymen would have to be permitted in the new church, however tightly it might be restricted and despite the fact that this had not been a Wesleyan custom. Some compensation for this major Wesleyan concession (without which it is certain that no scheme would have been successful) may be seen in the non-Wesleyan acceptance of the office of district chairman, but there is no suggestion in contemporary records that this was thought of as a momentous step. The chairman was conceived as the representative, not the ruler, of his fellow ministers in the district, and was expected to provide leadership rather than pastoral oversight.

Failure of Local Union

Some comment must be made on this institutional compromise. At the higher level it worked very smoothly. There was no drastic change of system. Final authority in the new church still rested in the representative conference, and if everybody was not familiar with a Pastoral Session, at least the term was self-explanatory, whereas the true mystery of the old Wesleyan Conference, the Legal Hundred, had been abolished. No important new organs of power were created. There was nothing in the history of the office of the district chairman to suggest that its wider adoption would prove revolutionary as long as the chairmen remained simultaneously superintendents of large circuits. All the uniting churches had possessed central departments which handled such matters as finance, youth work, social questions, and so forth; these were fused.

This leads one to ask whether the process was not a bit too easy, whether the new church was not too like the old. Little serious effort was made to take the chance offered by the negotiations to devise a form of Methodism more suited to the present century. If the chairmen, for example, had been immediately freed from circuit responsibilities and had been specifically charged with the job of making union a success on the local level, it is possible that in the first excitement of coming together much might have been achieved. The introduction of Separated Chairmen twenty-five years later was not at all the same thing. In any case, the success of the merger at the top was not paralleled by a successful merger at the circuit level; that is, at the level where ordinary Christians met one another. Such a statement may sound unnecessarily controversial, and it is therefore worthwhile making a long quotation from an article published recently by Dr. Eric Baker, in which he summed up his experience as president of the Methodist Church in 1959-1960. Dr. Baker has also been secretary of Conference for many years.

There is widespread impatience, especially on the part of our younger people, at the continued tolerance on the part of Conference of the redundancy which is steadily strangling our effectiveness. . . . Let me give two examples which are typical, not exceptional. There is one city which contains within its boundaries fifty-nine Methodist churches, considerably more than the Church of England possesses. Congregations are small and we could well do with half of them. I visited a town recently with a population of 17,000 where there are four large Methodist churches, none of which has an average congregation of fifty.... Methodist union took place twenty-eight years ago. When Conference decided that union at the circuit and society level would be a matter for local action, they could never have dreamed of such a sequel. The laity of the three churches ought never to have voted in such numbers for union unless they intended to consummate it locally. Ministers, of course, voted for it too, but not in such large numbers, and they are itinerant anyway. What can be done? I do not know. Conference has done everything in its power short of coercion, and unless new powers are sought from Parliament ... can do no more. In area after area, the appeal and often the direction of Conference has been flouted. Worship of bricks and mortar has supplanted the worship of the living God.[2]

It is more than possible, of course, that in many cases both ministers and laymen voted for the scheme because they did not intend to consummate it locally, and because they knew that nothing in the scheme would compel them to do so. The negotiators drew back from any attempt to determine in advance what should happen at the local level; there were no teeth in the scheme and it is difficult to see how there could have been; from any institutional point of view all churches are voluntary associations. There is a danger in such negotiations that a tide of opinion flow so strongly that in the end no one can withstand it. Many ministers and laymen seem to have voted for the scheme because they felt that they ought to do so. Once the vote for righteousness had been given they lost interest. Numerical majorities are not always a sure guide in church affairs. Although gradually at the local level many ex-Wesleyan, United, and Primitive Methodist churches drew together in what are called amalgamated circuits, this usually meant that all the chapels involved remained open, and that opportunities for efficiency and effective evangelism were not taken. In fact, union made the problem of redundancy worse, because situations which could dimly be defended in terms of the three churches became monstrous in terms of one united Methodism. To some extent, moreover, the financial benefits of union helped to support redundancy. The conclusion seems to be that in any future organic union in a country where overlapping is as considerable as it was in the case of the three English Methodist churches, the important step is to deal with the problem of local organization before union is implemented. The sequel of Methodist Union is a warning against the assumption that in such a case the unification of ministries and central departments will be sufficient to guarantee effective union where it really matters, where the Christian meets the non-Christian.

The Doctrinal and Institutional Difficulties

The second part of this essay is concerned with the doctrinal factors which provided the real difficulty in the negotiations. Although these factors were intrinsically important, concentration on them helped the neglect of more detailed problems. In this sense the Wesleyan opposition to union, although it did good work in clarifying and broadening the doctrinal statements, was looking in the wrong direction; in the long run the mistakes at local level proved more important than the improvements obtained at the doctrinal level.

What we are considering here is the section called "Doctrine" which stood at the beginning of the various draft schemes of union. The first paragraph of the section was meant to be the doctrinal standard of the united church. In the 1920 scheme the original draft of this paragraph ran:

> That the evangelical doctrines for which Methodism has stood from the beginning, as held by the three Conferences, and as generally contained in John Wesley's Notes on the

New Testament and the first four volumes of his Sermons, shall be the doctrinal basis of the new Church.

This must have seemed mild and natural to some, but to others it looked like a roadblock. They had been encouraged to base their preaching on the findings of biblical criticism, and now they were sent back to Wesley's Notes on the New Testament. One Primitive Methodist critic wrote: "Frankly, many of us do not believe what John Wesley believes." By February, 1920, A. S. Peake, himself both a biblical scholar and a member of the Union Committee, thought it wise to write a public article on the subject.[3] He appreciated the difficulty about the Notes on the New Testament. "I confess that I should have greatly preferred the omission of this reference ... [but] the loyalty of the Wesleyans to their great founder is such that the inclusion of the reference seems to be imperative." Peake underlined the importance of the word "generally" in the paragraph cited above: Of course Wesley must be criticized, his exegesis of the New Testament must sometimes be rejected, his interpretation of the Book of Revelation is "radically unsound." However, in 1919 the Wesleyan Conference itself had adopted a series of resolutions on doctrine, one of which said that the Notes on the New Testament "were not intended to impose a system of formal or speculative theology on our preachers," and, A. S. Peake suggested, this would be a reasonable basis for their interpretation in the united church.

It is clear, however, that Peake was not entirely satisfied, for when the Union Committee met in the first week of March, 1920, it appears that he had arranged in advance with Maldwyn Hughes, one of the Wesleyan leaders, to make a significant addition to the paragraph. He proposed:

> The evangelical doctrines for which Methodism has stood from the beginning, as held by the three Conferences, and generally contained in John Wesley's Notes on the New Testament and the first four volumes of his Sermons, sub-

ject to the authority of divine revelation recorded in the Holy Scriptures, shall be the doctrinal standard of the Methodist Church.[4]

In view of his earlier article it looks as though Peake's intention was to conciliate his own radicals by the introduction of the Bible as the decisive factor in the definition, for the new wording meant that anything which could be squared with the Bible need not be squared with the Notes on the New Testament. This left biblical criticism the arbiter, rather than Bengel modified by Wesley.

So much for the liberal attitude to the question of standards, which might be summed up in two heads: (a) an anxiety about the freedom of critical inquiry in the new church; and (b) the Primitive and United Methodist indifference to John and Charles Wesley, who were thought of as a peculiarly Wesleyan possession.

More important than the liberal reaction, however, was that of a powerful wing of the Wesleyan church. The leaders were ministers like J. E. Rattenbury and Amos Burnett, and laymen like Sir Henry Lunn and Kingsley Wood. They could count on the support of about one-third of the ministry and laity. They claimed to care especially for the links between Wesleyan Methodism and the Church of England; links which had been partly broken in the later nineteenth century, and which had no emotional appeal at all in the non-Wesleyan churches. (The Primitive and United Methodists could not comprehend, much less appreciate, a liturgical type of service and inherited a rather contemptuous assessment of Anglicanism.) Rattenbury and Lunn, however, did not really hold the Wesleyan theory of the ministry which had been associated with these sentiments in early nineteenth-century Wesleyanism and therefore lacked a completely coherent position. This was just as well, because they would have found even less sympathy if they had advocated a high view of the pastoral office. What they fastened on in the first paragraph of the section on Doctrine was (a) its satisfaction with a statement about Methodism quite divorced from any setting in the Catholic church, and (b) the absence of any appeal to the historical standards of the faith, either to the historic creeds or to such seminal epochs as the Reformation. Such omissions, the Wesleyan opposition said, would make any future reconciliation of Methodism to the Church of England much more difficult. Of course the mention of creeds was anathema to many non-Wesleyans, who were not in any case very much concerned about union with the Establishment. Their attitude was also deeply affected by what seemed at that time the unchecked progress of the Anglo-Catholic party in the Church of England; the Methodist negotiations took place during the unsuccessful campaign for the revision of the Prayer Book, a campaign which temporarily reawakened the old bitterness of Dissent. The 1920's were not the best time at which to advocate union between Methodism and the Established Church.

Two other points in the doctrinal section disturbed the opposition. In the 1920 scheme the statement on doctrinal standards was followed by a very brief reference to the nature of the ministry. No definition was offered. It was simply stated that "the office of a Christian minister depends upon the call of God.... Those whom the church recognizes as called by God, and therefore receives into its ministry, shall be ordained by the imposition of hands, as expressive of the church's recognition of the minister's personal Call." Such a rationalization of the laying on of hands hardly justified laying them on at all, but of course the Wesleyan introduction of this form of ordination in 1836 did not rest on any profound belief in its theological necessity, but on an anxiety to assert the reality of the Wesleyan ministry against the criticism of such Anglo-Catholic leaders as Pusey himself. Behind the rather vague brevity of this paragraph lay both the tumultuous history of nineteenth-century Methodism, in which the claim of the local preacher to be equal in status to an ordained minister played an important part, and also the growth of the popular picture of the Free Church minister as a cross between a highly rhetorical lecturer and a business man. (Spurgeon was a model.)

It was the ideal of the minister as a man amongst men. Here, however, the Wesleyan opposition were on weaker ground, for they had no very definite alternative to offer in place of the "representative" theory of the ministry.

The same difficulty oppressed them in their resistance to the last paragraph of the section on Doctrine. In this paragraph the negotiators tried to escape from the difficulties which surrounded the lay administration of the Holy Communion by a standstill agreement; the "general usage" of the uniting churches, it suggested, might continue. This could not be a final solution, because such a step meant federation rather than union, but the subject was very complicated at circuit level because there were wide differences of practice in the actual service, which even affected such details as whether the communicants received the elements kneeling or sitting, from the minister or from a lay poor steward or stewards. It was clear that without an agreement to allow most of these distinctions to continue for the time being no scheme of union would be acceptable. None of the schemes mentioned the actual order of the service. Even apart from this strong practical argument in favor of lay administration, opposition to it would have had to be based on a doctrine of the ministry in which the opposition did not really believe.

For a few months there was considerable optimism about the 1920 scheme and people talked as though union were imminent, but in May, 1921, the Wesleyan synods met and discussed the scheme. Only the Sheffield and Cornwall districts voted against it outright; at Leeds a similar resolution was lost by two votes. But the thirty synods which passed affirmative resolutions did so in very cautious terms, and optimism vanished. Burnett, Rattenbury, and Lunn were encouraged to raise the principle of union at the meeting of the Union Committee in June, 1921. Their defeat was decisive; the opposition could never hope to do more than amend the scheme. This was also evident when the opposition raised the issue at the Wesleyan Conference in July that year. The Representative Session accepted the 1920 scheme as a basis for further discussion by 341 votes to 57, which left a large block of neutrals. In the non-Wesleyan conferences there was no vote of any consequence against the scheme.

In the debate in the Wesleyan Conference both Rattenbury and Lunn referred with approval to a speech on the doctrine of the ministry which A. S. Peake had made at the Primitive Methodist Conference and which had been published afterward. They said that if Peake's speech represented the state of opinion in Primitive Methodism, they would have had little hesitation about the scheme. As it was, Rattenbury actually said that if the scheme were adopted "the religious life of the Methodist Church would be lowered." Peake had begun by saying that "there is no strictly defined doctrine of the ministry in the Methodist Church." His own views, he thought, resembled those of G. G. Findlay, a Wesleyan. What, then, was the source of the ministerial commission, and what was its significance?

> It comes to you through the Church and can come only in that way. Never forget that the divine source of your call does not render you independent of the Church. . . . You do not derive your ministry from the ministry of any succession which goes above the head of the Church and behind its back to Christ, for in all this He wills to trust His mystical body with the amplest powers and the fullest responsibility. You are therefore chosen representatives of the Church, possessing no privilege, no authority, which she does not possess, exercising no function which is not within her right, charged with no spiritual gift which is not already hers. . . . You have your ministerial significance only insofar as you are accredited representatives of the Church, holding her commission, dispensing her gifts and graces. You are priests, but so is every Christian, and your priesthood is not intrinsically different from that of your lay brother.[5]

It is perhaps a sign of how much things have changed that John Wesley would not have agreed with the limits set by Peake. He would have agreed with the rejection of the Anglo-Catholic position and he would have agreed that the pastor is the servant, not the master, of the church of which Christ is the Head. But he would have seen an unnecessary confusion in Peake's use of the term "Church." Within the meaning of this term there exists a fundamental relationship between pastor and flock, and this cannot be satisfactorily described by saying that anything the pastor does any member of the flock may do and that the pastor is the "representative" of the flock. To say that the ministry has no authority which the church does not possess is neither here nor there; the minister has authority within the church, but for Wesley this authority was given by God. He thought in extreme circumstances you might withdraw from one pastor and join yourself to another, but as long as you remain with him you must accept that he has authority.

The negotiating committee set to work again and produced a second scheme which was presented to the Conferences of 1922. Little was done to still the doubts of the Wesleyan opposition, and the Wesleyan Conference itself was obliged to draw attention officially to the loose drafting of the paragraph on the sacraments. It is interesting to compare this paragraph with the similar passage in the answer which the Wesleyan Conference made in 1922 to the Lambeth "Appeal to All Christian People." The Wesleyan Conference here affirmed its acceptance of the Apostles' and Nicene Creeds. "While claiming reasonable liberty of interpretation we heartily accept the substance of the teaching contained in both these venerable documents." [6] The Conference also said that Christ instituted two sacraments for his church. In the scheme for union this was put more loosely: "The Methodist Church recognizes two sacraments ... which from the beginning have been observed in the church and of which it is the privilege and duty of members to avail themselves. ... According to Methodist usage the sacrament of Baptism is administered to infants." There was no mention of dominical institution in either case, nor any clear suggestion to parents that they were under any kind of obligation to bring their children for baptism. There is no need to suppose anything very significant behind this unhappy piece of drafting; but the rather casual attitude to doctrinal questions

212

helps to explain the alarm which some critics felt about the doctrinal statements.

The scheme which was submitted to the Conferences of 1924 made no great alteration in the section on doctrinal standards; there was still no mention of the historic creeds or of the position of Methodism in the Church of Christ. The issue of baptism, raised by the Wesleyan Conference, was settled rather neatly by the insertion of the phrase "of Divine appointment and perpetual obligation" after the reference to the two sacraments. The phrase was taken from the Foundation Deed Poll of the United Methodist Church (1907), in the circumstances an unimpeachable source. The articles on lay administration, however, had grown extremely vague: "The general usage of the three uniting churches, whereby the sacrament of the Lord's supper is administered by ministers, shall continue to be observed. Exceptions to the general usage may continue until the Conference, with fuller knowledge of the needs and resources of the united church, is able to determine how to provide for all Methodist people to partake of the Sacrament with regularity and frequency." [7] As a formula, this guaranteed the *status quo* for the time being, left the final decision in the hands of a united conference at which the non-Wesleyan churches would be strongly represented, and conceded to the opposition the usage, rather than the principle, of ministerial administration.

At the same time one new paragraph made its appearance, an attempt to define the ministry.

> Christ's ministers in the Church are stewards of the household of God and shepherds of His flock. Some are called and ordained to this sole occupation, and have a principal and directing part in these great duties; but they hold no priesthood differing in kind from that which is common to all the Lord's people, and they have no exclusive title to the preaching of the Gospel or the care of souls. These are ministries shared with them by others, to whom also the Spirit divides his gifts severally as he wills.[8]

This was taken from a Wesleyan Methodist statement on church membership (1908). It is a good illustration of the historical truth that the Methodist idea of the ministry differs from the Anglican partly because it has always been affected by two institutional facts of some importance: the offices of class leader and local preacher; the first concerned with the cure of souls and the second with the preaching of the gospel. In Methodism these offices existed from the start, so that any discussion of Methodism must take them into account, whereas the lay reader is a recent innovation.

The circuits were now asked for a straight vote for or against the 1924 scheme. This was done in 1924-1925 and revealed a rather similar situation in each church. In the case of Wesleyan Methodism the figures were 650 quarterly meetings in favor, 101 against, and 11 ties; this meant that 85.3 per cent were in favor of union. When this was converted into actual votes, about 70 per cent of the laity consulted were in favor. In the case of the trustees about 69 per cent voted for the scheme. The Primitive Methodist figures were much the same: 578 (86.3 per cent) quarterly meetings voted for the scheme. This represented 11,627 votes for the scheme (75.5 per cent). In the United Methodist Church 280 quarterly meetings (80 per cent) voted for the 1924 scheme; there were 7,963 votes in favor (70.7 per cent). Although these figures implied an opposition of about 25 to 30 per cent in each denomination, the Wesleyan Conference was the only one in which this minority was represented at anything like full voting strength. The broad similarity of all forms of Methodism at this time is confirmed by the fact that 70 per cent of the Wesleyan laity was prepared to vote for the 1924 scheme.

It was clear to the United Committee, however, that concessions must be made if success was to be certain in the Wesleyan Conference, especially since it was agreed in 1925 that before legal powers were sought to consummate the union a vote of 75 per cent in favor would have to be obtained at each conference. A subcommittee was set up to discuss the doubtful points, and it reported to the executive of the Union Committee in March,

1926. Its proposals justified the delaying action fought by Rattenbury and his friends up to this stage. At the head of the section on Doctrine a completely new paragraph was inserted, which established Methodism in the continuity of the historic Church.

> The Methodist Church claims and cherishes its place in the Holy Catholic Church which is the Body of Christ. It rejoices in the inheritance of the Apostolic Faith, and loyally accepts the fundamental principles of the historic creeds and the Protestant Reformation. It ever remembers that in the Providence of God Methodism was raised up to spread Scriptural Holiness throughout the land by the proclamation of the Evangelical Faith. . . .[9]

This gave the "other side," as they were sometimes called, most of what they had asked: the Catholic Church, the Apostolic Faith, the historic creeds, and the Reformation tradition; the reference to Holiness was a welcome return to the first principles of Methodism in a period prone to accept the nineteenth-century heresy that the doctrine of assurance is the primary doctrine of Methodism. It is not so clear what was meant by the "fundamental principles" of the Protestant Reformation; the term "Reformation" covers a wide variety of attitudes, and in England the Protestant tradition had been predominantly Calvinist until the Wesleyan reaction gave a new respectability to the word "Arminian."

To balance these additions the subcommittee proposed to add two sentences to the definition of the ministry which had first appeared in the 1924 scheme. The purpose of the insertion, according to Scott Lidgett, was to convince the non-Wesleyan representatives that the Wesleyans had nothing "sacerdotal" in their minds. "The Methodist Church holds the doctrine of the priesthood of all believers and consequently believes that no priesthood exists which belongs exclusively to a particular order to men. But in the exercise of its corporate life and worship special qualifications for the discharge of special duties are required, and thus the principle of representative selection is recognized."

Finally, a change was made in the approach to lay administration of the sacraments. This was important, because the institutional and the theological cross at this point. The new section said once more that the "general usage" of ministerial administration would continue and went on: "Where, however, it can be shown that any church is deprived of a reasonably frequent and regular administration through a lack of ministers, the circuit concerned may apply to Conference for the authorization of persons other than ministers to administer the sacrament." [10] Two points arise. To begin with, for the first time it was implied that lay administration was simply a solution to a problem caused by a shortage of ministers. Since union was being recommended on grounds of increased efficiency, this was also to imply that the practice of lay administration would soon become unnecessary in the united church. The new paragraph, therefore, favored Rattenbury's point of view, insofar as it seemed more important to stop lay administration than to show its theological impropriety. The second important point is the phrase "persons other than ministers." This did not rule out the possibility of women administering the Lord's Supper. In fact, of the 156 dispensations granted in 1960, 38 were granted to deaconesses. There were, in 1960, 243 deaconesses at work in England of whom 62 were in pastoral charges. It is unlikely that anyone quite foresaw this development in 1926. Certainly the non-Wesleyan negotiators were satisfied.

There is no need to carry the story much further, for the 1926 scheme was the final compromise; its effect delayed until 1932 by the continued resistance of the Wesleyan minority. In the Wesleyan synods of 1926, one Representative and eight Pastoral Sessions voted against the scheme; in the Representative Sessions the vote was 66 per cent and in the Pastoral Sessions, 57 per cent. J. E. Rattenbury, J. H. Rider, and W. H. Armstrong now felt driven to persist. In the meantime, the Primitive Methodist Conference met in June, 1926; it passed the new clause on doctrine by 168 to 9 and the clause on the sacraments by 172 to 9; the final vote in favor of the scheme was 167 to 26. At the United Methodist Conference, which met in July just before that of the Wesleyan church, the majority in favor of the new clauses was 263 to 7.

The majority party in Wesleyan Methodism made a great effort. At the July conference J. E. Rattenbury's plea for further delay in view of the Synod results was rejected in the Representative Session. On this occasion the minority was reduced to less than 25 per cent, the lowest in the whole struggle. It is very obvious at this stage that the Wesleyan laity was forcing unity on the Wesleyan ministry. Hornabrook told the Pastoral Session, which accepted the scheme 377 to 159, that the Representative Session of the twentieth century would never sit down to a blockade by the Pastoral Session. Even so, the resources of the minority were not exhausted, and the leaders themselves were horrified when in 1927 the Wesleyan Representative Session carried by only 400 to 166 the resolution which would have initiated the legal consummation of the 1926 scheme. This was less than the 75 per cent majority which had been fixed as a target. Hastily the leaders of the minority, including both J. E. Rattenbury and Sir Henry Lunn, came to terms with the advocates of union. They did so because they had no further positive demands to make, and because they could hardly carry on what was rapidly becoming a civil war in Wesleyan Methodism. A compromise which did not affect the content of the 1926 scheme made union possible by 1932.

Conclusions

At first sight there was little to divide the three branches of English Methodism, and yet the struggle was intense, especially in Wesleyan Methodism. Why was this? The answer seems to be that for the Wesleyan minority, at any rate, the "church" meant the traditional kind of institution which they knew best through Anglicanism of the older, plainer, less Anglo-Catholic kind; an Anglicanism in which the relation between minister and the people was taken for granted rather than worked out theologically. It was psychologically impossible for a Wesleyan brought up against this background to imagine himself receiving the elements from the hands of a godly layman, and to tolerate those who did seemed a kind of treason. In the non-Wesleyan churches, on the other hand, there had evolved a very different ecclesiastical pattern; here the "church" meant a community wide open to lay influence at all points. There was a streak of Quakerism in Primitive Methodism which might be traced all the way back to the Connexional founder, Hugh Bourne. A Primitive Methodist of this generation might almost have been persuaded to accept episcopacy, provided the episcopate were open to the laity. A lay bishop was precisely the idea behind their lay vice-president. The Wesleyan minority felt that the non-Wesleyans would destroy any sense of order in the church; the non-Wesleyans felt that the "other side" wanted to impose an order for which there was insufficient theological foundation. The flaw in the position of the Wesleyan minority was that they had no basis from which to attack lay administration in principle; the general consent to lay administration, however restricted, made union possible.

The weakness of the non-Wesleyan position lay in a flabby doctrine of the Holy Spirit which assumed that the "spiritual" was always the spontaneous, the unrehearsed, the unwritten, the unread. Behind this again were two different forms of social organization, the one emphasizing the need for hierarchy, the other content with something more like a permanent "frontier" conception of society. At Methodist Union they united only the negative aspects of their respective principles. The clash is fundamental because the one tradition emphasizes that the Holy Spirit normally works through a social and ecclesiastical hierarchy, whereas the other emphasizes that the Holy Spirit is more likely to cut across existing social and religious institutions.

On the whole, this study suggests that the usual picture of Methodist Union in England is misleading. It is usually implied that doctrinal factors were unimportant; in fact, they presented

218   CASE STUDIES

the major difficulty the movement encountered. The general pressure in favor of union was so strong, however (and here the all-pervasive indifference to theology was probably decisive), that the Wesleyan minority was forced to abandon its hope of preventing lay administration of the Eucharist. At the same time, however, the apparent agreement on the institutional level was a little illusory; it worked all right at the departmental and college level, but became much less obvious at the equally important point, the local churches. This would have mattered less in a country where the uniting denominations had flourished primarily in separate geographical areas (as was the case with the Methodist reunion in the United States), but the three uniting churches were represented in every English town of any importance. Worse still, all too many villages had two distinct Methodist chapels, and some even had three. The resulting problem was one of human relations, rather than church relations. Insofar as these problems have been solved since 1932, the major cause is probably the steady growth of a common English culture, based on prosperity.

NOTES FOR ESSAY 9

1. *Proceedings of the Sixth Ecumenical Methodist Conference, held in Atlanta, Georgia,* 1931, p. 24.
2. *The Methodist Recorder,* xxviii, 24 July, 1960.
3. "The Doctrinal Statement," article by A. S. Peake, in *The Methodist Leader,* February 19, 1920, Old Style No. 2698, p. 121.
4. Report of the Union Committee, which met March 4, 1920, in *The Methodist Leader,* March 11, 1920, Old Style No. 2701, p. 164.
5. *The Methodist Leader,* July 7, 1921, Old Style No. 2770, p. 425.
6. *The Minutes of the Wesleyan Methodist Conference, 1922,* the section headed "Reply of the Conference to the Lambeth Appeal," pp. 85-89.
7. *The Minutes of the Wesleyan Methodist Conference, 1924,* section headed "Inquiry concerning Methodist Union," pp. 81-82.
8. *Ibid.*
9. *The Minutes of the Wesleyan Methodist Conference, 1926,* the section headed "Doctrine," pp. 81-82.
10. *Ibid.*

BIBLIOGRAPHY FOR ESSAY 9

Minutes of the Primitive Methodist Conference to 1930.
Minutes of the United Methodist Free Church Conference to 1930.
Minutes of the Wesleyan Methodist Conference to 1930.
The [Primitive] Methodist Leader. Weekly.
The Wesleyan Methodist Times. Weekly.
A. S. Peake: A Memorial Volume. J. T. Wilkinson, ed. (London: The Epworth Press, 1959).

10.
THE CHURCH
OF SOUTH INDIA

The intimate relationship
between Western colonial expansion and Christian missions was
in the beginning accepted so uncritically that in retrospect it is
largely forgotten. When Pope Nicholas V granted in 1452 to the
King of Portugal the power to conquer the kingdoms of the
pagans and to possess their temporal goods, he also insisted that
Portugal, while extending her dominions, should do her best to
spread the kingdom of God. When Col. Munro, British Resident
in Travancore and Cochin, invited the Church Missionary Society
to send missionaries to work under his direction and to establish
English schools in those two states, his clearly expressed intentions were twofold: (1) to educate the clergy of the ancient
Syrian Church in order to revive that Church from within and
to make it an effective instrument for the evangelization of India,
and (2) to diffuse English education and ideals among the leadership of society in order to strengthen and consolidate British
colonial power in India. Although Roman Catholics and Protestants used different methods, the available historical evidence does
not suggest that either of them found any conflict between the
expansion of Western power in Asia and their spiritual aspirations

by EUGENE L. TEN BRINK[1]

for the extension of the kingdom of God. When the mission of the Church was influenced by colonial relationships it was inevitable that it would also be affected by nationalism and the freedom struggle.

The Institutional Structure of the Mission Churches

In the context of colonial relationships the structure and function of the mission compound naturally developed into a highly paternalistic pattern of protection and patronage. This paternalism was reinforced on one hand by the Anglo-Saxon consciousness of the "white man's burden," and on the other by the feudalistic structure of Indian village life in which it was placed. Without really intending it, the missionary found himself slipping into the diverse roles of spiritual *guru*, petty *raja*, employer and paymaster, landlord, money lender, and one-man judiciary for settling disputes. When the mission compound was not only the source of many forms of benevolence, but also afforded powerful influence with the foreign rulers, it is not surprising that the loyalties of Indian Christians to the mission often transcended their loyalties to their nation and culture. In the institutional pattern set up by the missionary the Indian pastors and evangelists functioned as "Mission Agents," somewhat like the "Native Agents" of the East India Company. Though some Indians of ability worked more or less happily within this structure of subservience to foreigners, on the whole it did not attract men and women of high competence or encourage the development of dynamic Indian leadership. The "mission compound mentality" is slowly giving way to Indian national consciousness and a deeper sense of Christian responsibility under the double impact of national independence and the birth of the Church of South India, but many of the consequences of that pattern of dependency continue to plague the life of the church.

A sociological analysis of the structure and function of the mission in its relationships to its environment shows more or less the same forces at work in all the missions, regardless of church polity or theological convictions. The educational, medical, and industrial institutions of the missions soon became focal points of local vested interests and the struggle for power of dominant family groups. Regardless of the nature of the formal structures of authority or the expressed goals of mission institutions, the social dynamics of a colonial India transformed the character of all church polities and mission institutions. A written constitution, formulated in the context of atomized Western societies of individual families with long experience of political democracy, developed markedly different applications and functions in a society made up of large cohesive kinship groups in a subject nation. Even groups with a nonepiscopal polity could be dominated by "unconsecrated bishops" with unlimited power. Power of the purse among an impoverished and underdeveloped people gave a missionary all other powers besides. This pattern firmly established by the missionaries was usually perpetuated in other forms by their national successors. The larger kinship groups within a mission at first competed for power under the mission, but gradually marriage alliances between them facilitated a united front to make a bid for the power of the mission itself.

The Function and Role of Leadership in the Making of the Church of South India

Though in any social group leadership is exercised and decisions are made by a relatively small number of people, the role of leadership was especially important in the movement toward unity in South India. The missionaries exercised enormous power and influence, and the missions themselves were strongly dominated by a very few senior missionaries. Indian Christians not only lived under the double imperialism of colonial status and the mission compound, but had also been trained by centuries of tradition to accept without question the spiritual authority of the *guru* and the political authority of the *raja*. As in the historic meeting of Indian leaders in Tranquebar in 1919, the work of negotiating committeees was done by a very small group of leaders. The long theological debates about union were carried on by a handful of missionary theologians, Indian pastors, and British scholars to whom appeals were made by the various traditions. Although the final decisions were made by democratically elected church councils, their decisions were more often acts of faith in their trusted leadership than they were the expression of convictions arrived at through an understanding of the issues involved. There was a general consciousness of the scandal of Christian disunity as well as vague fears of loss of mission identity and foreign support, but the rank and file were for the most part willing to accept the decision of their representatives regarding unity and the means they adopted to achieve it. An Anglo-Catholic missionary reported that ninety-five per cent of the Indian members of his church did not know what churches were uniting. A Methodist missionary wrote in the *Methodist Recorder* in 1931 that "most of our Indian Christians know little or nothing about (the Scheme of Union); and, drawn as they are chiefly from the depressed classes, only just emerging from darkness and ignorance into the light of the Gospel of Christ, there is no reason why they should be troubled with the technicalities of a discussion which could only confuse them."

Sociological Factors

When about thirty Indian leaders and a few missionaries met at Tranquebar in 1919 to draw up a manifesto for Christian reunion, the world was rife with postwar idealism and optimism. The "war to end war" had been fought and won. It was an apocalyptic atmosphere where it seemed that anything could happen and no change was too great to be possible. Christian leaders who were drawing up the Tranquebar Manifesto for Christian unity were conscious of the fact that at the same time the leaders of the nations were meeting in Versailles to draw up plans for a League of Nations. Moreover, this new movement toward Christian unity was the extension of a union movement which had begun about two decades earlier. As a result of many years of missionary conferences held in the hill stations in the vacation month of May, missionaries of various denominations could discuss common problems, work out comity arrangements to avoid duplication of effort and conflict, and lay the foundations for the great union institutions which played an important part in the union movement. Most of the Indian leaders of that movement had studied in union institutions like Madras Christian College and the United Theological College, Bangalore, and had participated in the Student Volunteer Movement.

Thus the fellowship of missionaries which found in the face of a great non-Christian culture a sense of cultural and racial solidarity that was stronger than denominational differences, and Indian leaders who had studied together in union colleges, evolved similar patterns of work more or less based on the Henry Venn philosophy of missions. This strategy involved mission institutions for training up Indian leadership, who would take over from the missionaries in a process of devolution toward a self-governing, self-supporting and self-propagating church. Curiously enough this theory of the fading mission was developed at about the same time as Karl Marx was formulating his theory of the fading state in the same city of London. Venn thought of the mission as the scaffolding for the erection of the indigenous church, as Marx thought of the state as the temporary scaffold for the construction of a classless society. Neither theory took sufficiently into account the factor of human sin, particularly as love of power, or the resistance of established institutions to any change in function or structure. However, a growing similarity of outlook helped to bring into being a series of unions which eventually led to the Church of South India. The first was in 1901 when the work of the Reformed Church in America and the Scottish Presbyterians were joined together into the United Church. This was followed by a union of the work of the London Missionary Society and the Congregationalist churches of the American Board in Madura District. These two unions came together into the South India United Church in 1908.

This movement toward unity was also facilitated by the fact of increasing mobility of Christians in South India. The great famine of 1876 stimulated the dispersion of Tamil Christians, especially from the southernmost district of Madras. Some of them entered existing Anglican Churches, or started new ones, others found employment and membership in other denominations. Thus, family ties connected individuals belonging to many different churches. At the Tranquebar meeting Bishop Azariah made an eloquent appeal for unity on the basis of family ties: "Are we not all here brothers, brothers-in-law, fathers-in-law and sons-in-law!" As Rev. P. Sandegren, an eyewitness, has pointed out, it was in reality an appeal to each caste to leap over the boundaries of the churches.

The Influence of Indian Nationalism

After World War I the growing demand for self-determination began to be felt both in the nation and in the church. An increasing role in local government and inclusion of Indians in church committees marked the beginning of a transition from nineteenth-century colonialism toward democracy in both church and state. Even though few Indian Christians were directly involved in the freedom struggle, they were influenced by the aspirations and tensions in their society. The rising tide of nationalism and a renascence of Indian culture made South Indians more deeply conscious of their common Dravidian origins, even though they spoke four different languages. Parallel to the political movements of the time, an independence movement began in the church. As Indians gained political concessions in British India leading to a kind of diarchy and division of power, so Indian church committees vied for the power of the old "mission raj." The devolution of powers from mission to church, often too little and too late, intensified the conflict between them. Through the freedom struggle of the church from the mission there was a devolution of power, moving toward the distant goal of full integration of mission and church. This integration was sometimes

　　　　　　　　　　　　　　　　　　　CASE STUDIES

impeded by the fact that family or caste rivalries within the Christian community often kept a missionary in power as the only person acceptable to all parties.

This process of transfer of power was hastened by the "Quit India" campaign which Gandhi launched against the British in 1942. It was stimulated further when the first Japanese bombs were dropped along the Madras coast and the American consulate ordered all American citizens to leave India. These events strengthened both the movement toward Indian leadership and toward unity. The approach of independence carried with it the threat of the loss of favored minority status given the Christians under the British. The insecurity of the Christian minority was accentuated by the inner divisions among the Christians. The uncertainty regarding the future of missions in an independent India called for consolidation through unity in case foreign missionaries had to withdraw.

Caste and Mission

The all-pervading reality of the caste structure of Indian society has determined the patterns of social behavior for about two thousand years. For some groups of Christians caste blood is thicker than the water of baptism. One of the chief inhibiting factors against Christian unity is the persistence of caste in the church. Many of the Anglicans came from caste Hindu background. Their higher cultural level, stronger economic status, and group solidarity enabled great numbers of them to attain higher educational levels than the other Christians. Thus they were able to move more rapidly than others toward a middle-class urban orientation. Non-Anglicans came largely from a depressed-class rural origin. Christian unity confronted them with the prospect of return to the domination of the caste man which they had escaped through baptism. Moreover, marriage alliances and intimate social intercourse continued for the most part along traditional caste lines. Like race prejudice in the West, caste consciousness in South India tends to blunt the edge of the gospel, distort the character of the church, and hinder the cause of Christian unity.

Another factor which tended to inhibit the development of Christian unity was fear of loss of a distinctive character and ethos which had been built up in a mission tradition. One pastor coming from a mission that had built up a powerful administrative structure ended an impassioned plea against union with the words, "If union come, Methodism go to dog, India go to dog, world to dog!" Others felt that the acceptance of union meant disloyalty to their benefactors, the equivalent of saying to the mother Church, "We no longer want you, we have accepted a stepmother." Christians coming from American-supported missions often feared a loss of special privileges such as higher levels of subsidies and salaries and opportunities for scholarships and deputations to America. When a local group in one of the American churches registered "a most vigorous and solemn protest" against union out of a "fear of papacy" and hinted that these "dangerous developments" in South India would "affect the financial interest of our churches toward the mission work," the missionaries of that church voted to reassure the local group in America that as a mission they were not prepared to give assent to the scheme of union. However, the Board of Missions of that church pointed out that the mission had no authority in the matter, and it was for the church in India to decide for itself.

Shifts in Power Since Union

Before the independence of India and the inauguration of the Church of South India in 1947 the Indian outlook was strongly oriented toward the British Isles. Since a degree from a British university was the best passport to the higher ranks of public service, most of the Indian students who went abroad for higher studies went to the United Kingdom. Except for mission areas allotted by comity agreements to American churches, large parts of India had little or no contact with America. The achievement of independence marked a tremendous shift in the balance of influence from Great Britain to the United States of America. Large numbers of students began to go to America for their studies. With increasing financial integration American-supported projects began to be developed in areas of the church where they were hitherto unknown. Along with American money, American ideas and American personnel were more widely distributed in the life of the church. All this increased the complexity of the tensions in Indian society, such as the difference in the standard of living between Americans and other missionaries, the eagerness of groups in India to attract the attention of American benevolent organizations, the increase of American missionaries of a sectarian type, and the impact of the American way of life on Indian culture.

With church union and national independence has also come a more rapid shift of power from the mission to the church. However, many of the dioceses of the Church of South India are still in effect federations of mission fields rather than units of a united Indian church, because mission funds are still carefully earmarked for traditional work and church and mission workers continue in their old surroundings. Until the church is free to effect an interchange of personnel and a pooling of funds for most effective use in the total life and mission of the church, unity cannot become a full reality. However, this process of unification creates uneasiness among local vested interests and denominational power blocs. Local leaders who lose influence in a larger grouping sometimes go into opposition and become a disruptive influence.

The formation of larger and more heterogeneous groupings in a united church tends to shift the power struggles from the plane of rival family kinship groups to caste and linguistic groups. Owing to wide disparities in educational advancement union has sometimes increased the opportunities for the domination of underprivileged groups by more advanced communities of Christians, because of the breakdown of denominational barriers by which they were isolated from each other in the past. The re-alignment of state boundaries on linguistic lines has tended to intensify linguistic divisions among Christians. Sometimes the balance of power between two dominant minority groups is controlled by a much larger but unorganized and underprivileged group, somewhat like the uncommitted nations between the two major powers in the United Nations. Unable to achieve dominance over these better-equipped minorities, they can only decide which of the ascendant minorities shall dominate them. Secret fears of the effective techniques of an aggressive minority are sometimes the operative forces behind "theological" objections to "Anglicanization" of the Church of South India.

Conclusions

The positive factors for convergence in Indian society before 1947 overbalanced the negative trends toward distintegration, and therefore reinforced the movement toward Christian unity in South India. The common Indian struggle for independence from the British Empire united Hindu and Muslim, Brahmin and Dravidian, North and South, and suppressed latent conflicts which were to break out anew after Independence. So also the struggle of the Indian Church for freedom from foreign mission control united many diverse elements in Indian Christian society. The attainment of a united Indian Church was also the beginning of a fresh outbreak of Christian communal rivalries. In most of the Church of South India the roots of Christianity are about a century old, but the roots of caste go back two thousand years. Therefore the consciousness of ancient distinctions is often stronger than the sense of a shared Christian past. Caste and linguistic communalism, which are disruptive factors in Christian society, are only very slowly being permeated with the gospel and the goal of Christian unity. Moreover, the lingering patterns of foreign denominational mission support, which still bear the marks of nineteenth-century colonialism, continue to inhibit the movement toward real Christian unity.

The sociological factors which reinforced the movement toward unity have grown weaker after 1947, while disruptive forces have gained strength after that time in both the church and in society. In Indian society the forward movement of national development helps to check disintegration. In the church the unplanned retreat from outmoded mission institutions often has the demoralizing effect of a badly organized rear-guard action. But the very existence of the Church of South India is a gift of God's grace, an institutional reality in the life of the world. Although the reality of Christian unity awaits a collective change of heart concerning social distinctions inherited from a non-Christian past, the organizational structure of unity is altogether likely to survive.

Not only the missionary zeal and theological convictions concerning unity of Christians of South India, but also the historical forces of two world wars and the birth pangs of the second-largest nation on earth, went into the making of the Church of South India. It took the earth-shaking events of the twentieth century to shatter the institutionalized structures of Christian disunity. Now that Christian reunion has been institutionalized at a new level, involving both episcopal and nonepiscopal churches, it should not require such major earthquakes to achieve wider unity in South India, or to repeat the process in other parts of the world. In spite of the tensions, life together in this movement toward the one, holy, catholic and apostolic Church is a tremendous experience. This experience should make it easier for others to believe that such things are possible, even in a world where men's lives are determined, not so much by their formal confessions of faith, as by their uncritical acceptance of religious institutions inherited from the past, often from cultures other than their own. Just as the Great Schism in the Church in A.D. 1054 strengthened the spirit of schism in the Body of Christ, so also the Great Reunion of 1947 can strengthen and renew the spirit of wholeness throughout the broken household of God.

CHRONOLOGICAL SUMMARY

1858—First Hill Station Missionary Conference in South India in Ootacamund

1888—Lambeth Quadrilateral

1901—United Church formed from Reformed and Presbyterian bodies in South India

1905—Union of Congregationalists of the London Missionary Society and the American Board of Commissioners in Madura

1908—South India United Church formed by merger of two unions above

1912—India National Missionary Conference led by Dr. John R. Mott

1912—The Rev. V. S. Azariah became the first Indian Bishop.

1919—Tranquebar Conference and Manifesto

1929—First Scheme of Union, followed by six further editions

1941—Final Scheme of Union

1947, September 27—Inauguration of the Church of South India at St. George's Cathedral, Madras

NOTE FOR ESSAY 10

1. The author has made extensive use of Bengt Sundkler's excellent work, *Church of South India: The Movement towards Union, 1900-1947*, and R. D. Paul's *The First Decade*. His grateful thanks are also due to the following for their critical remarks which have been helpful in writing this essay: Principal J. R. Chandran, Dr. P. D. Devanandan, Rev. Paul Sandegren, Rt. Rev. H. Sumitra, and Prof. Chandran Devanesan.

BIBLIOGRAPHY FOR ESSAY 10

Grant, John W., *God's People in India* (Madras: Christian Literature Society; Toronto: Ryerson Press, 1959).

Hollis, M., *Paternalism and the Church: A Study of South Indian Church History* (New York and London: Oxford University Press, 1962).

Newbigin, J. E. L., *A South India Diary* (London: SCM Press, 1951). Am. ed., *That All May Be One* (New York: Association Press, 1952).

Paul, R. D., *The First Decade: An Account of the Church of South India* (Madras: Christian Literature Society, 1958).

Rawlinson, A. E. J., *The Church of South India* (London: Hodder & Stoughton, 1951).

Sundkler, Bengt, *Church of South India: The Movement towards Union, 1900-1947* (London: Lutterworth Press, 1954).

Ward, Marcus, *The Pilgrim Church: An Account of the First Five Years in the Life of the Church of South India* (London: Epworth Press, 1953).

11.
THE UNITED CHURCH OF CHRIST IN JAPAN

The Nihon Kirisuto Kyodan (hereafter termed Kyodan) is the United Church of Christ in Japan and represents the union of many denominational churches founded by mission endeavors since 1859. The Kyodan was established by resolution of the General Assembly in June, 1941, and was recognized by the Ministry of Education of the Japanese Government as fulfilling the requirements of the 1939 Religious Bodies Law. Orientation toward union, however, had been carried forward since the formation of the National Christian Council in 1923. A Commission on Promoting the Endeavor for Unification was established in 1928 through the encouragement of the International Missionary Conference held at Jerusalem. Through the study of this Commission a set of findings or proposals for unification were formulated and submitted to the Council. A decade passed. Surrounded by the atmosphere of military activity the National Christian Council's Fifteenth General Assembly in 1937 adopted the findings of the committee above with slight revision and projected the date of unification for 1940. This was the second step. However, the findings of the National

by KEN ISHIWARA

Christian Council possessed no inherent power to move denominational churches to take further steps toward unification.

On the other hand, the Government sent a draft of the Religious Bodies Law to the Diet in 1939 and succeeded in having it enacted. The law was to be effective after April, 1940. All religious organizations (shrines, temples, churches, denominations, and the like) were regulated under this law. As a consequence, Christian churches were moved to action, and their decision was to maintain existence under the aspect of state oversight. Thus, the United Church of Christ in Japan emerged. The emergence was not wholly the result of voluntary action. It was in part forced, and the NCC findings of 1937 were not central in guiding it. The polity of the Kyodan was regulated entirely by the Religious Bodies Law.

It was only when the Religious Bodies Law was revoked in the fall of 1945 that the Kyodan was free to establish her own polity according to her religious ideas and without governmental control. Such is the story behind the emergence of the Kyodan and the clue to her institutionalism. We shall first indicate in greater detail the historical conditions and character of her life and growth.

Founding of the Kyodan

The official date of the organization of the Kyodan is recorded as June 24, 1941, as already stated. The National Christian Council assumed the good offices of facilitating the organization of the United Church, following the completion of which task it was itself dissolved. In a sense, therefore, so far as the formal structure of the Kyodan is concerned, in order to meet the situation which existed at that time the National Christian Council itself seemed to be reorganized and enlarged as one Protestant Christian body. This may be called the mother-body of the Kyodan. There was, however, a specific difference between the NCC and the Kyodan. The former was a private institution and included in its membership a number of special Christian bodies besides the several

Protestant churches; the Kyodan became the one Protestant religious body recognized by the government, including in its fellowship all Christian churches and institutions in Japan. The government exercised some kind of control over the NCC, either by way of direct legal authority or by the exercise of administrative measures from the standpoint of national policy. But when the Kyodan was organized, the government extended to it legal public recognition but at the same time tightened control over its organizational life. This control, the result in part of the Religious Bodies Law put into force in April, 1940, grew increasingly severe during the years of the war.

The policy of the Japanese government in attempting to maintain control over religious bodies through legislation can be dated back to the early Meiji period. As early as 1899 the Meiji Government tried to gain parliamentary recognition for such legislation. Passage of such a law was attempted three times during the subsequent forty years. Each time, however, passage was blocked by strong opposition both in and outside of the parliament. Finally in 1939 the Hiranuma Cabinet barely succeeded in forcing passage of this legislation by the Diet under the guise of protecting religious bodies. Yet the law exercised government sovereignty over them to the end that "they render co-operation in the uplift of the spiritual life of the nation and for the unity of thought." The disguised intention was to exercise control over religion and to make use of it for the purposes of national policy through the instrumentality of making it a recognized institution. On the surface the Religious Bodies Law claimed to respect the freedom of faith of the religious people. In reality it was necessary for the religious bodies to secure the recognition of the Minister of Education. Furthermore, each religious body was forced to designate a person responsible to the government. Each separate denomination or independent church was required to have a director (or *torisha*) who was the elected representative of the religious body. Article 16 of the law states, "When the propagation of dogma or the conducting of ceremonies or religious rites constitute an obstacle to peace and order or cause failure in the faithful performance of the obligations of the citizen, the Minister of Education concerned may limit or forbid such ceremony or rite, may stop the function of the church minister, or cancel approval of the establishment of the religious body." In this way the law gave power to control the establishment as well as the activities of religious bodies not only to the cabinet minister in charge but also to local government officers acting under the prefectural governor. The article of the law which states that any religious rite or activity would suffer no restriction so long as the right of practice does not violate the public interest could be interpreted by local officers in accordance with their personal views and ideas.

The Religious Bodies Law was to be enforced from April, 1940, so that each Christian church and group had to make a final decision in relation to it. According to the law Christian bodies were to be called *Kyodan* and the separate denominations and churches of Christianity were to be united under three groups: the Roman Catholic, the Greek Orthodox, and the Protestant. No independent denomination or independent churches were allowed unless they had more than 50 individual congregations and 5,000 members. At that time there were only seven major Protestant denominations—the Japan Church of Christ (which was related to the Presbyterian and the Reformed Church boards), the Methodist, Congregationalist, Episcopal, Baptist (Union of Northern and Southern Congregations), Evangelical Lutheran, and the Holiness churches—which had sufficient numbers in both congregations and members to meet the letter of the law qualifying for continuation as independent denominations. However, it was strongly desired by the government that these churches should be united into one, to say nothing of the small denominations then in existence. Beyond this, among these major denominations were a large number of Christian laymen and pastors who thought it necessary in this critical period of political circumstance for all Protestant churches to unite in one body. Many conferences and negotiations took place after the early spring of 1940. Finally at the "All Christian Conference" held on

August 17, the proposal was made to request the executive board of the Japan National Christian Council to perform the good office of bringing about the union of all Protestant groups. A joint conference of all Protestant denominational leaders was called. This conference installed an official preparatory committee on church union and extended an invitation to all churches and related institutions to participate in the union of the Church. Accordingly each denomination held its separate general meeting to determine its position and on the occasion of the National Christian Assembly celebrating the 2600th anniversary of the nation's founding, held on October 17, 1940, the declaration of the "All-Protestant Union" was proclaimed. In the declaration there was stated the following sentence: "We, Christians of this country, in response to this great issue, and leaving behind the denominational differences, desire to come to unity and take our part in the guidance of the nation's spirit, to support the great rule of the Government and to pledge loyal performance of the essence of allegiance to our nation."

This declaration of the unity of churches represented only a formal expression in favor of union. There remained the technical negotiations of how the union should be realized, but no form of unity had been drawn up in relation to faith and theology. Even so, at that time it was stated in the declaration of union, "We expect to carry out the union of all the churches of Christ in Japan." The fact of the matter was that the Kyodan thus formed could be no more an essential or organic union than the National Christian Council had been.

However, the matter could not be left as it was. There was the necessity to become truly united. For this purpose a preparatory committee was designated to investigate the methods and means of achieving true unity. Nevertheless the committee failed to find a workable organizational plan which would be a "complete union of the whole." The matter was settled by adopting the federated, block system within the one Kyodan, leaving the matter of creed, administrative system, traditions, and rites to the discretion of each group in terms of their individual historical traditions, and focusing unity only upon the one order of the ministry, thus meeting the requirement of the Religious Bodies Law. In this way the formal organization of the Church Union was to be realized. On June 24-25, 1941, in accordance with the schedule, the constituting General Assembly met to organize officially the "United Church of Christ in Japan *(Nihon Kirisuto Kyodan)*."

Formal recognition by the Ministry of Education was given to the Kyodan as a legal religious body according to the Religious Bodies Law on November 24, 1941. The Kyodan represented the union of over 30 formerly separate denominations involving 1,534 churches and 388 congregations, with 2,697 ministers and over 259,000 members. The nation was divided geographically into 18 districts, including Formosa and Korea. Beyond this, three mission areas were designated as follows: Manchuria, North China, and South China. The denominations referred to above within the organization of the Kyodan were grouped into 11 sections (called *Bu)* as follows:

Section 1: The Japan Church of Christ

Section 2: The Japan Methodist Church, the Japan Methodist Protestant Church, and the Japan Seien Church

Section 3: The Japan Congregational Church, the Church of the Brethren, the Japan Evangelical Church, the Church of Christ, the Society of Friends

Section 4: The Japan Baptist Church (the Northern and the Southern)

Section 5: The Japan Evangelical Lutheran Church

Section 6: The Japan Holiness Church

Section 7: The *Nihon Dendo Kirisuto Kyodan* (including the Jesus Christ Church, the *Kyodo* Christian Church, the Christian Mission Church, the Society of Christian Mission, the Japan Pentecost Church, and the Japan Purity Church)

Section 8: The Japan Sanctification Christian Kyodan (including the Free Methodist Church, the Eastern and the

Western Branch of the Nazarene Church, the Alliance
Church, the Federated Christian Church, and the World
Mission Society)

Section 9: The Kiyome Church (Purification)

Section 10: The Japan Federation of Independent Churches
(including the Wesleyan Methodist Church, the General
Evangelistic Church, The United Christian Kyodan, the
Tokyo Christian Church, the Japan Bible Society, and the
Holy Ghost Church)

Section 11: The Salvation Body (Salvation Army)

In this way it can be said that the Kyodan with its federated
sectional system was in reality a kind of reorganization of the
National Christian Council, under the presidency of the "Torisha"
director, who was supposed to exercise control over the whole
Kyodan. However, as each section had its own annual meeting to
determine the business of the section, his position was not clarified, and he was only a nominal head. At the first General Assembly held in November, 1942, the resolution to dissolve the
sectional system was passed and was to be put into force in April,
1943.

In spite of the dissolution of the sectional system and of the
meaning which this act held in terms of "forward march" toward
organic union in a formal sense, the fundamental question of
Kyodan as a united church remained—the achievement of unity
of faith. The Second General Assembly in November, 1943, voted
to merge some of the 18 districts into a total of 9 districts for the
purpose of simplifying the administrative business of the general
office; and at the same time to the eight departments or bureaus
was added the new East Asia Department. This Assembly also
hesitated in the adoption of a creed, but by action of the committee on creed a catechism was adopted. In April, 1944, a director of the Orientation of Thought Bureau *(Kyogaku Kyoku)*
was appointed in order to carry out the urgent program of
Kyodan. Owing to the straitened conditions of the war situation,
it became increasingly difficult within the Christian world to

conduct free activities. This situation continued until the end of the Pacific War in August, 1945.

Reconstruction After the War

The conclusion of the war brought naturally at first a serious shock to the Christian churches in Japan, but at the same time freedom from control by outside powers, and the dawn of a new era of peace and bright hope. Within the two months following the close of the war the Religious Bodies Law was withdrawn, releasing Christian churches not only from legal regulations as regards matters of faith and doctrine, but also in relation to the conduct of religious worship as well as in the areas of church order, organization, and program. However, like the Japanese people at large, following the sudden release from war controls, the churches had not only failed to prepare for the most effective use of the opportunities of peace, but their resources, both material and personnel, even spiritual resources, had been exhausted by the ravages of war. At this time the churches were deeply grateful for the aid which was sent to them by Christian friends of many countries. This aid was a free expression of Christian fellowship but involved no inclusive and systematic plan of action and, hence, did not bear so much real fruit as it might have. Many new missionaries came to the country without adequate preparation in terms of knowledge of the Japanese character and Christian work in Japan. Hence, some denominations which were previously unknown were introduced, and other missionaries sought to re-establish old relationships with their mission boards, causing much disturbance within the Kyodan and leading to the withdrawal of some congregations from the union.

At this confusing time three attitudes were at work in the sphere of the United Church. The first opinion was reflected by those who considered the union simply as a matter brought about by the coercion of government through the Religious Bodies Law. Therefore, each Christian should be free to follow the guidance of his own conscience. The second opinion advocated the re-establishment of the former situation by restoration of the prewar denominational mission board relationships. The third opinion affirmed that even though the formation of Kyodan was in part the result of the Religious Bodies Law, it was also a providential opportunity for union of the churches in Japan, and in that sense efforts should be continued to maintain the union and to strive for further progress and the internal perfecting of unity by improving the order of the church. Obviously the first and the second, without recognizing the significance of Kyodan, shared a common desire and motivation, that is, to leave the Kyodan. Those who apprehended the ecumenical significance of the Kyodan and desired to support it were represented in the third group. As a result of these conflicting opinions the Japan Episcopal Church, the Evangelical Lutheran Church, the Holiness groups, the Oriental Missionary Society, the Baptist Federation, the Southern Presbyterians, the Salvation Army, the Society of Friends, the Nazarenes, and other minor denominations withdrew one by one from the Kyodan in 1946-1947. This same unsettled condition continued until 1950. In this way it was inevitable that some groups which had been comrades during the war years should have severed the ties with the United Church. Many, however, of the major churches remained to recognize the ecumenical significance of Kyodan and to constitute a union of Christian churches in Japan. The statistical report for the year 1955, ten years after the close of the war, according to the official year book of the Kyodan for the year 1957, is listed as follows:

> Churches and preaching stations: 1,507 (about one-third of the total number of Protestant churches in Japan)
> Ministers: 1,455 (one-third of the total number of Japanese ministers). Retired: 581. Total: 2,036
> Church members: 129,533 (a little less than one-half of the Protestant church membership)

In response to this situation in Japan the leading mission boards in the United States and Canada which had been sending missionaries to Japan since the beginning of Protestant evangelical work, gave very serious attention to the relationship of mission boards to the postwar Christian situation in Japan. As a result ten leading mission boards in North America united to form the Interboard Committee for Christian Work in Japan in November, 1947. This was done in order to lend strength and support to the Kyodan and its principle of church union in Japan. Also the Education Association of Christian Schools in Japan and the League of Christian Social Work Institutions were formed. At the same time there appeared with the close of the war the need to re-establish the National Christian Council *(Nihon Kirisutokyo Kyogikai)* in order to maintain the interdenominational work among the United Church and other Christian relationships. It was in June, 1948, that the NCC was reorganized.

It was generally recognized that the Kyodan, following the restoration of peace, must undergo some fundamental changes in terms of church structure, faith, and order. Another urgent project was the restoration of the churches which had lost their property and buildings. The memorable third General Assembly of the Kyodan was opened in June, 1946. In its session it was determined to repeal all laws and regulations established during the war period, and, further, to appoint a committee to prepare a draft of a new church constitution and regulations. The Assembly also repealed the system of the director and the General Control Office, setting up in its stead a moderatorship of the General Assembly, defining his function and power and assigning him to represent the Kyodan to the government as the *Kyodan Shukansha* (a governmental name given to the president responsible to the body as a person in charge). At the same time autocratic sections or bureaus within the general administrative headquarters of the church were eliminated and, instead, nine departments were established: General Affairs, Evangelism, Sunday School, Ministerial Affairs, Educational Affairs, Social Work, Women's Work, Youth Work, and Finance. As for the Executive Committee, 29 members were elected by the General Assembly and a number of committees were appointed, such as the Special Committees on Rural Evangelism, Church Reconstruction, Ordination,

Auditing, Ministerial Candidates, Creedal Preparation Committee, Hymnal Committee, Study Committee on the System of Theological Seminaries, the Allied Properties Supervision Committee, the General Committee for the Christ Movement for the Building of the New Japan.

The institutional structure described above not only represented the scope of activities possible in terms of the resources and energy of the church at that time of conflict, but also represented the program best-fitted for the church under the social conditions of extreme poverty and fatigue which prevailed at the close of the war. Therefore, when after some years the life of the nation in general achieved greater stability and order, the structure of the Kyodan also necessarily had to undergo change. The Sixth General Assembly of the Kyodan in 1950 determined to carry out such a reform. A proposal was drafted to rationalize the central administrative organization and to give greater power to the districts. The departmental system was changed to a committee system, with committees holding the power to determine and to carry out decisions and programs. Ten committees were organized as follows: General Evangelism, Faith and Order, Education, Ministerial Qualifications, Hymnal, Theological Seminaries, Social, Publications, Personnel, and Finance. A General Headquarters, presided over by the executive secretary with five assistant secretaries to handle the general business of different areas in the life and program of the church, was established. Some of the districts were merged so that the number dropped from 18 to 13, being determined geographically as follows: Hokksi, Ou, Tohoku, Kanto, Tokyo, Tokai, Chubu, Kyoto, Osaka, Hyogo, Chugoku, Shikoku, and Kyushu.

Although these changes indicated the general return to normality they left room for further criticism, and more changes took place but without fundamental reform. As regards the special commissions, there have been not a few changes and even some new additions. Especially was interest focused upon evangelism. The Seventh General Assembly (1952) inaugurated the Home Mission Society for the purpose of "stimulating a spirit of mission at large in the church and of strengthening a system of mutual church aid whereby evangelism could be vitalized both within the churches and without in the direction of non-Christian society." The Eighth General Assembly (1954) appointed a committee on Centennial Evangelism. It also established a special committee for pioneer evangelism in Hokkaido, together with a committee for the Labor Evangelism Program and others.

It is worthy of note that the same General Assembly voted to establish the Research Institute on the Mission of the Church. Its purpose is to encourage studies "both of a fundamental and of a practical character" on matters pertaining to "the various problems present in the area of the evangelistic life of the Kyodan and the area of church formation." Provision was made for five sections of the Research Institute: evangelism and theology; the policy of evangelism; the church and education; the church and society; and the church and international problems. In terms of plan and intention, the Research Institute was well conceived. However, problems relating to the life and program of the church are legion in character, and extend across the field of education, social work, and matters related to such institutions. All international problems which bear any relation to the mission of the church are involved. Hence, the danger of the Research Institute is to spread itself too widely, thus weakening its effectiveness.

Along with such reforms as listed above, amendments to church regulations were proposed from time to time. Amendments so proposed, however, could be put through the Assembly only with the greatest difficulty. The most noteworthy amendment to date was that passed by the Eleventh General Assembly in 1960, whereby the different committees and agencies for evangelism were brought together in a general forum involving redefinition of their specific programs as a part of one evangelistic outreach of the Kyodan. A position of general secretary for the Evangelism Committee was authorized by the General Assembly to exercise supervisory oversight in relation to the various committees and commissions on evangelism. The committee on Overseas Evangelism was elevated to the position of one of the official standing committees of the church. We know also that already by action of the earlier Eighth General Assembly the number of districts was changed from 13 to 14 as a result of the division of the Chugoku district into two sections. In recent years voices among some churches have called for greater autonomy on the part of the districts in church organization and program. Because of the many and complex problems involved in the concept of autonomy of the districts, however, no legislation has as yet been approved by a General Assembly of the Kyodan. This is not a problem that will be solved easily, since it involves the fundamental theological conception of the nature of the United Church.

Inner Consolidation

The most important problem for the Kyodan as a religious institution is to develop a definite standard of faith; so it was presumed from its outset that the Kyodan would have a creedal statement. However, as stated above, the National Christian Council had consciously avoided taking up for discussion the problems relating to a creedal statement. Not only this, but the constitution of the Council itself as adopted in 1923 stated, "It shall not be the business of the NCC to enter upon the matters of church creed or political opinions and any resolutions within these areas shall have no binding force upon the affiliated groups." When the National Christian Council undertook to promote the union of the churches, however, it was unable entirely to disregard the matter of creed or statement of faith. Furthermore the Religious Bodies Law required an official report to the government outlining the doctrinal position of the new United Church of Christ. Hence, the Preparation Committee for Church Union established in 1940 intended to prepare a draft confession of faith when they considered the structure of the United Church. In actuality, they could prepare only a brief and simple statement of faith, so-called 'Kyogi no taiyo' (Outline of the Doctrine of the Kyodan), and after securing its public recognition by the Minister of Education in 1941 as the official doctrinal position of the Kyodan, they presented this brief outline along with a statement of principles regulating Christian living to the assembly of churchmen. It was then left to the Bureau of Orientation of Thought. This Bureau presented to the Second General Assembly of the Kyodan (1943) a catechism designed to serve temporarily as a standard of faith until such time as a full statement of faith could be prepared.

Following the close of the war in 1946 the Fourth General Assembly of the Kyodan adopted its constitution containing in the third article an outline of the doctrinal principles of the church. The Assembly then appointed a committee to work toward the preparation of a creed. The Fifth General Assembly (1948) voted to accept the Apostles' Creed and to modify the second article of the Constitution by inserting "Confessing the Apostles' Creed." The Assembly further instructed the Department of Educational Affairs to formulate a correct reading of the Lord's Prayer and the Apostles' Creed in Japanese. This report of the department was brought to the next General Assembly in 1950. This same Assembly acknowledged the report and approved changes and revisions in the organization of the Kyodan as described in part above. These revisions involved the dissolution of the Department of Educational Affairs and the establishment in its stead of the Committee on Faith and Order. This committee then took up the work of amending the catechism and further designated a special committee to prepare a draft statement of a confession of faith. This draft statement was reported to the Seventh General Assembly in 1952, and, after continued study for two more years, was accepted by the Eighth General Assembly of 1954. At that time the Assembly voted to adopt the confession of faith along with a statement of principles for Christian living.

The character of this confession as a standard of faith for the United Church is still doubtful when judged from an ideal standpoint. Its adoption has not solved all the questions involved in the matter of a creed for the church as envisioned at the outset. It is certain, however, that the confessional statement by its proclamation will lend power to the continued development of inner life in the Kyodan. No one will question the sincerity of the Kyodan's attitude in establishing the Bible as the basis of faith and endeavoring to obey it. The act of proclaiming a confessional statement and incorporating into it the Apostles' Creed has given guidance to the interpretation of the Bible and has confirmed the resolve to maintain the faith of the early church and to conserve the reformers' understanding of the gospel.

Though there were several groups and individual ministers who, immediately after the cancellation of the Religious Bodies Law, returned to former denominational organizations, there also arose some groups who wanted the restoration of the sectional system for denominational activities within the Kyodan. These forces began to be heard in 1948-1949, when the disturbance caused by the withdrawal of several denominations had quieted down. The Committee on Faith and Order, which was asked to study the request for the sectional system, and which had made every effort to achieve a broad understanding, submitted its report publicly and clarified the point in question. This committee also continued to maintain negotiations with several denominational groups, such as a part of the former Japan Church of Christ (historically related to the Presbyterian and Reformed Church Mission Boards), with spokesmen for the sectional system, and with groups related to the Baptist *Shinseikai* (New Life Society) during an initial year of joint study aimed at a certain degree of common understanding. In spite of the efforts of the committee, however, early in 1951 some 50 congregations of the former Japan Church of Christ withdrew from the Kyodan. The former Free Methodist group also withdrew into closer relationship to their companion denomination overseas. In the case of the former Baptists, the larger number remained in the Kyodan. These matters must be remembered as unfortunate incidents in the history of the formation of the United Church. At the same time, however, we must note that these incidents offer a sharp warning against too hasty treatment of the matters involved and excessive eagerness in bringing about the desired result of formal union.

The Kyodan must necessarily continue its efforts toward the

realization of union and unity within. Of primary importance is the proper ordering of the constitution of the church upon the basis of the confession of faith. Following the Eighth General Assembly (1954), which adopted the confession, study was naturally begun to change a portion of the constitution, and an amendment was so proposed to the Ninth General Assembly (1956). It was to be expected, however, that in response to the demand for further comprehensive study, the matter was entrusted to the Faith and Order Committee. This report was submitted by the Faith and Order Committee to the Tenth General Assembly in 1958, which then appointed a Special Constitutional Revisions Committee to prepare a draft of the amendments, which was presented to the Eleventh General Assembly in 1960. The proposed change was not accepted. Because of strong objections to the character of the districts in the structure of the Church, decision was postponed until later. We have not yet achieved full understanding about the nature of the church within the Kyodan.

Institutional Structure of the Kyodan

The Kyodan is the largest body among Christian churches and institutions in Japan, but it is not the only body. There are many denominational as well as sectarian activities in Japan at present. Our survey is limited to the Kyodan under present conditions.

When Japan was defeated in 1945, Hirohito's Empire was torn into pieces along with her authority over religious institutions, including Christian churches, both Roman Catholic and Kyodan. The Religious Bodies Law was abolished according to the Potsdam Declaration. So, the Special General Assembly in June, 1946, discarded all wartime offices and systems, and formed a new constitution and regulations. The General Assembly was made the highest governing body, the moderator of which was to represent the Kyodan until the following General Assembly, supervising all offices and the secretariat. The secretariat was divided into nine divisions, each division having a chairman, a secretary, and a committee for consultation.

Kyoku. Geographically speaking, the Kyodan was divided into 18 Kyoku (districts) which in 1950 were rearranged into 13, and later became 14. Each local church directly belongs to a district and is supervised by the District General Assembly. The moderator of the District General Assembly represents the district and presides over district politics and evangelism. This institutional system has never been changed basically. There is a voice calling for more authority for the districts. but it has not won a strong response so far.

The Ministry and the Laity. The superior status and important role played by the ministry should be noted here. According to Protestant principles, the minister is only a believer, having no superiority over the laity within the church. Yet, it cannot be denied that the minister is called to the office of feeding the flock and receives special seminary training to aid the congregation. Moreover, in a non-Christian country such as Japan where the church is comparatively young, many lay people are not trained sufficiently to fulfill their part in the ministry of the church. Moreover, they are busy in their own work. It is the minister who assumes almost all responsibility, such as management and education in the church at large as well as in the local church. Democratic regulations of the Kyodan, of course, provide the way; and lay people are eligible for participation in church government as well as management. As a matter of fact, one half of the delegates of the Kyodan General Assembly are lay people.

This is not so at the district level. The number of lay delegates at the District General Assembly is small, and their influence is limited. Moreover, most secretaries of the General Secretariat and the chairmen and members of the committees are ministers. Lay people are chosen when their professional knowledge or skill is essential to the office. This limited degree of lay participation may be permissible during a time of transition. Even so, the situation should be changed in the nearest future. Unless lay people are given more opportunity, lay leadership will never come into existence in this country.

Kyodan and Mission Boards. Though the Kyodan is independent of any mission board, the relation is very intimate and close. Mission boards respect the Kyodan because of her ecumenical character. Ten mission boards formed the Interboard Committee for Christian Work in Japan (IBC). IBC, together with the Education Association of Christian Schools and the League of Christian Social Work Institutions, organized the Council of Co-operation (CoC). CoC aids these three suborganizations, and is highly regarded by the Kyodan.

Kyodan and NCC. Following World War II, the National Christian Council was reconstructed in 1948, and is quite active in co-operative endeavors and in information exchange. The Kyodan herself is a united church, but certainly she can not replace the NCC. Although the Kyodan is in reality one church among over one hundred denominations and churches in Japan, she is aware of her responsibility in being the largest, most influential, and most contributory member in the NCC fraternity. That is the present situation of the Kyodan.

BIBLIOGRAPHY FOR ESSAY 11

C. W. Iglehart, *A Century of Protestant Christianity in Japan* (Tokyo: C. E. Tuttle Co., 1959).
The Japan Christian Year-Book, 1951 (Tokyo: Kyo Bun Kwan, 1952). (Also the subsequent issues)

12.

BAPTIST-DISCIPLE CONVERSATIONS TOWARD UNITY

The Baptists and the Disciples in the United States once worked together in their churches and associations, but after a rather short relationship, characterized by considerable conflict among the leaders, the two bodies separated. They have made many attempts to accomplish a reunion or *rapprochement* during more than one hundred years. Although it is a simple matter to answer how the most recent conversations between these two denominations came about, there is still general conjecture as to why they did not succeed. Nevertheless, it is possible to identify some of the forces which played on the conversations and to attain insight into the nature and workings of denominations such as these when they are drawn into unitive considerations.

Who Are the Baptists and the Disciples?

The Baptists represented in this study are the group commonly known as the Northern Baptists, but presently designated officially as the American Baptists. They are organized as the American Baptist Convention and their missionary enterprise is carried

by FRANKLIN E. RECTOR

on under the direction of the American Baptist Home Mission Societies and the American Baptist Foreign Mission Societies.

The Disciples are that group officially organized under the International Convention of Christian Churches (Disciples of Christ) and their missionary enterprise is carried on under the direction of the United Christian Missionary Society. Before 1956 the name of the convention of these churches was officially listed as the International Convention of Disciples of Christ.

The local churches of both Baptists and Disciples operate under strict congregational government and authority, including the authority of ministerial ordination. The Baptists number some 6,300 local congregations, and have just over 1,500,000 members in 36 states and the District of Columbia; the Disciples record 1,900,000 members in some 8,000 congregations, located in 41 states and the District of Columbia. The Baptists gave more than $80,000,000 for the annual support of their churches and missionary enterprise in 1959-1960; the Disciples gave $84,941,000 for these purposes in that year.

A word should be said on the matter of congregational autonomy in these two denominations. Recognizing that there should be no inference whatsoever that either of these communions is of a mind to change from the congregational form of government, it is still true that they both consider the independence of the local congregation to be a mixed blessing. Both have experienced considerable increase in the number of "independent" churches, or those churches which will not co-operate in some or all of the enterprises of program planning, missionary endeavor, and strategy for church expansion. Since co-operation in such enterprises is voluntary on the part of the local congregation, all proposals must be examined carefully with respect to the degree to which they may be expected to elicit or discourage co-operation in the thousands of local units across the nation. The block of "independent" churches for both denominations is quite large; and, theoretically, every local church is potentially capable of being driven toward independency by an unwise proposal in program or an unpopular decision on the part of the denominational convention or its agencies. Such an insight into the polity of the Baptists and Disciples is important, for it has direct relevance to any move toward unity on the part of either denomination.

The autonomy of the local congregation goes even farther for both Baptists and Disciples, in that the relationship of the congregations to the convention of the two denominations is entirely voluntary. In the case of the Disciples, any member of any congregation who registers and attends the International Convention may vote on business matters or resolutions, whereas in the American Baptist Convention only those who are delegates of the congregations may vote. However, in neither convention is the action of the convention authoritative or binding on the local congregation. Even though the action of the conventions may be taken as advisory to the congregations, such actions are, in the last analysis, little more than the majority agreement of those present and voting.

On the other hand, the conventions of both denominations function as a kind of "opinion forum," and it is in these conventions that an action or protest group may be heard most effectively. And if the congregations do not or are not bound to accept the actions of the conventions, those in administrative and policy-making positions in both denominations are quite sensitive to the mood, voice, and resolutions of the conventions. Even a strongly vocal minority may, in some instances, use the democratic process of the conventions to force consideration of the minority position in future policy decisions, actions, and resolutions to later conventions.

Recent Efforts Toward Merger

An intensive period of overtures between the Baptists and Disciples began in 1928. In that year Dr. Edgar DeWitt Jones, a Disciple minister in the city of Detroit, was the fraternal delegate to the Northern Baptist Convention. In his address to the convention Dr. Jones broached the matter of the union of Baptists and

Disciples, and his suggestion was received with considerable enthusiasm. As a result, a Joint Commission of Baptists and Disciples was appointed to discuss the matter further. This commission presented identical reports to the two bodies, including twelve specific recommendations. The Baptist Convention of 1929 received the report and assigned it for further study to a special committee. The International Convention of the Disciples of Christ meeting in the same year received the report and adopted it unanimously, an action which has not been rescinded by any subsequent Convention.

At the Baptist Convention in 1930 the work of the special committee came before the delegates in the form of two reports. The majority report was favorable to union with the Disciples, but the minority report, written and championed by the late Dr. F.L. Anderson of Newton Theological Institution, rejected the union. The minority report was adopted by the convention, which said, "This convention respectfully and affectionately declines to recommend said unity of program with the Disciples so long as they hold to baptism for the remission of sins."

This decision will be discussed a little further for two reasons. First, at no time, before or since, were the Baptists and Disciples so near to reunion as at that convention. The Disciples had already adopted the report a year earlier, and approval on the part of the Baptists would have meant that it was possible to proceed with negotiations for implementing the union. There also was considerable sentiment for the adoption of the majority report of the special Baptist committee, so that only strong and sometimes painful debate caused the convention to adopt the minority report.

The second reason lies in just this fact of strong Baptist support for union. The quotation above from the report would indicate that a doctrinal issue was the deciding factor in the vote of 1930, but there is evidence to the contrary. Light is thrown on this issue by the terminology used in support of the minority report. It was argued that union *"would destroy the harmony* of the Northern Baptist denomination" and, more importantly, it "would *weaken* the convention's stand with the Southern Baptists ... and affect the *raising of our budgets* for several years to come." [Italics added.] In reviewing the history of the attempts at union between his people and the Disciples, Hillyer H. Straton says of this incident:

> The burden of Dr. Anderson's plea was that if Northern Baptists continued to talk or possibly united with the Disciples, it would jeopardize very seriously Northern and Southern Baptist relations. It was hoped that Southern Baptists and Northern Baptists would reunite in the foreseeable future, and if Northern Baptists and Disciples effected a union, then this would impede the possibility of Northern and Southern Baptists uniting.[1]

It is thus apparent that factors of institutionalism were present and operative in the frustration of unitive efforts at the 1930 convention. These were (1) a threat to harmony, involving the independency inherent in congregational autonomy; (2) a threat to status and ethnocentric interests which might accrue from a larger united Baptist denomination; and (3) a threat to the *status quo*, if not the vested interests, of the larger organizational agencies of the denomination, through the withholding of financial support. This last point also has a nexus with autonomy and independence.

The issue of unity between the Baptists and Disciples lay dormant until late in 1944, when a joint committee appointed by the two denominations began to meet again. The realization of this joint committee was preceded, however, by at least three unitive "transfusions." The first of these was in 1936, when again a fraternal delegate to a Baptist Convention delivered an address which stirred the matter into some degree of new life, even if very temporary. Dr. George A. Campbell, a Disciple minister in St. Louis, reviewed the Baptist action of 1930 and called for the appointment of a new Baptist committee to meet with a similar committee from the Disciples to restudy the matter.

The newspapers in St. Louis where the convention was held, stated in their issues of May 24, 1936, that "merger ... seems a remote possibility," and that "Northern Baptist Council dodges offer of merger." On the same date the *New York Times* carried a story which stated that the Baptists were "silent on church union." This was not quite the case, but the action of the General Council was that the incoming officers of the convention be a committee to confer with Dr. G. A. Campbell regarding the implications of misunderstanding between the Disciples and the Baptists. It is significant that the committee was authorized to speak only with Dr. Campbell, an individual, concerning this matter. Furthermore, the notice of this action which was handed to the public and religious press carried a *nota bene* which stated, "Positively no implications concerning merger. Do not mention such." [2] It would appear that as of 1936 the climate of opinion among the Baptists was not favorable to conversations with the Disciples.

This matter was again opened up by a fraternal delegate of the Disciples to the Northern Baptist Convention in 1940. On this occasion Dr. Raphael H. Miller, Sr., of Washington, D.C., addressed the convention, making an extremely strong plea for unity of the two groups, and receiving a standing ovation at its conclusion. Out of this effort the convention authorized the General Council to appoint a committee, this time to study *relations* between the two groups, not unity. From all evidence this committee remained within the structure of the General Council, for it was the Council which reported back to the 1941 Baptist Convention, recommending further co-operation with the Disciples.

This was a period of co-operation between the two groups. For some time they had been co-operating in preparation of their graded church school materials, and at the 1940 Baptist Convention, in addition to his statement on unity, Dr. Miller had announced a joint project for the purpose of compiling and publishing a hymnal. This hymnal, entitled *Christian Worship, A Hymnal* was published in December, 1941. There followed other co-operative ventures in publications, particularly that of the joint publication of devotional and family magazines, *Secret Place* and *Hearthstone*.

So far as the Baptists were concerned, it is apparent that there was a change in terminology with respect to conversations with the Disciples which completely avoided the term *union* and used instead the terms *relations* and *co-operation*.

The matter remained in a state of good relations or co-operation for the next few years, and in December, 1943, an article written by Hillyer H. Straton of the Baptists and calling for reconsideration of the position of the Baptists and Disciples on unity was printed in the *Christian-Evangelist* (Disciple). This was the third of the "transfusions" mentioned earlier, and it resulted in the appointment of the joint committees which began to meet in December, 1944. The result of their meetings were, however, still little more than further co-operation between the two denominations, or at least between their ministers. Three-hundred-and-fifty ministers representing both groups spent a week in conferences and fellowship at the Northern Baptist Assembly Grounds in Wisconsin in August, 1945.

This was essentially the state of the affair until 1947. The joint committees which were appointed in 1944 had continued to meet, but in 1946 the Disciples committee again precipitated the matter of union by asking the Baptist committee whether their objective was to explore the possibilities of union. As a result, both committees went to their respective conventions in 1947 with identical requests that (1) the committee membership be enlarged to 15, (2) the status of the committee be raised to that of a commission, and (3) they be authorized to study the content of faith and polity of the two bodies in order to discuss intelligently the possibility of union. Both conventions granted this request and a Joint Commission on Baptist-Disciple Relations was born, which had a special standing and prerogatives to discuss the matter of union. In the case of the Baptist Convention of 1947, there was a unanimous vote that the commission explore *again* the possibility of union with the Disciples of Christ, the word again being purposely included.[3]

In December, 1947, the Joint Commission met and the following three subcommittees were created: (1) on cultivation and education (pulpit exchanges and other educational fellowship devices); (2) on theological questions; and (3) on missions, publications, pensions, conventions, and other agencies.

A new tide of enthusiasm and optimism rose with respect to possible union. The Joint Commission was very active and vocal, and encouraged discussion of union in many ways, including articles in the regular publications of both denominations, and publishing informational brochures from time to time.[4] Interest was so high and the climate so apparently favorable that the Baptist magazine *Missions* printed an editorial in January, 1948, headed "The Eventual and Inevitable Merger of Baptists and the Disciples of Christ."

As the result of suggestions by the Joint Commission, the holding of simultaneous conventions in the same city was also planned. The Commission had hoped that this might be done in 1951, but it ultimately was planned for 1952 in Chicago, at which time certain joint sessions of the two conventions would be held. One of these joint meetings was to be a communion service. In reporting plans for the 1952 convention the *Watchman-Examiner* (Baptist) said, "It was agreed by those present to hold simultaneous conventions in 1952 as a *preliminary to a merger* vote, probably the following year." [5]

The two quotations from Baptist sources would indicate that harmony and progress toward union were inevitable when the two conventions got to Chicago, but certain events transpired which nullified all hope of progress in 1952. The first thing was the inclusion of a timetable leading toward the consummation of unity, which had been worked out by the Joint Commission, in the report of the Baptist section of the Commission to the 1949 Baptist Convention. After a stormy session on the floor of the convention, the Baptists approved the report, including the timetable, rejecting an amendment which would have both deleted the timetable and delivered what amounted to a reprimand to their section of the Commission.

It was then necessary for the Disciple section of the Commission to take the same timetable before the 1949 International

Convention as its official report. Here the report was approved, and the timetable adopted.

The five steps of the timetable were as follows:

1. A conference of Northern Baptists and Disciples of Christ at Green Lake, Wisconsin, in 1950.
2. Simultaneous conventions in the same city in 1952.
3. A report to be presented at the respective conventions in 1953 which would read somewhat as follows: "The Joint Commission of Baptists and Disciples recommends that we present to our conventions for consideration in 1954 'A Basis of Union.'"
4. The presentation of "A Basis of Union" in 1954.
5. A vote on the proposal of union of Baptists and Disciples in 1955, on the basis of the previously presented "Basis of Union."

Again it would appear that with the approval of the plan of the Commission by both conventions, the conversations toward union would be operating in a very favorable climate, and that the 1952 simultaneous conventions in Chicago would produce some significant advance in the unitive process. Owing to intervening actions this was not the case, however. These actions and other events which led to the breakdown of conversations will be discussed in a later section.

The simultaneous conventions were held as planned, with the two conventions meeting separately during the day and joining for the evening sessions. A communion service had been planned for one of the joint sessions, to be held on the third evening of such sessions. The communion service was held as planned, but not as a *joint* communion service. It developed that the Baptists were opposed to holding communion services as a part of conventions, even their own, feeling that this was a function of the local church in its worship. The matter was settled finally by having the service as a communion service of the First Baptist Church of Evanston, Illinois, although it was held in the largest exhibition hall in Chicago, and the Disciples were "guests" at the service.

Very little was heard in either convention about the matter of union of the two bodies. Both the Baptist and the Disciple sections of the Joint Commission reported to their respective conventions, but they did not submit identical reports. The Baptist section included a recommendation in its report which requested "that after one further meeting for evaluation the Commission be discharged and all future work be carried on through the Committee on Relations with other Religious Bodies of the General Council (Baptists), and the Association for the Promotion of Christian Unity (Disciples)." This recommendation was adopted by the convention, an action which had been rather definitely determined by the action of the 1950 convention and the Baptist discussions of the matter which had taken place in the intervening period before the Chicago conventions.

The report of the Disciples section to its convention made no such recommendation, but the report does reveal the uncertain state which prevailed when the report was prepared. It was as follows:

> These conventions are not intending to propose the union of American Baptists and Disciples of Christ. Through the years, however, both churches have discovered their kinship and have experienced a strong affinity.... The recommendations which the Commission will make to the respective conventions about its future will be determined after the current conventions, at a meeting to be held perhaps in June.
>
> Whatever the future holds for the American Baptists and the Disciples of Christ in their relations to each other, both communions will be enriched by the experience of these conventions and both will be sensitive to the leading of the Holy Spirit.[6]

The Joint Commission did meet officially one more time on November 6, 1952, in the city of Cleveland. Here it was discovered that only the Baptist section had been voted out of existence by its convention, but it was readily agreed that the Disciples should take a similar step, since the then Association for the Promotion of Christian Unity (now the Council on Christian Unity) of the Disciples had carried on such activities as that outlined by the action of the 1952 Baptist Convention, previous to the creation of the Joint Commission in 1947, and could assume the responsibility again.

At this final meeting a statement was drafted to be presented to both denominations, recommending, among other things, that (1) reports of the committees of the two bodies be reviewed annually, and (2) a study of appraisal of Baptist-Disciple negotiations be made to discover and analyze obstacles to union which had appeared. Neither of these two recommendations has been carried out.

Breakdown of the Conversations

The most promising and fruitful period of Baptist-Disciple conversations toward unity flourished and waned in the three years between 1947 and 1950. The period extends from the conventions of the two bodies which raised the status of their joint committees to that of Joint Commissions, to the 1950 Baptist Convention in Boston which reversed the 1949 vote of approval of the timetable leading to decisive consideration and a possible vote on merger.

In this period of time the work of the Joint Commission was organized and its subcommittees produced favorable results in their assignments to explore the possibility of union. Considerable enthusiasm was raised among both Baptist and Disciple congregations, and literally hundreds of pulpit exchanges were arranged between their pastors. College and seminary youth groups entered into several ventures of united fellowship, and the ultimate union of the two denominations was promoted by these groups. Ministerial fellowship and Bible study retreats were sponsored with considerable response from both denominations. Worship and study aids were produced and published jointly. On the local level, at least six united churches were formed by former Baptist and Disciple congregations, and the matter was discussed and studied in other places, nearly all these being east of the Mississippi River. Simultaneous state conventions of Baptists and Disciples were held in Nebraska, Illinois, and Pennsylvania, a joint visitation and evangelism program was carried on in Cleveland; and there was considerable co-operation between the two groups in many scattered cities and associations.

In the face of all this progress toward unity and co-operation, however, severe opposition was spreading among many local churches, particularly in the Midwest and West. The voices which were raised against the work of the Joint Commission were individual voices, and most of them belonged to Baptist ministers. Although it was widely stated that *both* Baptist and Disciples churches opposed the union, there was no instance of concerted action to cease the work of the Disciple section of the Joint Commission, nor any faltering on the part of the successive International Conventions of the Disciples in approving the recommendations of the Commission. Neither is there more than an occasional letter of inquiry into the work of the Commission or the processes involved in local Baptist and Disciple unions in the files of the Disciples section of the Commission. There were frequent expressions of doubt that the move toward union was "getting anywhere with the Baptists," but no Disciple correspondence reflects doubt as to whether the effort should be made.

Another striking fact is the lack of opposition on the part of the national leadership of the Baptist Convention. There is evidence that these leaders tried to stand aloof from the work of the Commission for the most part; to let the Commission carry the responsibility as an appointed body of the Baptist Convention; to refrain from membership on the Commission or overt activity in its deliberations; to express opinion only when advice or counsel was sought; and in general to take a "wait and see" attitude. Such leadership may be accused of excessive timidity and sensitivity to a quite vocal minority, but it did not act overtly to disrupt or suspend the work of the Commission because of its own opposition to the idea of merger, *per se*. At least there is no documentary evidence of such action.

What occurred is what the opposition itself would like to describe as a "grass roots" movement. The opposition accused not only the Commission but the national leaders and "the Eastern churches" of trying to push through a merger without regard to the desires of the churches out across the rest of the country. The voices raised against the Commission purported to be the voices of the churches and of the "true" Baptist faith. They insisted that (1) Baptist churches wanted to remain Baptist churches; (2) a move toward merger would force an already divided denomination into further divisions and schisms—that some churches would remain as they were, some would go into the merger and some into the Southern Baptist Convention; (3) the Baptist World Alliance would be placed in jeopardy as a fellowship of Baptist bodies; and (4) the hope of merger between Northern and Southern Baptist Conventions would be ended.

Chronologically, the first concerted opposition to the work of the Commission was raised in the Northern Baptist Convention of 1949 in San Francisco. Here the Baptists were first introduced to the time schedule which the Commission had proposed. When this time schedule was introduced, a young Kansas minister sought to amend the report of the Baptist section of the Commission by deleting the timetable, and thus perhaps beginning the processes which would dissolve the Commission. The amendment was defeated on the floor of the Convention, but only after a loud minority support that caused the chairman of the Baptist section to call for a standing vote in order to clarify the issue. This vote was overwhelmingly in favor of approving the report of the Baptist section, including the time schedule.

In September of 1949, *Crusader*, a Northern Baptist news magazine, held a round-table conference on the matter of Baptist-Disciple merger, and this report was published in November of that year. Although this publicity served to evoke much favorable comment on the merger, it now appears that it tended to crystallize the feeling against it. Letters in the files of the Baptist section of the Commission, as well as those to the editor of *Crusader* in succeeding weeks, strongly opposed further pursuit of the matter.

One of the participants in the *Crusader* conference was the same Kansas minister who had led the opposition in the San Francisco convention. He made a strong case against merger in the published report: (1) at least 75 per cent of the Baptist churches of Kansas would sever their relations with the Northern Baptist Convention if the Baptists and Disciples were to unite, (2) great numbers of churches in other states, particularly southern California, would withdraw and probably go into the Southern Baptist Convention, and (3) the people in the churches of the denomination were not well enough informed about ecumenicity in general and about the merger in particular to be in favor of union.

Shortly after the *Crusader* round table was held, the Kansas Baptist Convention was in session and the same minister introduced a resolution calling for the dismissal of the Commission on Relations with the Disciples of Christ "in the interest of harmony and co-operative endeavor within our Baptist Fellowship." Not only was this resolution adopted, but the minister who introduced it was elected president of the Kansas Convention for that year.

The resolution was approved by several local congregations in Kansas, was introduced and adopted in the Baptist Associations of Southeastern Iowa, was introduced but withdrawn in the interest of harmony in the Iowa Baptist Convention. A similar resolution was adopted by the Los Angeles Baptist Association, and the Illinois Baptist Convention voted "not to unite with the Disciples." All these actions were taken in the month of October, 1949, except that of the Southeastern Iowa Association, which was dated September 15, 1949. This would seem to indicate that the Kansas resolution had been released ahead of its adoption in Kansas, for the wording was essentially identical, and was introduced by some correspondent in Southeastern Iowa.

Only in the Los Angeles Association was there any mention of a doctrinal or theological issue in the matter of union. This brief reference stated, "Whereas, the existing differences in doctrine and polity make such union impossible; and whereas. . . ." Other issues included those mentioned earlier, namely that the harmony of the denomination was threatened; relations with other Baptist bodies were threatened, as was the existence of the Baptist World Alliance; there were differences in geographical boundaries and numerical size of the two conventions; and that the "Commission has exceeded its original authorization to explore 'again the possibilities of union' by presuming a framework of organic union which does not exist and is not authorized."

Little has been said about the activities of the Joint Commission during this period of rising opposition. This very period was, in effect, the period of most active and productive work on the part of the Commission. Its study committees had completed their work and the two brochures, *Shall Northern Baptists and Disciples Unite?* and *The Theology and History of the Disciples and Baptists* were printed and prepared for circulation. These along with the reprint of the article "Three-Fourths of a Loaf" by A. T. De Groot and a copy of the *Crusader* round-table issue were mailed to all ministers and leaders in both denominations in the early weeks of 1950. Here one must assess the importance of timing, for the most effective material produced by the Commission was not put in the hands of the churches at large until *after* serious opposition had begun to arise. This was most unfortunate. Had such material been in the hands of a wider selection of Baptists at an earlier time, there would have been a broader base for appraisal of the issues raised by the opposition throughout the year 1949.

Once the material had been circulated, requests for additional copies began to come in from both Baptist and Disciple groups which wanted to study the matter of merger. Some of these studies were carried on in single churches, and others were joint studies by members of both Baptist and Disciple churches. Still other requests for materials were for panel or study sessions in state conventions of Baptist churches. It should be said, however, that these convention requests came only from the eastern portion of the United States. Some of these studies and the general enthusiasm for the material produced by the Commission came as late as 1950 and 1951, when the fate of the Joint Commission had already been decided by the 1950 Baptist Convention, and when plans for the dismissal of the Commission were in the making.

Also, in 1949 and 1950, joint groups of Baptist and Disciple ministers met for study and fellowship at the Northern Baptist Assembly grounds at Green Lake, Wisconsin. These meetings were well planned, with nationally known Protestant ministers and lecturers as study leaders, and more than 200 ministers of the two bodies were in attendance in the two meetings. The meetings were sponsored by the Joint Commission and were the result of the planning of the subcommittee on cultivation. Pulpit exchanges were also sponsored by the Commission and in the years 1948 through 1951 they involved more than 200 churches per year. In 1948 there were 130 officially reported exchanges, in 1949 there were 144 exchanges with 273 ministers and 288 churches participating, in 1950 more than 200 exchanges, and in 1951 119 exchanges.

Enough has been said to indicate that although some strong opposition to merger arose in 1949, the work of the Commission continued and considerable interest and activity was evident among the churches until as late as 1951. Indeed, many factors pointed to the promise of further progress toward unity in the simultaneous conventions of Baptists and Disciples in Chicago in 1952. In fact, many persons came to Chicago expecting something significant to happen. Those, however, who were close to the Commission and who knew the actions taken by the American Baptist Convention in the years following 1949 were aware that not only would little be done to further the union of the Baptists and Disciples but that the Baptists would be voting to close the work of the Commission altogether.

It is important to understand that the Northern Baptist Convention of 1952 did not spontaneously rise up to repudiate and terminate the work of the Commission, but actually was voting on a *recommendation of the Commission itself*, that it be discharged. This recommendation was included as a part of the report of the Baptist section of the Commission to the convention, and it was approved. Thus, the work of the Commission was ended without a fight on the floor of the convention, and without disharmony or schism in the ranks of Baptist churches. It was ended without the Convention as a body ever facing the issue of actual merger with the Disciples. In short, by dismissing the Commission, the convention *was not asked to declare itself on the work of the Commission toward unity*, since the recommendation inferred that *further relations with the Disciples would be carried on* by an existing committee of the General Council of the convention.

It is therefore important to understand how it was that the Commission recommended its own demise. The recommendation made in Chicago by the Baptist section of the Commission was one which arose out of the confusion and fear of schism in Baptist ranks which was first introduced in the 1949 convention, when its report on the suggested timetable was challenged by amendment. The opposition to merger caused enough concern among the leadership of the American Baptist Convention that the Commission was counseled by both friends and Convention leaders to slacken the pace with which it was leading to a decision on merger. This resulted in the recommendation of the Commission to the 1950 Baptist Convention that the timetable be dropped and then, two years later, the recommendation that the Commission be discharged.

Theological and Institutional Factors

During the conversations over more than thirty years, only one factor which may be termed theological in nature was ever raised. "The Disciples are sacramentarian with respect to baptism—they believe in baptism for the remission of sins." It was at least in part because of this imputation of sacramentarianism that the Baptists voted not to merge with the Disciples in their 1930 convention.

Although the matter of the place of baptism in the conversion of the individual person was much discussed during the period of the 1947-1952 conversations, it was never an issue of determination in the proposed merger. It did not come to a vote by any official group or convention of record. One Baptist leader carried on a personal campaign on the matter, but there was wide doubt of his "findings" that Disciples ministers were convinced of the necessity of baptism for the remission of sins. At best, those findings showed that *some* Disciples thus understood the meaning of baptism and that as a whole they believed that immersion was the acceptable form of baptism for them to practice. The Disciples had no official creed, hence no official statement on the matter. There was considerable liberty of opinion, and this left considerable latitude for the interpretation of Acts 2:38 by a religious group whose early history was steeped in biblical literalism. . .

The Joint Commission on Baptist and Disciple relations dealt with this question as well as many others in its brochure on *The Theology and History of the Disciples and Baptists*. Here the position of each denomination was stated, the latitude of opinion in both was indicated, and it was asserted that there were essentially no differences between Baptists and Disciples on the question of baptism.

No issue, theological or institutional, ever came before the Baptists or the Disciples in the form of a vote on merger. The only issue ever decided was that the Commission should not continue, which meant the breakdown of the conversations. In this decision virtually all the issues were institutional. These issues were projected against a background which consisted of a lack of cohesion in the locally autonomous fellowship of American Baptists, the rife competition between American and Southern Baptists, and a loosely organized Baptist fellowship in the Baptist World Alliance.

To this must be added the fact that the strongest opposition came from sections of the country where the Disciples were strongest, and from sections closest to Southern Baptist territory, in which territory the Disciples were also rather strong. Local congregations which for many years had been in competition with the Disciples, now saw the possibility of having to join forces with them. These churches, or at least their ministers, were of the opinion that it would be difficult to get Baptist churches to accept this situation and to continue their association with the American Baptist Convention. Thus a type of colloquial nationalism, which may more simply be called sectionalism, operated to prevent union of the Baptists and Disciples. There is no doubt that the eastern sections were more favorable to such union than the western and southwestern sections.

A related but inconclusive factor is the exchange of ministers between Baptists of the American and the Southern Conventions. The exact extent of this cross-fertilization is not known, but it was fairly large and moved mostly in the direction of Southern Baptist ministers who had taken fellowship and charges in the American Baptist Convention. At least two of the ministers in active opposition to the merger were former Southern Baptist ministers or had been reared in Southern Baptist teaching. Although their activity may be described as typical of persons who had been subjected to the Southern Baptist position that theirs is the original if not the "true" Christian church, it is difficult to assess the importance of their early background, since many less conservative American Baptist ministers are also former Southern Baptist ministers. Indeed, the chairman of the Baptist section of the Joint Commission was such!

Foremost in importance in institutional factors was perhaps the desire to maintain the *status quo* in the American Baptist Convention. It has already been pointed out that there was considerable independence from the Baptist Convention on the part of many local congregations, and that fear of further schism was great. The threat that a large segment of Baptist churches would not accept merger was a real one, and the loss of such churches was a risk that could not be easily faced. The article by De Groot, "Three-Fourths of a Loaf," argued that it was better to go on to a larger fellowship between Baptists and Disciples, even if only three-fourths of the churches would be included. De Groot suggested that the churches in opposition were those which were already in fact not closely associated with either Baptist or Disciple Conventions. However, this position was not accepted by leaders in the American Baptist Convention, and they counseled against any move which would further divide their fellowship.

It should be emphasized that this factor related only to the divided state of the Baptists and to their fear of further alienating churches. It did not apply to the *status quo* as represented by the leaders, executives, or agencies of either the Baptists or Disciples. The Joint Commission had appointed subcommittees to investigate the difficulty in the merger of agencies and their reports were favorable. Excerpts from some of these reports follow:

> Foreign Mission Representatives—"We see no major obstacles in the way of a merging of our total mission task, if this should be indicated as a part of our closer fellowship and co-operation."

> Subcommittee on Schools and Colleges—"There would not appear to be any problem as to the mutual relations of their schools and colleges should the Disciples and Baptists merge. They have the same general plan of incorporation and government."

> Subcommittee on Publication—"The members of the staffs of our respective publishing agencies are in complete agreement concerning the desirability of such a co-operative publishing program, and study is being given to formulate the content of the suggested Christian Family magazine by the respective editorial staffs."

> Statement of the Pension Boards—"The study of the two pension plans revealed that they differ in almost every

272

aspect. We believe it was our judgment at the time of the conference that in the event of the union of our two bodies the responsibilities of both boards as contemplated would have to be completed. From the date of union it would be necessary for either one plan or the other, or a third plan to be instituted, to provide for the incoming ministry of the larger fellowship."

There seemed to be no insurmountable barriers at the organizational level, and there is no evidence of any attitudes at those levels which would have precluded the merger. Furthermore, the Baptists and Disciples appeared to be alike in many other respects:

- There was no appreciable difference in the size of the two bodies, although the Baptists had somewhat fewer local congregations than the Disciples.
- The levels of financial support for all causes in the two denominations were essentially the same.
- There was no ethnic or language barrier between them.
- They had essentially the same form of church government, convention, and missionary structure.
- There was no definitive difference in social stratification, when the two constituencies were taken as a whole.

It would seem, therefore that the conversations were frustrated almost entirely by institutional rather than theological factors, and a psychological climate of extreme denominational fear and insecurity.

One thing is certain about the conversations from 1947-1952. They did not end in a decision *against* merger. Neither convention was presented with an opportunity to decide that question. What was decided was that the Baptists and Disciples should stop talking about merger, which, to be sure, may be construed as deciding not to merge. In any event, nothing more has been heard about the matter since the simultaneous conventions of 1952. The Baptists have not raised the issue again, and the Disciples have turned their affections toward other possible mergers.

NOTES FOR ESSAY 12

1. Statement made before a round table on "Should Baptist and Disciples Unite?" in *The Crusader* (Baptist), November, 1949.
2. A copy of this notice, along with other valuable material on Baptist-Disciple relations, has been furnished the author from the official files of a leading religious publication.
3. See statement of Hillyer H. Straton in *The Crusader, op. cit.*
4. Three brochures were released officially by the Commission. Two of these were written at the request of the Commission by members of its own subcommittees. They were: *Shall the Northern Baptists and the Disciples of Christ Unite?* and *The Theology and History of the Disciples and Baptists.* A third brochure was the reprint of an article by A. T. DeGroot under the title of "Three-Fourths of a Loaf," which the Commission authorized to be printed and circulated.
5. Issue of May 5, 1949. Italics added.
6. *The Year Book of Christian Churches* (*Disciples of Christ*), published by International Convention of Churches (Disciples of Christ), 1952, p. 86.

BIBLIOGRAPHY FOR ESSAY 12

Gates, Errett, *Early Relation and Separation of Baptists and Disciples* (Chicago: The Christian Century Company, 1914).

Harrison, Paul M., *Authority and Power in the Free Church Tradition* (Princeton: Princeton University Press, 1959).

Roberts-Thomson, E., *Baptists and Disciples of Christ* (London: The Carey Kingsgate Press, 1951).

13.

THE METHODIST UNION IN THE UNITED STATES

Church union negotiations are likely to involve conflicts of institutional interests as well as theological disagreement; and, when they do, political processes similar to those of civil governments are necessary for a solution. The goal of these political processes in church union questions is reconciliation of the divergent interests in formal patterns of behavior that will be stable and uniform in church life after union.

In the union of three branches of American Methodism in 1939 the most difficult problem was the protection of certain minority interests. The three bodies were almost identical in their official doctrinal positions. Although theological issues are inherent in some of the problems that were debated (relation of laity and ministry in church government; race; the episcopacy), the concern over minority interests focused on the form of church government. The problems were seen therefore in predominantly legal and political terms. The present study does not attempt to give a complete account of Methodist Union. Instead it concentrates on the place of minority interests as the crux of the institutional issues in this instance. On the basis of this examination some

by JOSEPH L. ALLEN

concluding comments will be made on the political role of the leaders in the negotiations.

The Three Uniting Communions

At the time of union two of the groups were rather large, and the third was relatively small. A year before union the Methodist Episcopal Church (MEC) reported 4,490,658 full members in 24,317 congregations in the United States and its territories, plus another 657,857 members in 2737 congregations outside the United States.[1] The Methodist Episcopal Church, South (MECS), was smaller but still of comparable size, with a membership in the United States of 2,895,090 members in 16,970 congregations, plus an overseas membership of 24,107, in 166 congregations.[2] The third communion, the Methodist Protestant Church (MP), in 1936 had 148,288 members in the United States, constituting 1498 congregations.[3]

All three denominations came from a common source, the Methodist Episcopal Church, arising from the organization of Wesley's societies in America under the leadership of Francis Asbury. They thus shared a predominantly Anglo-Saxon ethnic background. In America, however, the Methodists soon included Negroes and eventually some of the nineteenth-century immigrants from continental Europe. The three groups also had in common the circuit-rider tradition from the early decades of Methodist work in America, and they all reflected the trend toward a more settled ministry and toward increasing attention to the towns and cities. Furthermore, all three possessed the system of conferences characteristic of American Methodists. The basic body in each denomination was the Annual Conference, generally covering a state or a smaller area. Over these was the General Conference, a legislative body of representatives from the Annual Conferences meeting every four years. Below the Annual Conference level were found District Conferences and Quarterly (local) Conferences. In many other features of polity they were very similar and in official doctrine, as we have noted, they were almost identical.[4]

Geographically the two larger bodies occupied different sections of the nation at union, whereas the third overlapped these two sections. The MEC's strength was in the northern and to a lesser extent western parts of the nation, those areas outside the eleven former Confederate States. Most members of the MECS were in the former Confederate States and the adjoining border states. These two denominations overlapped geographically in three ways. First, after the Civil War a large number of Negroes left the MECS to join the northern branch, which then continued to bring in southern Negroes by its missionary activity. By 1939 over 300,000 Negroes, living mainly in the South, were members of the MEC.[5] The second instance of overlapping occurred in the border states, particularly Delaware, Maryland, Kentucky, Missouri, and Oklahoma. Both groups were relatively strong in these areas after the separation in 1844, and competition between them was a problem until (and after!) union. Third, as time went on both denominations extended their work in areas occupied by the other group. By 1939 the MECS had conferences in Illinois, California, and the Pacific Northwest. The MEC, on the other hand, established a number of churches for whites in the South, especially in eastern Tennessee and other nearby Appalachian areas.

At its origin in 1830 the MP Church was strongest in Maryland. By Union one large group of MP members lived in an area stretching from Maryland and West Virginia northward and westward through western Pennsylvania and into Illinois. Another strong area was central North Carolina, and smaller groups were found in several states of the South. This distribution meant that the Methodist Protestants did not wholly identify themselves with the sectional interests of either of the other two groups.

Institutional Problems in the Original Divisions

The problem dealt with at union in 1939 essentially reflected the issues in the original separations, necessitating a brief account of these early divisions. Two separations are pertinent to this study. The first came in 1830, when a group which had left the original Methodist Episcopal Church formed the MP Church. In 1844 the second occurred when the Methodist Episcopal divided into northern and southern bodies.

Both these divisions occurred because of disagreements about the nature of the church government. The MP group was defending the right of the laity to representation in the church government, the rights of the ordinary traveling preacher over against the bishop, and the right to criticize the church government. The MECS in the 1844 division supported the authority of bishops over against the General Conference and of a minority region's representatives in the General Conference over against the will of the majority. Both crises centered on the place and form of authority in the church government, a problem which arose early in American Methodist history, as is shown by events leading up to the Methodist Protestant division.

Several times before 1830 leaders of "Methodist Reform," as it was called, had protested against the existing form of church government. The first major protest was the O'Kelly movement, resulting in the departure of some of the reformers in 1792 and their formation of the Republican Methodist Church, later named the Christian Church. Numerous reformers remained in the Methodist Episcopal Church, and they continued to voice their dissatisfaction, particularly over the power of the bishop, a concern stimulated by the autocratic procedures of Bishop Francis Asbury. They were too weak to prevent a major victory by the defenders of episcopal power in 1808, when the General Conference wrote into the church's constitution the "third restrictive rule":

> The General Conference . . . shall not change or alter any part or rule of our government, so as to do away

episcopacy or destroy the plan of our itinerant general superintendency.[6]

In 1820 and 1824 the protest against episcopal power led to further General Conference struggles. The issue was the manner of choosing presiding elders, ministers who since 1792 have been chosen by bishops to assist them in their supervisory tasks. After an initial success the reformers were finally defeated on this issue in 1824.

These skirmishes had helped to unite the reformers and increase their discontent. Subsequently they were incensed by the expulsion of several laymen and local preachers from a local church in Baltimore. The charge was that they had criticized the church government in an unfair and injurious way. In late 1827 a convention of reformers drew up an appeal to the next General Conference. Their main request was for lay representation in the church government. Moreover, they defended a member's right to trial by jury within the church and his right to criticize freely the church's practices. The 1828 General Conference only offered them assurance against further expulsions and granted the dubious right to those already expelled to return upon admission of their errors. Dissatisfied with the result, the reformers made plans to withdraw from the denomination, and in 1830 there convened the first General Conference of the Methodist Protestant Church. The new denomination adopted a presbyterian polity with a president instead of bishops and established equal representation for laymen and clergy in the church government.[7]

A distinction must be made between the institutional issues over which this division arose and the conditions of the social environment which contributed to these factors. The institutional issues of broader representation in government, right to trial by jury, right of free speech (in criticism of the church government, particularly), right of appeal against arbitrary rule, all sound peculiarly like the concepts of democracy defended in the United States by the followers of Jefferson and Jackson. These issues in MP division represented a conflict between the American democratic ideal of that day and a clergy-dominated, moderately autocratic church government.[8]

The departure of the Methodist Protestants did not end disputes over the form of government of the Methodist Episcopal Church. The restrictive rules of the 1808 Constitution had placed certain policies outside the legislative authority of a General Conference and thus had set the stage for the later struggle over the relative authority of bishops and General Conference. Already in the debate over the appointment of presiding elders in the early 1820's the southern Annual Conferences more readily defended the authority of bishops than did the northern. This sectional difference became much stronger when national tension heightened over slavery. Methodists had long-standing official statements condemning slavery, but they also had found it expedient not to emphasize this position among southern members. In 1836 after long debate the General Conference condemned "modern abolitionism" by overwhelming majorities.

In 1844 the agitation over slavery could no longer be repressed. The main occasion for debate was the fact that Bishop James O. Andrew, who lived in Georgia, was legally a slaveholder. A motion was put "that he desist from the exercise of this office so long as this impediment remains." [9] Debate over the motion raised the question whether a General Conference could legally discipline a bishop, particularly when no trial had taken place. Was the General Conference able to take any action it wished if it could muster a majority? Furthermore, who was to decide the constitutionality of a General Conference decision? Was it judge of its own actions? Debate did not settle these constitutional issues. The Conference finally approved the resolution by a vote of 111-69, with most northern delegates voting for and almost all southern delegates voting against.[10] The southern delegates then lodged a protest and recommended to the Conference that a plan for division of the church be drawn up. In a few days the Conference approved a Plan of Separation which provided that the Annual Conferences in the slaveholding states could

280

unite in a separate denomination, should they so desire, and arranged for the division of church property. On the basis of this Plan of Separation delegates from fifteen southern Annual Conferences met to form the Methodist Episcopal Church, South, in May, 1845, and convened in their first General Conference the following year. After the division most of the members and Annual Conferences were in the northern denomination. A large minority—far larger than in the MP division—went into the MECS. Both denominations maintained an episcopal polity, though in the MECS the bishop's authority was not subject to change by General Conference legislation, whereas in the MEC the General Conference became in actual practice much more nearly the supreme governmental authority.

Although the debate and separation of 1844 dealt with the institutional problem of governmental authority, a narrowly legal-constitutional interpretation does not reveal the depths of the issue. The division was obviously inseparable from the political problem of the southern minority versus the northern majority in the General Conference. Whether the General Conference majority had complete legislative authority was not an abstract question, but a matter vital to the Southerners' understanding of their interests, just as it was to the Northerners' view of their moral responsibility in the face of slavery. As in 1830 the institutional problem of 1844 reflected an issue in the wider society, this time slavery, which eventually split the nation as well as the church. The way the delegates took sides on the constitutional issue paralleled for the most part the division between slave states and free states. It cannot quite be argued, though, that there was nothing to the constitutional issue save a defense of regional interests over slavery, for the constitutional question went back at least to 1820, when the same regional cleavages on the question had begun to be evident apart from any reference to the question of slavery. The Southerners saw their position on the authority of the General Conference as a matter of constitutional principle. It was slavery, though, which made their views compelling to them and prevented a solution of the constitutional question.

Outline of the Negotiations Leading to Union

The process of seeking a solution extended over nearly seven decades, once friendly relations were re-established. The following chronology of the main events in this process supplies a frame of reference for a discussion of institutional issues in the negotiations:

1848 A fraternal delegate from the MECS to the MEC is not received.

1866-1867 The MECS and the MP Church (southern branch) negotiate unsuccessfully over union.

1869 Fraternal delegates from the MEC exchange notes with the bishops of the MECS.

1876 The Cape May Commission declares the fraternity and equality of the MEC and MECS.

1877 The northern and southern branches of the MP Church reunite, having divided in 1855-1856.

1898 A joint commission of the MEC and MECS is organized and recommends various co-operative actions.

1910-1916 The Federal Council of Methodism seeks unsuccessfully to solve the problem of competition of the MEC and MECS in home and foreign fields.

1910-1911 A commission with representatives from the MEC, MECS, and MP Church makes suggestions for union.

1916-1919 Commissions from the MEC and MECS work out a plan of union with provision for seven regional conferences, one for Negro members.

1920-1922 General Conferences of these two bodies acknowledge considerable opposition to the plan and endorse further negotiations.

1923	The renewed negotiations produce a plan calling for union with two Jurisdictional Conferences, one northern (including the Negro Annual Conferences) and one southern.
1924	The General Conferences of both denominations approve the 1923 plan.
1925	The Annual Conferences of the southern church give the plan a majority vote but fail to pass it by the necessary three-fourths. The plan thus fails of passage.
1930	The MEC and the MP Church begin further negotiations.
1934-1935	Representatives from all three denominations agree on another plan with six Jurisdictional Conferences, five of them geographical divisions and one for the Negro Annual Conferences.
1936	The Plan of Union is accepted by the General Conferences of the MEC and the MP Church; their Annual Conferences subsequently approve the Plan.
1937	The Annual Conferences of the MECS approve the Plan by more than the required three-fourths vote.
1938	The General Conference of the MECS approves the Plan.
1939	These three Methodist groups unite to form The Methodist Church.

Institutional Problems in the Negotiations

The task of achieving union required first that the Methodists solve the problems that had originally divided them. After nearly a century most of the same institutional questions remained prominent. For better or worse, however, the situation was not the same. Some new conditions increased the chances of union. The nation had been reunited, slavery had been abolished, and gradually over the years the cultural cleavage between the South and the rest of the nation was being overcome. Within the churches bishops frequently acted less autocratically than in the past; for instance, they more often conferred with pastors and congregations in making appointments. Other changes made the problem more rather than less difficult. Although slavery had vanished, racial segregation had taken its place, and union was impossible without agreement on the status of Negro members. Furthermore, the very act of dividing had provoked additional problems which stood in the way of union. The two episcopal bodies did not accept each other on an equal basis for many years, and competition between them in the border states and overseas increased their mutual ill-feeling. Lastly, the denominations themselves developed sizeable bureaucratic structures which had to be combined in any union, but which if combined might help to hasten a sense of unity.

Fortunately for the union all three bodies remained quite conscious of the tradition they had in common—a common founder and origin, a common body of doctrine, similar polity. Repeatedly in the negotiations references were made to this shared tradition. It was a constant source of discontent over their divided state. Into this situation the three denominations came seeking to overcome the institutional problems which now demanded solution: (1) the continuing demand for democratization of the church government; (2) the new question of the equal and legitimate status of each denomination; and, above all, (3) the southern concern over protection of its interests as a minority and the many structural questions connected with that problem.

The MP Church and the Desire for Democracy. The history of the negotiations shows a gradual reduction in MP prerequisites for union. Shortly after the Civil War the MECS leaders suggested a merger with the southern branch of the temporarily divided MP Church. The MP reply was a list of fifteen demands,

CASE STUDIES

including a change in the name of the denomination, abolition of the presiding eldership, an increase in the number of bishops to one for each annual conference, the right of a minister to appeal his appointment, denial of veto power to bishops. It may be that these conditions were set by people who did not desire union at all. At any rate negotiations proceeded no further.

By 1910, when the MP Church joined the other two groups in discussion of possible union, it had sharply reduced its demands and showed a marked increase in desire for union. A speech in 1911 by the MP president made four requests: equal representation for laymen on the annual conference level and above; an elective presiding eldership; provision to review the plan of appointment of ministers; and election of all local church officers by the church membership. Even though the list was reduced, these points still substantially embodied the long-standing MP concern for democracy in church government.

As the negotiations proceeded, the MP concern focused on one point: equal lay representation. When the three groups returned to negotiations in the 1930's, this principle was fixed in the final Plan of Union. The other three MP demands made in the name of democracy were not granted. MP efforts did help to bring a change in the name of the denomination, leaving out the word "episcopal," but omission of the term did not change the fact. The MP Church still was returning to episcopal polity. MP desires also were benefited by establishment of a Judicial Council as the new denomination's authority on constitutional questions. This action removed any possibility that either a bishop or a General Conference could make a ruling without appeal.

In spite of the few concessions it received, the MP Church entered the union, meeting opposition only from some of its theologically very conservative members. It entered without constitutional clauses to protect its own members' rights or to give them any distinct status. Former MP members are now indistinguishable from any other Methodists in governmental rights and privileges. The MP Church's struggle in the negotiations was not in its own behalf as much as for the rights of laymen and ministers in any of the three uniting bodies.

Why was the MP Church willing to enter the union so easily? No complete answer is available, but some reasons may be suggested. Time and custom had healed the breach between the MP Church and the others much more thoroughly than that between the two episcopal bodies. Democratic procedures had become generally acceptable to the society at large and were not attacked in principle by any significant social group. Changing customs in church government, plus the few concessions the MP's did receive, relieved most remaining fears. Also the fact that the MP Church's membership was small and lately had been declining encouraged a merger with the two much larger, growing Methodist groups. Union therefore was in the interest of the denomination and posed no threat to the customs of most of its members. The wider society encouraged unity rather than division and thereby made the institutional issues relatively easy to solve.

The Two Episcopal Bodies and the Problem of Equal Status. Following the division of the MEC and MECS came a period of increasing alienation between them. The bone of contention was institutional status—the refusal of the northern denomination to accept the southern on an equal basis, and the Southerners' claim to be an equally legitimate body. In 1848 the General Conference of the MEC rejected a fraternal delegate from the MECS, Dr. Lovick Pierce, with the declaration that the southern body had violated the 1844 Plan of Separation and had seceded from the church. Dr. Pierce replied that any further communications between the two bodies would have to be renewed from the northern side.[11] No further communication took place between the two denominations for twenty years—until after the Civil War and the re-establishment of national union. Meanwhile competition increased in the border states. The bitterness was increased by long litigation over the division of church property, for if the southern body had seceded, as the MEC claimed, all denominational property legally belonged to the North. The United

States Supreme Court settled the legal question in 1854, ruling that the 1844 Plan of Separation had in fact divided the church. In civil law, then, the MECS did not secede; rather the church divided itself. Legal statement of this principle did not mean that the North accepted it. In 1869 a delegation of northern bishops indicated that they still looked on the MECS as secessionists, and in reply the southern bishops took their northern colleagues to task for their attitude.[12]

Finally in 1876 the two denominations agreed on the principle which the MECS had maintained ever since 1844. A conference of officials from the two churches at Cape May, New Jersey, issued the following statement:

> Each of said Churches is a legitimate branch of Episcopal Methodism in the United States, having a common origin in the Methodist Episcopal Church organized in 1784.
>
> Since the organization of the Methodist Episcopal Church, South, was consummated, in 1845, by the voluntary exercise of the Southern Annual Conferences, ministers and members, to adhere to that communion, it has been an Evangelical Church, reared on Scriptural foundations, and her ministers and members, with those of the Methodist Episcopal Church, have constituted the Methodist family, though in distinct ecclesiastical connections.[13]

This agreement meant that fruitful negotiations were now possible. Neither now had the prerogative to ask the other to accept its polity and practices as a condition of union. Because the two (and later three) were negotiating as equals, the method of union logically became *reorganization*, rather than the return of one to the other.

Minority Interests. From the time serious negotiations toward union began in 1910, almost every major problem was a variation on the same institutional issue: the authority of the General Conference versus the protection of regional interests. The commissioners faced this issue most directly in their debates over the jurisdictional system; but they were still wrestling with it in their decisions about the episcopacy, the Judicial Council, and the status of the Negro Annual Conferences.

The exponents of protection for regional interests, as in 1844, were the Southerners; those most zealous for a strong General Conference were from the North. Both sides desired union; both agreed that it should come by reorganization of the church government, not by absorption of one denomination into another. The MECS, however, wanted union to allow the southern minority explicit constitutional protection for its distinctively regional interests. They wanted assurance that they would not be ruled by outside opinions in specifically regional concerns. The MEC commissioners, though willing to grant some protection for regional interests, did not want to jeopardize true union. They wanted the General Conference to be the chief policy body of the denomination, whatever minority rights might be recognized. The commissioners clearly expressed this disagreement as early as 1911. The problem was whether actual unity was compatible with southern demands for minority protection.

The jurisdictional system was the Southerners' answer to this problem. From 1910 to the time of union some kind of regional conference system was a prerequisite for any plan the South would even discuss, and northern commissioners soon accepted this situation as unavoidable. Several types of jurisdictional arrangement were proposed. Briefly, all of them were plans which divided governing responsibility between the General Conference and several regional conferences, intermediate in size between the General Conference and the Annual Conference. The final plan provided for six Jurisdictional Conferences. Five are divided by geographical areas, with two of them primarily in formerly MECS territory; the sixth, the Central Jurisdiction, is made up of the Negro Annual Conferences formerly in the MEC. The final Plan of Union limits the General Conference's legislative authority to "matters distinctively connectional," a phrase still being debated.[14] The Plan reserves to the Jurisdictional Conferences the authority to elect and assign bishops, to select representatives to the general boards and agencies and, if desired, to set up its own program to promote the work of those agencies. This compromise system makes possible unified policy and action in most aspects of church life but allows regional differences when they are demanded.

Debates both during the negotiations and since 1939 have implied that "distinctively regional interests" might be numerous and might appear in any section of the church. Whatever the theoretical possibilities, only one clear difference has appeared—racial customs. In 1939 as in 1844 the race problem was the crucial condition in the church's social environment which led to demand for protection of the minority region. Other distinctive interests in the South are difficult to discover. Bishop John M. Moore, probably the most influential of the southern commissioners, stated the matter correctly when he wrote that "any movement or trend that might change this condition was disturbing and was regarded with suspicion and opposition. This philosophy of race relations was deep-seated and stronger even than any church affiliations." [15] When the leaders of the MECS spoke of protection of regional or minority interests, they always had the race problem in mind, whatever other possibilities might have occurred to them. Professor V. O. Key has commented about southern politics that it "revolves around the position of the Negro." [16] The church politics of the southern Methodists reveals a similar obsession.

This interpretation of the function played by the jurisdictional system for southern Methodists is reinforced by northern reactions to the system since union. The recent Commission to Study the Jurisdictional System reported that in areas outside the South, Methodist leaders called the system "unnecessary, economically wasteful and in some respects a divisive addition to the church structure." [17] In these nonsouthern jurisdictions very little use is made of the Jurisdictional Conference except for those functions required by the constitution, for those areas apparently do not feel the need to defend any distinctively regional interest.[18]

The other major institutional issues in union—the episcopacy, the Judicial Council, and the status of the Negro Annual Conferences—were all closely related to the same demand for protection of southern interests. At the insistence of the southern commissioners two important changes were made in the episcopacy. First, the manner of electing bishops was changed. Since 1792 all Methodist bishops had been elected by the General Conference. The southern Methodists knew that if this procedure were continued after union, they could not be sure of selecting bishops sympathetic to their own ways. In the Plan of Union, therefore, the right to elect bishops resides with the Jurisdictional Conferences. Second, a parallel change occurred in the assignment of bishops to episcopal areas. Since union, bishops preside over Annual Conferences only in the jurisdiction in which they were elected, unless another jurisdiction requests their services and a transfer can be arranged.[19]

The establishment of the Judicial Council was much more than a reflection of the minority-interests concern, but it aided that cause, nevertheless. The Southerners had maintained since 1844 that the General Conference that year acted unconstitutionally in its resolution about Bishop Andrew, but there had been no established body with higher authority than a General Conference to interpret constitutional questions. The Judicial Council today has that authority and thereby assures minorities of their constitutional safeguards, just as it protects individuals against arbitrary and unconstitutional action in many forms.

The decision about the Negro Annual Conferences gives further evidence that racial segregation was the dominant minority concern of southern Methodism. In the pursuit of their minority interests some of the representatives of the MECS first explored the possibility of setting up a separate organization for the Negro members of the MEC.[20] When the northern delegates would not hear of this arrangement, the Southerners then pushed for a special jurisdiction for Negro members with Negro bishops limited to overseeing Annual Conferences in that jurisdiction. The Plan of Union allowed Negroes to be represented both in the General Conference and in the general boards and agencies on equal standing with whites, but the separate Negro jurisdiction

CASE STUDIES

enabled the MECS to continue its racial segregation practices on other levels of church life in the South.

The separate Negro jurisdiction is often defended by southern Methodists today on the grounds that it gives Negroes more representation on general boards and in the Council of Bishops than they likely would have if they were part of the geographical jurisdictions. It is interesting to note, however, that this point is usually made by whites rather than Negroes. When the MEC voted on union, the main opposition came from the Negro members and from their staunchest sympathizers among the whites. Many of these members felt that continued disunion was preferable to union with a separate Negro jurisdiction. Defense of white southern minority interests, not Negro interests, was the primary goal of those who wrote the Central Jurisdiction into the union. The concern was not "minority interests in general," but some very specific interests of a particular minority.

Unlike the MP Church, the MEC and MECS represented two sides of a fairly deep social cleavage, based on the difference in dominant racial customs in the two regions. Under the circumstances some form of regional autonomy was probably the only alternative to complete failure of the negotiations. In the final plan the two groups made some room for both positions. The Southerners' racial customs were respected in the establishment of the Central Jurisdiction and in the division of powers between General and Jurisdictional Conferences. The racial views of the MEC were recognized in the principles that the union would include the Negro members and that no arbitrary limitation would be imposed on Negro representation in the General Conference.

Deciding which side compromised its interests the most, depends on understanding what each side most desired. A distinction must be made between the peripheral and the vital interests of an organization. Peripheral interests can always be sacrificed for more desirable goals; vital interests are not subject to compromise nor can they be used in bargaining. Questioning the peripheral interests of another group is largely compatible with continued good relations and with a sense of mutual acceptance;

attacking the validity of another group's vital interests is tantamount to rejection of the group itself. There is of course no absolute distinction between the two types; the crucial question is how the group itself interprets its interests. The MECS commissioners believed that the maintenance of segregation within the church was a vital interest, more vital to it than union or various other goals. Before they would have bargained with it they would have broken off the negotiations. For the MEC most influential church leaders apparently preferred union to the elimination of racial segregation in the church. Granted the principle of racial equality in representation the northern leaders could accept segregation.[21] The sides taken on the major institutional problems therefore reflected what each group of commissioners understood to be the vital as opposed to the various peripheral interests of its denomination. These interpretations in turn were strongly conditioned by the prevailing value preferences of the two regions.

Persistence of Old Institutional Problems Since Union

Since union the institutional issues discussed in the negotiations have attracted varying degrees of attention. Some have almost disappeared from sight as objects of debate. The issues raised by the MP Church, for example, were subject to substantial agreement at union and have provoked little discussion since then. The Judicial Council likewise met with widespread favor in the negotiations; its existence has not been a cause of disagreement.

The jurisdictional system has continued to evoke disagreement because of its segregating Central Jurisdiction and its effects on the episcopacy and the denominational life. The General Conferences of The Methodist Church have made statements condemning racial segregation and discrimination, and most of the denominational agencies have eliminated discriminatory practices in their own work. Until 1956, however, the church did not make any changes in the jurisdictional system itself. That year the

General Conference took two steps. First it passed a constitutional amendment, subsequently approved by the Annual Conferences, allowing local congregations and Annual Conferences in the Central Jurisdiction to transfer into another Jurisdiction, given the permission of both conferences affected by the transfer. This move has provoked an extended debate over the transfer of whole Annual Conferences from the Central Jurisdiction to white Jurisdictions. The amendment, however, is wholly permissive about the transfers; the southern white Jurisdictions know that no transfers will take place in their areas without their consent.

The second action in 1956 was the establishment of a commission to study all problems related to the jurisdictional system and to report to the 1960 General Conference. The commission recommended few changes in 1960, and few were made. The General Conference did approve a constitutional amendment to have the Jurisdictional Conferences meet at the time of the General Conference, so that bishops could at least be consecrated at the General Conference and so that they could be assigned outside their own jurisdictions when such moves were desired. This amendment was defeated in the Annual Conferences, however.

In the light of such meager modifications it is worth asking whether the system protecting southern minority interests can be changed significantly. The answer depends on the same issue on which establishment of the system depended: how the self-conscious groups of the denomination interpret their interests. Many of the white southern Methodists are still concerned to protect the racial customs of their region. Any move to abolish the Central Jurisdiction in large areas of the South or to abolish the jurisdictional system would confront these Southerners with a test between two of their interests—denominational unity and racial segregation within the church. As long as the racial concern remains a vital interest for white southern Methodists, then they will demand a structure similar to the jurisdictional system as a requirement for the maintenance of union.

Retention of some such protective structure is likely for some time, but it is not the only possibility. Southern church members are undergoing a slow but perceptible change in their racial views. This change is encouraged by the denominational structure itself, particularly the boards and agencies. The Woman's Division of Christian Service and the Methodist Youth Fellowship, for instance, frequently raise questions within the South about its racial patterns and repeatedly involve southern Methodists in nondiscriminatory interracial church activities.

A far more powerful force for change is the influence of the surrounding society. The challenge to segregation which is being made through legal and political channels over the nation encourages those within the church to join in the changes. Many southern Methodists instead support the resistance to these changes. The denomination in the South is likely to revise its views about the need for constitutional protection only when the region itself has become less concerned to defend racial segregation. The church can influence such a change in the surrounding society, but it can be only one, and not the strongest, of many converging forces.

Conclusion

The argument of this study has been that the most difficult problems of Methodist union were institutional issues surrounding the demand of the southern white Methodists for protection of their regional interests. In the discussion of this and related problems the following conclusions have emerged:

• The concern was not for minority interests in general, but for the interests of a specific minority. This minority kept the problem uppermost in the negotiations, and the interests of other minorities did not receive comparable attention.

• The form and intensity of the Southerners' demand for protection of their interests cannot be explained apart from the significance of racial segregation in the wider society in the South and the cleavage over this issue between the South and the rest of the nation. It is fruitless to argue over whether the issue in

1844 and 1939 was race or whether it was the problem of the authority of the General Conference versus other authorities. The constitutional questions were the institutional issues requiring solution; the problems of race and region brought the constitutional questions to a head. Neither was merely incidental to the problem.

• In spite of the cleavage the considerable common tradition of the three groups played a major part in keeping alive the desire for union and the willingness to continue negotiations, and in providing a sizeable area of agreement.

• Agreement by the commissioners came much earlier than acceptance of their solution by the denominations. This was particularly true in the MECS, which rejected the 1923 plan in spite of its concessions to regional interests, and where even in the General Conference of 1938 a last-ditch fight was waged by a small body of opponents of union.

• Although a solution was found which made union possible, along with preservation of district regional practices, union has not brought a full sense of unity. After more than two decades the same regional groupings still exist and some of the same differences regularly arise.

• Union nevertheless set in motion forces within the church which are increasing the sense of denominational unity over against sectional loyalties. The success of these forces is likely to depend on whether there are similar forces in the wider society which will break down the sectional and racial antipathies.

• The political nature of the negotiations over minority interests helps to explain why the results were as they were. The negotiations present a sharp contrast between the conciliatory MP commissioners and the persistent demands of the MECS. The different responses of these two denominations, both of them in the minority though enormously different in size, cannot be explained in moralistic fashion by ascribing agreeableness to one group and stubbornness to the other. Nor can one attribute a mysterious force to racial or geographical cleavages which makes them more difficult to solve than any other kind. The policies of each group, as well as of the MEC commissioners, reflect an assessment of its own conditions and values, and each group had a different set of factors to weigh.

The MECS representatives, for example, faced such questions as the relative value of union and of continued denominational independence, the importance of agreement with their own region's racial customs compared with their obligation to the Negroes, their responsibility to represent their denomination's expressed interests compared with their need to convince their people to modify their views, and the importance of personal advancement or popularity over against the good of the whole denomination. They had to decide not only what things were important, but how important—how much they were willing to sacrifice in other values; and they had to find some way to express this assessment in concrete proposals. In the negotiations all three groups were attempting to represent fairly the interests of their own denomination. If any one thing made the MP group more conciliatory than the MECS, it was that their interests were more clearly served and much less sharply threatened by union. If the MEC commissioners appear to have compromised the most in agreeing to a segregated Negro jurisdiction, they too were reflecting the great interest of their denomination in union and the fact that for many of their members the pain of denominational division was sharper than the pain of racial segregation. In church negotiations, as in civil government, politics involves this complex task of assessment of conditions, interests, and values.

The answers which emerge from this kind of assessment are not part of a deterministic system. They could have been different. To say that the commissioners were necessarily involved in their own concrete situation still allows room for criticism of their decisions in one or both of two ways. One way is to show that the negotiators did not adequately understand all the actual facts relevant to the situation. It may be charged, for example, that theological considerations were not explicitly discussed even at points where they were crucial to an understanding of the church's nature, or it can be claimed, as another example, that the southern commissioners did not sufficiently understand the needs and desires of another minority, the Negro members of the MEC. A second form of criticism is to argue that the negotiators valued the wrong thing or valued something to the wrong degree. Thus the extent of the Southerners' desire to conform to the mores of their region is often questioned.

The institutional problems surrounding the issue of minority interests presumably could have been solved in more than one way, but the solution still had to come by some kind of political process, involving negotiation, conflict, compromise, and other activities political in nature. Whatever issues dominate the negotiations, church union requires the service of people who are discerning Christians and are skilled at applying their faith to the conditions within which the church acts.

NOTES FOR ESSAY 13

1. *Minutes of the Annual Conferences of the Methodist Episcopal Church,* Fall Conferences, 1938, pp. 492-495, 500-503.
2. *General Minutes and Yearbook of the Methodist Episcopal Church, South,* 1938-1939, Curtis B. Haley, ed., p. 433.
3. U. S. Department of Commerce, Bureau of the Census, *Census of Religious Bodies,* 1936, II, 1084, 1108ff. The figures for these three groups are not entirely comparable.
4. Doctrinal variety was certainly present within Methodism, much more so than the negotiations indicated; but this variety was not expressed in official doctrinal statements, nor did it lead to issues in the negotiations.
5. The Negro members of the Methodist Episcopal Church constituted only a small minority of Negro Methodists in the United States. The African Methodist Episcopal Church and the African Methodist Episcopal Church, Zion, took form as a result of Methodist divisions early in the nineteenth century. The Colored Methodist Episcopal Church (now Christian Methodist Episcopal Church) originated after the Civil War from former members of the Methodist Episcopal Church, South. By 1936 these three Negro denominations had among them well over a million members (Department of Commerce, Bureau of the Census, *Census of Religious Bodies,* p. 1084).
6. *Discipline of the Methodist Episcopal Church,* 1808, pp. 15-16.

7. Edward J. Drinkhouse, *History of Methodist Reform* (Norwood, Mass.: Norwood Press, 1899), II, 296.

8. James R. Williams, *History of the Methodist Protestant Church* (Baltimore: Book Committee of the M. P. Church, 1843), pp. 326-327. In 1830 Methodist Episcopal members totaled around 475,000.

9. *Journals of the General Conference of the Methodist Episcopal Church* (New York: Carlton and Lanahan), II, 1844, 65-66.

10. *Ibid.*, II, 1844, 84; *Report of Debates in the General Conference of 1844*, pp. 190-191.

11. *Journal of the General Conference of the Methodist Episcopal Church, South*, 1850, p. 190.

12. *A Record of All Agreements Concerning Fraternity and Federation Between the Methodist Episcopal Church and the Methodist Episcopal Church, South* (no publisher, no date), pp. 6-10.

13. *Ibid.*, p. 17. In 1910 representatives of all three denominations reaffirmed this same principle, including in it the Methodist Protestants.

14. See Nolan B. Harmon, *The Organization of The Methodist Church*, rev. ed. (Nashville: Methodist Publishing House, 1953), p. 108. Northern and southern Methodists continue to differ over the relative power and importance of General Conference and Jurisdictional Conferences in the church government. Constitutions, for all their apparent clarity, often can be interpreted to support either side of issues they were written to settle.

15. John M. Moore, *The Long Road to Methodist Union* (Nashville: Abingdon-Cokesbury Press, 1943), p. 137.

16. *Southern Politics in State and Nation* (New York: Alfred A. Knopf, Inc., 1949), p. 5.

17. *Report to the 1960 General Conference of the Methodist Church by the Commission to Study and Recommend Action Concerning the Jurisdictional System* (no publisher listed, 1960), p. 9.

18. Bishop Nolan B. Harmon suggests that a reason for setting up the jurisdictional system was the size of united Methodism and the "difficulty in operating and efficiently administering its vast work through one enormous General Conference" (*The Organization of The Methodist Church*, p. 172). Although this argument was indeed set forth by the southern commissioners in the negotiations, Methodism already had structure to take care of that problem—the Annual Conference. It is difficult to see why the commissioners would have felt any need for further administrative machinery of this kind except for the difference between northern and southern racial customs.

19. One major change in the power of the bishop was not a matter of regional difference in the negotiations. Since union, bishops have exerted increasing power over church policy through their membership on the

denominations' boards and agencies. The growth in denominational bureaucracy has produced a growing competition in power between bishops and board executives.

20. *Joint Commission on Unification of the Methodist Episcopal Church and the Methodist Episcopal Church, South* (New York: The Methodist Book Concern, 1918-1924), II, 108; Moore, *Long Road to Methodist Union,* pp. 115-116.

21. The northern Methodists actually were not departing from their own church's practices in accepting racial segregation in the union. Although the MEC had Negro bishops, none had presided over a white conference. Negro members, except for an occasional few, were already segregated in separate Annual Conferences from the white members, even where the Negro and white Annual Conferences overlapped geographically.

BIBLIOGRAPHY FOR ESSAY 13

Culver, Dwight W., *Negro Segregation in the Methodist Church* (New Haven: Yale University Press, 1953).

Harmon, Nolan B., *The Organization of The Methodist Church,* rev. ed. (Nashville: Methodist Publishing House, 1953).

Joint Commission on Unification of the Methodist Episcopal Church and the Methodist Episcopal Church, South, 3 vols. (New York: The Methodist Book Concern, 1918-1920).

Moore, John M., *The Long Road to Methodist Union* (Nashville: Abingdon-Cokesbury Press, 1943).

Neely, Thomas B., *American Methodism: Its Divisions and Unification* (New York: Fleming H. Revell Co., 1915).

Tigert, John J., *A Constitutional History of American Episcopal Methodism,* 6th ed. rev. (Nashville: Publishing House of the Methodist Episcopal Church, South, 1916).

A Working Conference on the Union of American Methodism (New York: Methodist Book Concern, 1916).

14.
PRESBYTERIAN-EPISCOPALIAN NEGOTIATIONS IN THE U.S.A. (1937-1946)

Although history never exactly repeats itself, it is interesting to note that Episcopalian-Presbyterian negotiations looking toward union date back to the 1880's. The so-called Chicago Quadrilateral of 1886 (later, in 1888, becoming the Lambeth Quadrilateral) had gone forth as part of an invitation to other Christian bodies. The Presbyterian Church in the U.S.A. alone responded. The history of the negotiations which then took place still makes profitable reading, inasmuch as the unsolved issues raised seventy years ago are unsolved issues to this day. There were no permanent results. Conversations faded into polite exchanges of resolutions of friendship. The fact, however, that these two churches had once enjoyed a brief courtship is probably one of the main lessons for the second courtship forty years later.

The Two Churches

Both churches are transplantations of religious fellowships existing in Great Britain. The Episcopal Church essentially derives from the Church of England and the Pres-

by GIBSON WINTER [1]

byterian Church from the Church of Scotland. Both established their American organizations after the Revolution and approximately at the same time. The national organization of both churches was influenced by the type of political thinking which produced the American Constitution. Thus in each case a fellowship which began as a state church had been transformed into a denomination with government influenced by American political thought.

The movement for union began with several factors in its favor. The churches were comparable in size; the Episcopal Church had about a million and a half communicants, the Presbyterian Church perhaps two million. In most communities the two churches represented similar economic and social levels in the population; there was both a kinship and sometimes a certain rivalry. Both churches had high educational standards for the ministry. Each had a definite theological tradition and there were accepted formularies, so that negotiators on each side could begin with some objective knowledge of the tradition of the other church in doctrine, discipline, and worship.

Three principal motives seemed to impel the leaders who began the union movement and worked diligently for it. (1) Certain leaders in the two churches were close personal friends and had been educated together. (2) There was a deep theological interest in the ecumenical movement after the Oxford and Edinburgh conferences of 1937. (3) Many lay leaders, but some clergy also, were interested in the practical aim of avoiding duplication on the local level and providing a common ministry in mission fields, at home and abroad.[2]

A Short History

The second chapter in the story of unity negotiations—with which we are primarily concerned in this essay—begins with the General Convention of 1928. No less a person than Bishop Brent, then a symbol of the ecumenical cause, introduced a resolution inviting representatives from four communions to meet with a newly formed Joint Commission to "study matters of Christian Morality looking toward organic unity." The four invited churches were the north and south "branches" of the Methodist Church and two branches of the Presbyterian Church. The Commission (Bishop Parsons of California, Chairman) issued its first report in 1931—an innocent report, as it reads in retrospect. Only the northern Methodist and Presbyterian U.S.A. sent delegates. Substantial agreement seemed to exist on matters concerning the Christian home (the divorce problem receiving only passing attention), international peace, race relations, economic evils, and education. A minority report, signed by a caustic layman, Judge George F. Henry of Iowa, saw so little value in these polite generalities that it argued against further talks. "The subject of organic unity between the churches," so the Judge complains, "was avoided, *as it will always be avoided by wise men....*" In this prophecy, however, the Judge was mistaken. The Commission asked to be continued, and "to be given authority to confer on other lines." The request was granted, thus opening the way to stormy days.

The (Episcopal) Commission's report for 1934 was again innocuous, though it is interesting to note that the Lutheran Church had, in the continuance resolution of 1931, been added to the communions invited to confer. One recommendation of the Commission deserves attention, since it applies to the present as well as to the year 1934—namely, that unification ought to take place among General Convention commissions themselves. Confusion had resulted, so the Commission complains, by the fact that three commissions were dealing with unity problems, the two rivals being the Commission on the World Conference on Faith and Order and the Commission on Ecclesiastical Relations. Overlapping was deplored and a unifying remedy sought. It needs seeking still today.

The Commission's title, by 1937, had become awkward to the

point of embarrassment: "Joint Commission for Conference with the Methodist, Presbyterian, and Lutheran Churches on Christian Morality in Relation to Organic Unity and Confer with the Representatives of These Other Communions upon Lines of Approach to Unity Other than Specifically Moral." It deserved the new title by which it has been known ever since—namely, "The Joint Commission on Approaches to Unity."

The Report for 1937 was itself once more brief and innocuous. Negotiations with Lutherans and Methodists are mentioned, but, as the report of 1940 will say, these communions were so busy with their own unification that larger ecumenical considerations were in abeyance. Presbyterians, however, had stood by. Hence, concentration upon this one communion appeared to be indicated. At any rate, it was at this Convention that the Commission, alluding to the fact that "hitherto for fifty years we have conferred from time to time with representatives of the Presbyterian Church," presented the now famous though controversial resolution "to achieve organic union between the respective churches." So far as the Journal of the Convention of 1937 indicates, the resolution was adopted without opposition, and even without debate.

By the time of the General Convention of 1940, however, controversy, both within and without the Commission was clearly in the offing. In the interval between Conventions, the Commission had published a pamphlet containing a proposed Concordat between the two churches. This Concordat (by a strange omission, not printed either in the Journal of 1940, or any later Journal, but existing only in pamphlet form) is discussed at length in the Commission's report, though no vote on it was asked for. The *Concordat* contained a document called *Things Believed in Common*—possibly the most permanently significant part of the pamphlet, and one which may still serve a useful educational purpose and may well deserve reprinting. It also contained a section on "Things That Might Be Undertaken in Common"—once more, a document deserving renewed attention today. A third section, which proved to be of only ephemeral value at the time, envisioned a mutual recommissioning of ministers of the two churches so as to permit co-operative ventures in "unity-churches" in rural areas.

This report of 1940 laid before the Church for the first time some of the basic issues which all unity negotiations with non-Episcopal communions inevitably underscore. But since it asked for no decisions, it received none. The Commission was merely given permission to continue.

The General Convention of 1943 saw controversy out in the open, symbolized unmistakably by the presence of a very frank Minority Report. By 1943, the *Concordat* had proved itself ephemeral. It had been replaced by a more searching and fundamental document called *Basic Principles*. Here, at last, the final issues involved in the problem of union with a non-Episcopal church were fully exposed for debate. Neither majority nor minority, however, felt the time quite ripe for debate or vote. A "continuance" resolution was once more presented and adopted.

The story of the General Convention of 1946 is still so fresh in memory that it need not here be repeated. Suffice it to say that the document entitled, in 1943, Basic Principles, had now received an even more challenging form as a Proposed Basis of Union. This was submitted by the majority report "as worthy of the serious study of the Bishops, Clergy, and Laity of our Church . . . looking forward to decisive action by the General Convention of 1949." The debate on the resolution, however, soon made clear that postponement of a decision was not welcomed by a large section of the Convention. The resolution was lost.[3]

The Structure of Communication

The negotiations between the Presbyterians and Episcopalians began with considerable promise and terminated without clear decisions on the part of either body. This fact alone makes this venture in unity significant, for it suggests a breakdown in the structure of the negotiations. The lack of a clean break in discussions can, of course, disguise a division over substantive issues, as when parties agree to disagree by dropping a subject. However, in this case the conversation was dropped as well as the particular subject, and, in fact, the subject was not officially dropped, although further negotiation seemed fruitless.

Responsibility for the collapse of the conversation is attributable to the Episcopalians. The time had come in 1946 for the Episcopal Convention to indicate its intentions to press further with the negotiations; its unwillingness to decide this question automatically brought the negotiations to a halt. Since the Episcopal Church initiated the negotiations and terminated them by default, this report will try to see the negotiations primarily from the perspective of the Joint Commission on Approaches to Unity of the Protestant Episcopal Church. However, differences of perspective will be introduced, where they are relevant, as seen from the Department of Church Co-operation and Union of the Presbyterian Church; moreover, this perspective is assumed primarily for clarity of exposition and should not be interpreted as implying a passive role of the Presbyterian Department.

This analysis treats the negotiations as a problem in the processes of communication. No assumptions are made as to the desirability of the negotiations or the rightness of any particular decisions. The substantive issues are subordinate to questions of process. Although differences on issues may well have been the principal cause for the failure of the negotiations, the mode of termination suggests a concomitant breakdown of structure which deserves consideration.

Three aspects of the process of communication are isolated for special comment: (1) the social and cultural climate in which the negotiations were initiated and terminated (an historical perspective); (2) the basic difference in the principles which give continuity to the negotiating bodies (an ecclesiastical perspective); (3) an evaluation of the procedures employed in the negotiations (an interpretation of method).

Social and Historical Context of Negotiation

The Declaration of Purpose (1937) and the *Concordat* (1939) appeared in the 1930's—a period of social revolution in the United States. American life underwent a radical shift in mental climate with the approach of World War II; in fact, as Samuel Lubell has noted, no important social legislation was accomplished under the New Deal after 1938. The beginning of World War II marks the end of an era. If we assume a certain congruity between social and cultural processes, a Declaration of Purpose to achieve organic union is consonant with the social transformations which were effected in the 1930's.

World War II thrust the United States into a phase of heightened productivity and intensified nationalism. A single facet of the internal life of the country has significant bearing on the negotiations: the internal life of the United States was subject to increasing strains with the frustration of the prolonged military engagement and the radical changes in social stratification which were occurring as a consequence of increased productivity. The racial question is the most obvious of these internal issues which emerged with the war. Difficulties between labor and management in dividing up the spoils of the war effort were likewise a constant problem. The churches and other large organizations were marking time on programs of expansion during the catastrophe and ministering as well as possible to their memberships.

In this changed atmosphere of World War II, the negotiating commissions had been pursuing their task. Although the *Concordat* does not appear in the Journal of the 1940 Convention of the Episcopal Church, it had been worked through to a document known as *Basic Principles* which was presented in 1943. This latter document stated the fundamental issues confronting these churches in achieving organic union. Here was the crucial document around which the churches might have debated their intentions and possibilities. The Episcopal Convention of 1943 received the majority and minority reports of the Joint Commission without comment, continued the Commission, and directed it to carry on negotiations with the Presbyterian Church U.S.A. Bishop Parsons notes later that the desire to maintain concord within the Episcopal Church in the crisis of war caused the Commission to postpone debate of *Basic Principles* (1943). The issues in this document were obviously controversial for the Episcopal Church. The year 1943 can be seen in retrospect as the turning point in the fortunes of the negotiations, for the external strains of war created a climate of appeasement within the religious organization —in this time of crisis we stand together by avoiding discussion of differences. Failure to debate such a fundamental document as *Basic Principles* meant that the Episcopal Church came away from the Convention with a sense of latent division and conspiracy. The highly vocal minority of the Commission now made a broadside attack on the Presbyterian negotiations in the church press and increased anxiety in the House of Deputies at the 1946 Convention in Philadelphia. Peace at any price in the 1943 Convention proved very costly in 1946; the lean years of heroic resolution were rapidly giving way to the fat years of organizational expansion.

The third major shift in historical context coincides with the termination of the negotiations between the Presbyterians and Episcopalians. The General Convention of the Episcopal Church met in Philadelphia in 1946 after the conclusion of the devastating war. The rapid elimination of the Office of Price Administration in this era gives some indication of the mood of the United States as it turned from the stringencies of a war prosperity to a peace boom. The rapid demobilization is likewise symptomatic of the mood. Korea was already in preparation. The United States was about to launch upon a "binge" of prosperity which was tempered only by the Marshall Plan.

Social collectivities such as labor organizations, political parties, and churches undertook a crystallization of identity during these postwar years. The labor unions engaged in struggles for fringe benefits, pension plans, and work rules; these are generally measures which solidify the loyalty of memberships. Great corporations extended their empires. Churches undertook the greatest building program in their history. After the discipline of the co-ordinated war effort, each turned to his own garden. The decision at Philadelphia in 1946 to have the Commission prepare a statement on bases of negotiation for intercommunion and organic union which could be reviewed by the Lambeth Conference (1948) was symptomatic of this period of organizational consolidation; the Episcopal Church was looking away from the Presbyterians and to its own solidarities. The Presbyterian Church had already begun to press the other party for evidence of their serious intention, so that the critical moment approached with no further possibility of evasion. It was *not* what was *done* at Philadelphia which is fundamental to the termination of the negotiations. The majority of the Commission had requested the submission of the *Proposed Basis of Union* (1946) to the Church for study and report. The minority considered this document repugnant to the mind of Christ and opposed its submission to the Church. This minority felt that each new step meant a more binding commitment. The General Convention (1946) was unwilling to postpone a decision on the *Proposed Basis of Union* until the 1949 Convention, as recommended by the majority of the Commission, and turned the attention of the Commission in quite a different direction. The Episcopal Church was ready to tend its garden. This new direction reveals the struggle to confirm its own identity as a segment of the Anglican communion. It had now become evident to the Presbyterians that the Episcopalians were uncertain of the ground on which they were pursuing their original Declaration of Purpose and the negotiations ceased, although the Presbyterians expressly answered the 1946 Convention by a statement of willingness to pursue the original purpose, thus leaving the door ajar on their part.

The third stage of negotiations, termination, is thus seen to coincide with the era of organizational expansion in the United States. This organizational interest dominated the churches after

World War I; William Adams Brown noted a similar pattern of religious development in the early 1920's when the promise of the Interchurch World Movement dissolved before the drive of the denominations to organizational growth.[4] Without taking a deterministic view of historical processes, it is still possible to feel the weight of this postwar struggle for organizational expansion. The decisions of the Philadelphia Convention in 1946 are clearly congruent with this trend. There is some feeling that the presence of the Archbishop of Canterbury at the Philadelphia Convention strengthened this trend in the minds of the Deputies, not so much in anything that he said, although he did hold out promise of unity through intercommunion (a good excuse to drop the *Proposed Basis*), but more distinctly by his presence as a symbol of Anglican solidarity. At the very least, his presence encouraged the Deputies to cast their eyes toward Lambeth, which is to say inward rather than outward.

The Presbyterian-Episcopalian negotiations coincided stage for stage with three distinct periods in the recent history of the United States. (1) The heroic Declaration of Purpose came in the era of social revolution. (2) The postponement of the hour of decision (1943 consensus of silence) came when attention had turned away from internal differences and outward upon a common enemy. (3) The revulsion at earlier dreams and the desire to restore the safe outline of a traditional identity came with the cessation of external threat and the promise of organizational prosperity. The United States moved from the era of the New Deal through the hell of war to the era of the Big Deal. The Presbyterian and Episcopal Churches moved simultaneously from a period of sacrificial concern through a period of troubled discussion to an era of separate expansion. The congruity of these stages suggests, at least, the importance of *kairos* in great undertakings. It also suggests that organizations need permanent, well-established instruments of negotiation if they are going to pursue great matters without becoming subject to rapid shifts in social and cultural climate.

Difference in Institutional Pattern

Sherman Johnson notes that there were ambiguous provisions in the document, *Basic Principles* (1943). These provisions were agreed upon and yet understood differently by Presbyterians and Episcopalians; and, in fact, agreements were more apparent than real. This difficulty in the negotiations extends to the problem of a common basis for communication. If communication is conceived in linguistic terms, it can be said that a common language provides symbolic consensus for communication. Actual communication enlivens and transforms the consensus, but it presumes a common language. Communication, as in the negotiations between these Churches, helps to build a consensus, but the lack of a minimal consensus is itself a major problem in negotiation.

A careful review of the documents in the negotiations, including such statements as "Things Believed in Common," might reveal some interesting points of semantic divergence whose source could be traced to underlying differences of orientation to religious life and experience. However, it may be useful in this report to indicate a divergence in orientation which may have affected the House of Deputies at the General Convention of 1946 more than any particular provisions in the documents. This divergence arises from the distinction between the Episcopal Church as a cult church in contrast to the Presbyterian Church as a confessional church.[5]

Distinctions of this kind are, of course, typological and refer to differences in emphasis, and yet they can create a significant cleavage in the value consensus. Such differences reflect the existence of different religious languages. Such a cleavage, if it can be validated, has broad significance for the problem of negotiation between churches which fall on different sides of this split. The problem of maintaining order in the membership during negotiations becomes very serious when words become too ambiguous, for clarification on the negotiating level cannot touch anxiety on lower levels.

The distinction between cultic and confessional churches centers in a difference in principle of continuity. The cultic church maintains its continuity essentially through its liturgical unity. The Anglican communion has, on the whole, tended to this cultic type of identity: hence, the immediate reversion of all discussions of union with Anglicans to the problem of orders of ministry. Similarly, questions of Scripture, the Creeds, and the Sacraments as well as the Episcopate are treated in the context of liturgical continuity. The Quadrilateral is after all a cultic frame for negotiation. The ambiguous position of the Offices of Instruction, Thirty-Nine Articles, and the Catechism in the Episcopal Church reflects the pre-eminence of the cultic principle of continuity. Alden Kelley, at one time a member of the Joint Commission on Approaches to Unity, notes this characteristic when he says that "the faith of the Episcopal Church is to be found implicitly in its worship rather than explicitly in an historic 'confessional' document." [6]

Distinctions of this kind are easily exaggerated, and yet there is evidence that the Presbyterian Department sensed this difference in the negotiations. Presbyterian continuity, to be sure, involves cultic tradition; however, the Presbyterian point of zero-tolerance as a Church comes at the threat to pure doctrine and confessional orthodoxy. Irregularity of doctrine is, in principle, more threatening than cultic nonconformity. Cultic and Confessional churches will, of course, have to negotiate over the whole range of creedal, cultic, disciplinary, and communal problems; but each type tends to focus the crucial issues around problems which are central to its own principle of continuity. This difference appears in a letter from the Department of Church Co-operation and Union of the Presbyterian Church to the Joint Commission of the Episcopal Church on December 13, 1945; the Department notes that the *Proposed Basis of Union* in the most recent revision by the Episcopal group omitted "the Confession of Faith and Catechisms from the first paragraph under section 1, on Doctrine." [7] The mere fact of such an omission by the Episcopal Commission tells more about the fundamental difference in ethos between the churches than the way in which the omission was handled. The cultic church is preoccupied with ministry and practice; the confessional church works from true teaching to proper discipline and practice almost by implication. Broadly speaking, the confessional approach is more rational and, therefore, more easily communicated in negotiation.

It would be a mistake to exaggerate this cleavage in ethos; nevertheless, it has important bearing on the negotiations. Each party to negotiation can, of course, gain richness and depth in its own life by confronting dimensions of religious experience which it tends to scant; for example, the Episcopal Church has probably never enjoyed such a clarification of its own teaching as it derived from the negotiations with the Presbyterians. However, the significance of terms is quite different in the two types of churches. Suggested changes of practice may seem minor to a confessional orientation and yet pose radical threats to a cultic body. For example, Bishop Parsons notes in a letter of February 19, 1959, that the use of the term "presbytery" in the *Proposed Basis of Union* was a real threat to Episcopalians in 1946. Clearly the use of the term bishop would present a real problem to rank-and-file Presbyterians, as R. W. Lloyd has noted, and yet the problem is how such terms impinge on the continuity of the two bodies.[8] A change of terms, and to some extent therefore of forms of continuity, requires a long process of assimilation in a church of the cultic type. A change of terms in a confessional body involves the difficult but more rational process of clarifying the relation of the new term to the doctrinal position of the body. Again, the rationality of the confessional structure facilitates change, whereas the cultic body resists changes in symbols since it maintains its ethos by organic continuities that are less accessible to rational manipulation. Moreover, this resistance is intensified in a cultic church which is uprooted from the cultural soil in which it originated and upon which it has depended for support.

These relative distinctions between cultic and confessional types touch the fundamental principles of organization of religious bodies. One aspect of this is the differential problems of communication within the memberships of each type. The more organic, cultic type of continuity offers more resistance to rational manipulations even in directions which are consistent with its own ethos. For example, the *Proposed Basis* (1946) would fuse Episcopate and Presbytery as "functions," but the cultic type of church reacts more to this change as a symbolic threat than to the obvious similarity of function. The rational understanding of the negotiators spreads to the membership very slowly, whereas the threat to continuity is posed immediately. Rational consistency is much less important in churches of a cultic type than continuity of external forms; in fact, doctrinal "drift" does not seem to trouble such bodies. All churches cling to tradition, but those of the cultic type do so more than others. Moreover, this devotion to form is intensified in cultic churches such as the Episcopal, which have been uprooted from the cultural soil in which they were nurtured, for they depend thenceforth upon a few symbols for a sense of organic continuity.

Apart from the more radical question raised by this distinction, the emphasis on symbolic continuity in the cultic type may account for the vulnerability to panic in the Episcopal Convention of 1946. Even George E. DeMille, who has written a very Anglo-Catholic account of these negotiations in his little volume, *The Episcopal Church Since 1900*, notes that the conservatives did not trust the House of Bishops in the 1946 Convention and pushed through a precipitate discussion of the *Proposed Basis* (1946) in the House of Deputies. This stampede in the House of Deputies, despite the fact that they had waited for guidance from the upper house in 1943, is indicative of the level of anxiety. The important point, however, is that the rational propositions in the *Proposed Basis of Union* provide little defense against the feeling that changes in symbols are destructive of organic continuity. This lack of access to reason creates special problems for negotiation with a cultic type of church.

Dean Sherman Johnson suggests that unofficial projects in common during preceding years and other modes of working together might have furthered the negotiations. Such reciprocities seem essential for negotiation with churches of the cultic type. The shift in the General Convention of 1946 toward emphasis upon intercommunion may also be taken as a clue to a pattern of negotiation with a cultic type of church. Negotiation, in other words, need not be simply by committees which attempt to formulate rational statements and plans. Such formulations are obviously useful and even essential, but they form the less important mode of negotiation for a cultic church. Common action, joint patterns of worship, and so on form the principal modes of negotiation for the cultic type of church. To the extent that this is true, the Convention of 1946 represents the culmination of a divergence in ethos which was not taken seriously enough in the mode of negotiation, even though the divergence was constantly present in the content of the discussions. To state the issue too simply, the negotiations were conducted with a rationalistic bias which is inconsistent with the basic ethos of Anglicanism. The minority members of the Joint Commission of the Episcopal Church symbolize this inchoate and yet profound resistance to rational manipulation.

Ralph W. Lloyd notes a cultic resistance in Presbyterian ranks to the Prayer Book liturgy of the Episcopal Church. He also notes that the availability of an option in liturgies generally quieted anxiety on this question. By contrast, the foregoing analysis would suggest that the Episcopal group would not consider that they had moved toward union until they had moved toward common worship in their tradition. Options in liturgy, in other words, would be much more difficult to assimilate, despite the great diversity in the history of the liturgy, than vagueness in doctrinal formulation.

The drive to organizational expansion and consolidation of identity after World War II coincided exactly with the Episcopal Convention of 1946. The tent stakes were being driven more deeply into the ground. Consolidation of identity in a cultic church means exaggerated emphasis upon forms of worship and validating symbols of continuity—a period of cultic positivism.

As Ralph W. Lloyd has noted, the problem of Orders and Episcopate created the big hurdles in the negotiations. In brief, the principle of cultic continuity was coming into even greater prominence with the postwar consolidation.[9] The House of Deputies (1946) reflected this mood in their decision to refer the matter to the guardians of the tradition—the bishops gathered at Lambeth.

Procedure in Negotiation

Bishop Edward Parsons noted the trend to secrecy in negotiation after 1943, although he hesitated to make mention of this fact for fear of seeming critical of his successors.[10] The causes for secrecy may be very complex; for one thing, the Commission had made its position clear and now needed a firm ground for union; in fact, this question of method in negotiation is of extreme importance and deserves consideration in light of the preceding analysis of divergence of ethos. It seems clear from the "Blue Book" of the General Assembly of the Presbyterian Church in 1944 that their Department was having difficulty in maintaining confidence among the constituency during the unproductive years of the negotiations. The split in the Joint Commission of the Episcopal Church with majority and minority reports in 1943 and 1946 testifies to difficulties in the Episcopal ranks. The problem represented on both sides is one of procedure in the conduct of negotiations between bodies which operate through a representative democracy.

A representative democracy has difficulty with secret diplomacy, because the withholding of information inhibits the democratic process. Responsible voting requires an informed body of voters. Consequently, increased secrecy decreases the responsibility of the voters. This generally known phenomenon is a source of particular difficulty in negotiations between bodies like the Presbyterian and Episcopal Churches. Bishop Parsons believed in open negotiation and kept the Episcopal Church informed at each stage of the discussion with the Presbyterians. In fact his

CASE STUDIES

policy of open discussion and churchwide study gave rise to widespread criticism in the church press, but he viewed such difference of opinion as essential to the clarification of issues. His method of open negotiation was partially shelved after 1943. In fact, the *Proposed Basis for Union* (1946) had been made available only a few months before the General Convention of 1946 (in the summer months). Bishop Parsons is convinced that this secrecy did much to aggravate the situation at the Philadelphia Convention (1946). However, the difficulty may well have been the shift from open to closed negotiations rather than the mere fact of confidence in the last few years of the discussions. When the Joint Commission ceased to inform the Church of its activities, enough anxiety had been generated among the conservative groups so that pamphlets and articles against the proposed union were circulated throughout the church. In other words, the Commission withdrew from the field of public debate at the very moment when public concern had developed in the church.

Confidence in negotiation also becomes difficult in reporting to a General Convention or a General Assembly. For example, the Joint Commission had made public enough information so that it had to report even when this meant the presentation of majority and minority statements. The commission would have preferred to work on the problem long enough to arrive at a consensus, but Conventions do not wait upon a consensus. If negotiations have been relatively public, demand grows for public clarification. The public character of the negotiations, to this extent, boomeranged on the Commission. When the Commission withdrew from public debate after 1943, it was too late to take such a step and, in fact, confidence at this stage aggravated the problem.

Public debate during negotiation may accentuate the feeling that change is coming too rapidly. Dean Johnson notes the widespread feeling that things had moved too rapidly; Episcopalians felt that they were being led to a union without a courtship. The charge of undue haste may be partly true, and yet 1937 to 1946 had only produced a *basis* of union—some points for discussion. If one reads through the series of documents, a reasonable unanimity on major points appears from the very first and much that follows is clarification. This is not to say that the unanimity would be acceptable to either body or even that all negotiators shared this common mind. Nevertheless, the years from 1937 to 1946 were largely a period for clarifying ways of handling problems of order. The sense of "haste" emerged in two dimensions: (1) consensus on a *basis* of union was emerging among the majority of the negotiators; (2) the full seriousness of the negotiations was gradually dawning in the consciousness of the constituencies. Despite the assurance that no substantive steps on union would be taken without consultation with Lambeth, the Episcopal constituency *felt* a stepping up of the tempo of the negotiations. Public debate engendered a growing disquiet.

Another consequence of public debate is the sense that one is being committed further through continuing discussion; negotiation itself presumes an understanding. Dean Johnson refers to this as one of the most important factors in the decision for a new tack at Philadelphia. Bishop Parsons has observed that the tentative discussions from 1928 to 1937 had convinced several leaders that no real progress would be made until definite commitments to action were undertaken. These leaders had come, after a period of nine years in regular discussion, to an awareness of the importance of definite commitments. It seems evident that the representatives of the Episcopal constituency in the Convention were just becoming aware of their commitment after nine years of negotiations. Public debate had slowly created this awareness; and, once aware, they felt that further negotiation meant deeper commitment.

Two consequences have, thus far, been attributed to public debate of the union of these bodies: (1) growing anxiety which issues in a sense of undue haste in the negotiations; (2) a dawning sense of being entangled in something which one has not clearly understood or anticipated. These two consequences are damaging to negotiation, however necessary such tension may be at some later stage in the process. These feelings seem to have been important factors in the termination of the negotiations. The ques-

CASE STUDIES

tion, then, is how to maintain the flow of information—an essential procedure in representative bodies—without engendering panic, for public debate without adequate understanding increases anxiety without directing it toward significant problem solving.

One is hard put to see any simple way out of this dilemma in democratic process. The democratic process presumes open negotiations, and yet anxiety rises when information is circulated without an understanding of all the facts. Much that is discussed in the early stages of interdenominational negotiation, especially where more questions than answers are available, can best be left to the commissions. This is not to say that the constituency could not handle these problems but only that they give so little attention to the issues. In terms of the state of understanding and awareness of commitment of the constituencies, it is evident that the negotiators were moving too rapidly. However, the central problem was *not* the tempo of the negotiations but the kind of public debate which was created through this method of negotiation.

A few generalizations may be hazarded on the basis of the foregoing discussion of public and private negotiation. Democracy hardly requires that every statement in a long process of negotiation should be shared throughout the churches. Furthermore, when statements are shared with the churches, this process needs to be carefully implemented in order to assure widespread discussion and understanding of the real issues. Any other method simply plays into the hands of those who wish to use the statements in order to create a panic. When one realizes how little the constituencies realize what resolutions are passed by the denominational bodies, even on crucial issues, it becomes clear that ingenuous notions about democratic process can do great harm in negotiations between the churches.[11] When the negotiators are ready to make a formulation which can be pursued, this can be given the widest possible distribution for discussion. Until that point is reached, reports to the Convention or Assembly can better be left to the effect that "negotiations continue."

This evaluation may apply more in the case of the cultic type of church than the confessional, for it is possible to reassure a membership of a confessional church by producing propositions which coincide closely with their doctrinal position. This interpretation should not be understood as suggesting the manipulation of memberships by committees. The problem is how a commission can maintain and deserve the confidence of the membership, for they may undermine the confidence of the membership by means of inadequately formulated statements. When a commission is ready to have its continuation tested by its findings, as a cabinet standing on a formulated policy, then public discussion is in order and the commission should be ready to face the consequences. Premature sharing of formulations, however, seems to have undermined the confidence of the Episco-palians in the work of their Joint Commission. However justified or unjustified this loss of confidence, it seems to have come partly from an injudicious use of the democratic process.

Conclusions

If the process of communication had been ideal in the Presbyterian-Episcopalian negotiations, it is conceivable that the two bodies might have agreed to disagree. In actual fact, the Episcopalians are still open to negotiations according to the mandate of the General Convention (1946), and the Presbyterians are still open to discussion according to their reception of the 1946 resolutions.[12] The termination of discussion, therefore, was a temporary cessation of conversation rather than an open rupture. The processes of communication broke down in the midst of the negotiations, so that there is no way to know what might have eventuated from adequately structured communication between the two bodies. The preceding analysis of communication has only looked at factors which seemed to contribute to this structural breakdown, passing over many of the factors which made the discussions as successful and encouraging as they were. There

CASE STUDIES

is no reason to assume that fuller communication would have led to organic union, nor is there reason to feel that full communication is impossible. The negotiations from 1937-1946 give no answer to these questions, since they ceased prematurely.

The lack of a common basis in values—the cultic-confessional split—suggests that prolonged discussion, other modes of negotiation, and great caution in publicity would have been required for a successful prosecution of the Declaration of Purpose. It looks very much like bad faith on the part of the Episcopal Church when one reads the action of the Philadelphia Convention (1946) in the light of the Declaration of Purpose (1937), and yet the resolutions of 1946 only disclosed the enormous distance between these churches, a distance to which the Presbyterian Department was sensitive from the first.

There is fruitful complementarity in these religious types—the cultic and confessional. Ecclesiastical fundamentalists fail to appreciate confessional strengths, even as confessionalists are all too likely to interpret cultic devotion as idolatry. The union of spirit and body implies a fundamental union of confession and cult which may be seen as complementary aspects of religious life. These differences, however, can be complementary only when they are joined in the rich diversity of an ecumenical church. When these aspects polarize, as they did in the Reformation, the churches are impoverished. The preceding discussion has attempted to identify a comparable polarization which occurred in the Presbyterian-Episcopalian negotiations. The failure to take serious account of this difference of ethos in its bearing on the procedure of negotiation led in time to polarization. This difference could have led to complementary development, but such an eventuality would have required long and patient negotiation. These churches will be much richer expressions of the Church, according to the present writer, when this reunion is accomplished.

The moral of this story has already been pointed in the course of its telling. The enthusiasm of the Declaration of Purpose (1937) gives some hint that the social and cultural similarity of these churches and the friendships among the leaders had been mistaken for similarity in ethos and orientation. It took less than a decade to realize that the cleavage to be overcome lay much deeper than the superficial similarities. In R. W. Lloyd's words, "the hurdle to organic union is higher than they hoped and believed." When the negotiators were ready to deal seriously with this basic cleavage, the Episcopal commission had lost the confidence of the membership; at least, the historical context in 1946 and the spread of panic had cooled the ardor of 1937. The diversion of attention to Lambeth was a way of shifting the burden of negotiation away from those who were dealing directly with the Presbyterians. The Department of the Presbyterian Church made a statement of receptivity to further discussion but they seemed to realized that negotiations were closed with the decision at Philadelphia.[13]

It is important to acknowledge the accomplishments of these negotiations. The documents produced during these years paved the way for recent statements which augur much for the future in the way of unity. The South India plan has also contributed to this advance. Reading the documents from the Presbyterian-Episcopalian negotiations, one is repeatedly struck by the wisdom and insight of these negotiators. Ground has been laid in these documents for much of the work of unification which confronts the churches. On the Episcopal side, the churches owe a great debt to the vision, devotion, and perseverance of Bishop Parsons in initiating and guiding these negotiations until his retirement. Bishop Parsons and Henry Sloane Coffin accomplished together some initial steps toward things in common which may bear much fruit in the movement toward unity.

NOTES FOR ESSAY 14

1. This essay draws on two reports which were written for the Commission on Institutionalism by two participants in these negotiations: Dean Sherman E. Johnson, Church Divinity School of the Pacific, Berkeley, California, and President Ralph W. Lloyd, Maryville College, Maryville,

Tennessee. The references to these contributors relate to their mimeographed reports.

2. Sherman Johnson, report, p. 2. Exception is taken with justice, by R. W. Lloyd, to the simple parallelism between Episcopal and Presbyterian development.
3. Unpublished report of T. O. Wedel to the Unity Commission, January 5, 1951, "Unity Negotiations with The Presbyterian Church in the U.S.A." (mimeographed).
4. *The Church in America*, p. 121.
5. This emphasis in the Anglican communion is noted in "An Anglican View of the Concept of the Church," by T. O. Wedel, *Journal of Religious Thought*, Vol. IV, No. 1, 1946-1947, pp. 53-66.
6. "The Episcopal Church and Church Unity" by Alden Kelley (mimeographed); it is evident that Presbyterianism and Lutheranism originally maintained much more balance between cult and confession than they were able to preserve through the later periods.
7. Mimeographed statement to Rt. Reverend R. E. L. Strider from Reverend William B. Pugh, Stated Clerk.
8. R. W. Lloyd, report, p. 10.
9. R. W. Lloyd, *ibid.*, p. 9-11.
10. Bishop Parsons alludes to this in George De Mille, *op. cit.*, pp. 156f, and in correspondence, February 19, 1959, with Gibson Winter.
11. See "Fellowship for Whom" by Herman H. Long, Board of Home Missions of Congregational Christian Churches; Long finds 7.0 per cent to 18.0 per cent of lay officers with a clear understanding of denominational resolutions on race.
12. After the completion of this report, the 1961 General Convention of the Protestant Episcopal Church accepted the invitation of the Presbyterian Church to join with them in inviting the Methodist Church and the United Church of Christ to discuss union.
13. The statement released by the Presbyterian Department, March 18, 1947, is somewhat ambiguous, since it reveals receptivity and yet a sense that the Episcopal Church is deferring further conversation.

BIBLIOGRAPHY FOR ESSAY 14

Brown, William Adams, *The Church in America* (New York: The Macmillan Company, 1922).

DeMille, George E., *The Episcopal Church Since 1900* (New York: Morehouse-Gorham Co., 1955).

Long, Herman H., "Fellowship for Whom," Board of Home Missions, Congregational Christian Churches.

Parsons, Talcott, Bales, Robert F., and Shils, Edward A., *Working Papers in the Theory of Action* (Glencoe, Ill.: The Free Press, 1953).

Wedel, Theodore O., "An Anglican View of the Concept of the Church," *Journal of Religious Thought*, Vol. IV, No. 1, 1946-1947, pp. 53-66.

15.
THE UNITED CHURCH OF CHRIST IN AMERICA: ACTUALIZING A CHURCH UNION

Church union negotiations and procedures in the United States are often very different from each other. For example, during the years when the Lutheran Church, Missouri Synod, was in discussion with the American Lutheran Church, the major point of attention was a common basis of doctrine. In the discussions between Presbyterians and Episcopalians the order of the ministry and the liturgy were especially important. In the negotiations between the Congregational Christian Churches and the Evangelical and Reformed Church, neither doctrine nor liturgy and ministry were as important as church polity. Indeed, questions of a common statement of faith and liturgy were to be pursued after the formal unification of the denominations.

This order of events hardly makes sense to many churchmen. Some would question whether the Congregational Christian is a "church" at all, since it has no confessional basis of membership binding for all its congregations. Some would view this union as analogous to the merger of two free associations, for example, two foundations for charity or two groups of trade unions. They might interpret it as a manifestation of the democratic and

by JAMES M. GUSTAFSON
(Assisted in research by Hugh Wire)

practical character of American culture, and of the nondoctrinal character of "liberal" Christianity. A more complete analysis could interpret the procedures in the light of such questions. The present study is more limited in intention. It isolates national agencies of the two denominations in order to see what occurs as they seek to combine their work after formal unification of the denominations has occurred.

The Denominations Involved

In order to understand a small part of the union, it is necessary to have a synoptic picture of the denominations. They are the Congregational Christian Churches of the United States of America, and the Evangelical and Reformed Church (henceforth designated as CC and E and R, respectively). In 1953, the CC denomination numbered 5287 congregations, with a total membership of 1,263,472 persons. The E and R Church had 2718 congregations, with 750,463 members. The Congregational Christians are located most heavily in the northeast portion of the United States, with 38.4 per cent of the congregations and 42.8 per cent of the membership in that region. They are almost as heavily concentrated in the North Central portion of the country; 38.9 per cent of the congregations and 37.8 per cent of the membership being in that region. The E and R Church is most concentrated in the North Central region: 49.8 per cent of the churches, and 53.2 per cent of the membership. In the Northeast region there are 36.7 per cent of the E and R congregations and 36.0 per cent of the members. Both churches are proportionately weaker in the South and West, though the Congregationalists are much stronger in the West than the E and R Church (12.2 per cent of its membership compared to 1.1 per cent of the E and R membership).[1]

The Congregational Christians have been dominantly long-time Anglo-Saxon residents of America. Many proudly trace their ancestry back to the Pilgrim and Puritan immigrations of the seventeenth century. In recent decades many acculturated sons

326

of immigrants from many countries have joined the CC churches. The E and R members are dominantly of German ancestry. Many congregations were bilingual until recent decades. A Hungarian synod belongs to the E and R Church just as a German Conference belongs to the CC Churches.

The CC Churches have traditionally been governed by a congregational polity, though it has never been so radically congregational as that governing many Baptist groups and the Disciples of Christ. Indeed, there have been times and places in which the polity has been virtually presbyterian, for example, in Connecticut under the Saybrook Platform in the eighteenth century. The E and R Church traditionally has had a modified presbyterian form of government. The union has been acclaimed as the first major one in America in which churches of these divergent polities have been joined together. The Congregationalists have previously united with three smaller denominations: the Evangelical Protestant Churches, the Congregational Methodist Church, and the General Convention of Christian Churches. The E and R Church is a union of the Reformed Church in the United States and the Evangelical Synod of North America.

The Congregational tradition stems from seventeenth-century Puritanism. Its theology was Calvinistic covenant theology; its polity was determined by the Cambridge Platform of 1648. In New England the Congregational churches were the established churches in the towns and colonies. During the eighteenth and nineteenth centuries the evangelical revivals of America had a deep impact upon Congregationalism. Two theologian-preachers typify these revivals: Jonathan Edwards in the first awakening, and Charles G. Finney in the second. In the nineteenth century New England, and particularly Massachusetts, was torn by the Unitarian controversy, which led to the separation of many congregations and members. Also that century was characterized by co-operative missionary efforts in which Congregational sponsorship and participation was of great importance. In the latter part of the century Congregationalists were leaders in the emerging social concern of the churches. The two movements of the social gospel and liberal theology had had deep and continuing impact on Congregationalism. The denomination has no creed on the basis of which membership is defined.

The Reformed Church in the United States consisted chiefly of Palatinate immigrants from Germany. They followed the Reformed order of worship, and used the Heidelberg Catechism. This Church made a notable contribution to American theology and church life (Mercersburg theology) through the seminary that is now located at Lancaster, Pennsylvania. The Evangelical Synod in the main represented immigration to America a century later than the Palatinates who constituted the Reformed Church. Whereas the Reformed group had its dominant strength in Pennsylvania, the later immigrants migrated to the Middle West, particularly in the St. Louis region. They represented in a large measure the Prussian Union Church in background, and thus bear the marks of both the Lutheran and Reformed traditions, with strong strains of German pietism. The E. and R Church, constituted in 1934, holds its doctrinal standards to be set forth in the Heidelberg Catechism, Luther's Catechism, and the Augsburg Confession.

Negotiations for the union of the E and R Church and the CC Churches began officially in 1942. The union was delayed by a lawsuit on the part of dissident Congregational Christian churches. In 1953 a court decision made possible the continuation of negotiations, and in 1957 the two denominations met in Uniting Synod on the principles of the Basis of Union and Interpretations. The Second General Synod of the United Church of Christ was held in 1959. Thus far it is the *General Council* of the CC Churches which has united with the E and R Church. The union must be implemented by continued negotiations, by the approval of the constitution and a statement of faith, and the respective ratification procedures of the two denominations. These procedures must be in accord with resolutions on the "structure" of the new church (the "structures resolutions") passed by the General

Council of the CC Churches and the General Synod of the E and R Church in their 1956 meetings.[2]

The dissent is strongest among certain groups and persons in the CC Churches. A National Association of Congregational Churches has been formed to "preserve the Congregational way." The major issue of dissension is ostensibly that of polity. The loss of the autonomy of the local church and traditional freedoms is feared. There is no doctrinal consensus among the dissenters; some are fundamentalists and others represent extreme liberal theology. Recent events indicate some consensus on very conservative political views. The extent of the schism is not yet clear.

The union is the result of stubborn and dedicated leadership on the part of men and women in both churches. The CC leaders persisted in the light of uncertainty and opposition on the part of many congregations and prominent pastors. The E and R leaders and churches were patient and firm during long months of legal and informal argument in the CC Churches. The union was aided by the flush of ecumenical enthusiasm among American Protestants immediately following World War II. The glow of euphoria had dimmed by the time of the uniting Synod, and the remaining steps are being taken in a serious determination to complete the union. The revival of interest in Reformation and biblical theology among both denominations has given impetus to some of the support in both churches. Commitment to the union, however, is theologically inclusive in both groups. The traditional ethnic identifications of both groups have probably been a hidden factor in suspicion of the union in some areas, particularly in the Middle West.

The complete study of this church union remains to be written. The present study intersects a time of rapid change in the administrative structures of the churches. From the time of the beginning of the present study to its completion in the spring of 1959, a period of eight months, some decisive changes were made. By the time of its publication more will occur. Thus all that can be accomplished is a definition of some of the processes and factors at work during a church union procedure.

A Case Study of Administrative Merger

A small part of a long and vast union process is here limited for intensive study. It has a clear starting point: 1957, when the denominations joined to form the United Church of Christ in America. Its finishing point is not fixed; the institutional amalgamation is underway, but its final form is not precisely defined. There are projected patterns, but these have to be worked out through procedures of negotiation, and through processes of common work. The plans and procedures must be in accord with the Basis of Union and the "structures resolutions" passed in 1956. These resolutions were drawn up in the light of the lawsuit tried in the Federal Court in New York, and affirm the necessity of maintaining present structures insofar as possible while engaging in co-operation. The denominations are faced with the dilemma, on the one hand, of denying the reality of the union, by holding the present administrative and institutional patterns insofar as possible; and, on the other hand, of integrating the organizations too fast and consequently being charged with bad faith by enemies of the union.

Within the United Church a small segment of the total process has been isolated for study, namely, the unification of the staff and work of the Division of Church Extension and Evangelism in the Board of Home Missions of the CC Churches, and the Board of National Missions and the Commission on Evangelism in the E and R Church. The units under study have comparable areas of responsibility in the work of the denominations. The titles immediately indicate that there are differences in organizational structure; church extension is a part of the CC Board of Home Missions, and is affiliated with evangelism work; church extension is the total function of the Board of National Missions in the E and R Church, and evangelism is the responsibility of a separate commission.

The question here addressed is: What are the variable factors in the structures and functions of the agencies of the two denominations that foster or hinder the process of unification? An answer to this question requires reflection on a mass of information gathered from documents and interviews. An historical narrative of the union will not provide the answer. Rather, the interest lies in the institutional factors that exist in this church union, and may very well exist in other unions. Although this study centers on a segment of the CC and E and R union, its findings probably reveal aspects of the total organizational process involved in the United Church.

The main issue appears to be that of uniting a church with presbyterian polity with churches of congregational polity. Indeed, one level of the tension is the problem of clarification of the lines of authority and power in the formal, legal, authorized structure of church government. Hovering over this question are theological questions about the nature of the Church, on which there have been historical differences between the two groups. For the present study, however, the theological question is interestingly irrelevant. When churches develop their administrative organizations, whether this is done with care and self-consciousness, or whether the organizations emerge out of processes of occasional repair and addition, the institutional factors take on a certain autonomy of form and function. When administrative agencies are to be integrated, the question is not primarily what the mind of Christ means for the order of administration. Nor is the question one of what pattern of administration immediately corresponds to the theoretical political organization of the church. The issue is more one of the *effective allocation of personnel and resources in order to expedite certain tasks* to which the churches are committed. The administrative structure must be functional with reference to specifically defined tasks of the church: for example, the organization and development of new congregations; the raising and loaning of funds for church building; the requirements of effective administration at the regional levels, and the best relationships to local congregations. Efficiency in the use of resources is not the only point of reference in the determination of administration. Other considerations are involved. One is the conception of the nature and mission of the Church that guides the institutions. Another is how to find a working relationship that acknowledges the integrity of the two denominations. A third is how to combine operations in which the job definitions of staff persons overlap, or in which there is significantly different interpretation of what the job is. A fourth is the preservation of confidence and good will between persons during the stresses and strains of changing patterns of organization. Others could be named, but it is sufficient here to notice that church unity at the institutional level requires processes of negotiation, ordering of resources and personnel, and development of patterns of administration and work that are in many respects as complex as doctrinal definitions of the unity of the Church in Jesus Christ. Thus the oneness that is affirmed by a uniting Synod is not institutionally actualized until many other factors are explored and adjusted.

In order to indicate some of the difficulties that occur after church union has been consummated at the highest echelons of denominational life, five areas have been isolated for analysis. The resolution of these difficulties requires not only processes of negotiation, but also patience and sufficient time in which familiarity and confidence can grow. The areas isolated are (1) differences in conception of mission and "style of life," (2) difference in the personal influence of key personnel, (3) differences in understanding the function of particular offices or positions, (4) differences in the patterns of intra-staff relations and the relation of staffs to their boards, and (5) differences in the patterns of relations between denominational staffs and local churches.

Differences in Conception of Mission and "Style of Life"

At a number of points differences in conception of purpose appear to separate the agencies involved in the union. At others the understanding of purpose is similar enough not to be a point of difficulty. Attention here is turned toward the differences.

Evidence indicates that the E and R Board of National Missions understands its work to be concentrated on the welfare of the denomination. It is a servant of the denomination in a more sharply defined way than the comparable CC agencies. The CC staff and program appear to be influenced deeply by a conception of the Church's mission to diffuse aspects of American life. Its program is often experimental, indeed dramatic, in such a way that the importance of extending the influence of the Church into all aspects of contemporary culture is illustrated. The mission to the "beat generation," the esoteric cultural sect of young Americans centering in San Francisco, is the most prominent illustration of church extension and evangelism moving into situations in which institutionally defined goals of success are not important. Another such dramatic gesture is the support given to the Church of the Nazarene in Brooklyn, where large sums of money are being spent in an effort to develop new patterns of life in an established congregation in order to meet the needs of the "inner city." The writings of imaginative staff persons in the Board of Home Missions become institutionally developed in these missionary programs.

In contrast the E and R Board of National Missions confines its activities in the main to the establishment of new churches within the normally accepted procedures and goals for such a program. To be sure, it has given support to a number of special projects, such as a work among fishermen in the Back Bay Mission, a rural community center in the Ozarks, a mission to off-reservation Indians in Wisconsin, and a number of interracial projects. These projects have not been so dramatically publicized as the CC programs. They tend to reflect the traditional E and R concerns for ameliorative social work and forms of personal service, rather than a penetration of the wider cultural and social milieu. One E and R staff member suggested that the differences supplement each other, and ought not seriously affect the union.

Though there is a difference in the conception of mission at this point, it is important to note that the financial resources of the CC agencies are far greater than those of the E and R Board. Thus imaginative leadership in the CC group has an affluence of resources that enables it to take risks that the E and R Church cannot afford.

A brief survey of the evangelism literature of the two denominations indicates something of the same difference in outlook. CC literature is published in the finest style, with format and art work appropriate to men of cultured tastes. It is often and exposition of ideas about the need and nature of evangelism in contemporary life—the arts, literature, suburbia, the inner city, and higher education. In contrast, some of the E and R literature is similar to instructions given in the CC programs for lay visitation and membership recruitment. It describes steps that can be taken to reach new people for church membership.

Not so much a matter of difference in mission, though related to it, is the vague but perceptible difference in "style" between the agencies of the churches. This can be seen in the format and content of the publications distributed, and particularly in the reports distributed to the churches. The CC Board of Home Missions, like the whole denominational administration, has an obvious public relations consciousness. The CC reports are printed in an elegant and expensive manner, comparable in appeal to the publications of the Standard Oil Corporation, or *Fortune* magazine, the leading American business journal. They are designed for eye appeal and readability. A Canadian Anglican remarked upon looking at some of the literature, "You will never get the proletariat to read that stuff." E and R literature does not have the professional public relations style; it is prosaic, printed with economy in view, and assumes that the reader will not mind all this because he is interested in what is said.

This difference in style suggests that the leadership of the two denominations differs in affiliation with patterns of social symbols that now pervade American culture. There is "middle highbrow" up-to-dateness in the CC style that indicates the acceptance of many current cultural values, and the consequent importation of them into the life of the denomination. The E and R leadership is clearly not impressed with many currently accepted patterns in American institutions, and sees no need to import them into

334

denominational life. This difference may further reflect the orientation of the CC agencies toward a pattern of cultural values more characteristic of American middle class suburbs, and the E and R agencies' orientation toward a solid, stable pattern less affected by the swiftly changing life of the society.[3]

A more specific difference in interpretation of task can be found in the concentration of the E and R staff on mission churches, whereas the CC staff and funds are directed to all churches in the denomination. This can be seen in the allocation of loan funds. The CC funds are available for any congregation that can make a good case for its needs. Well-established congregations needing money to expand their physical facilities are as eligible as new congregations buying a lot for their parsonage. The E and R funds are available only for mission churches, and the attention of the church extension staff consequently is directed to such churches.

The isolation of significant differences in the sense of mission, style of work, and focus of attention ought not imply that there are no areas of common vocation. There are many; for example, both denominations have a strong concern for town and country churches and state their purpose in this area in a similar way. Both concentrate staff time and money on the establishment of new churches. Such points of common purpose cannot be described fully in this study.

Importance of Key Persons on the Staffs

Both denominations have benefited from the influence of distinguished leadership. At the staff level one finds at least three types of persons whose presence is always felt, even when such persons are absent from a meeting. One is the "charismatic" leader, who provides the center of loyalty, enthusiasm, and many of the ideas for the staff. Another is the competent administrator with long experience, whose prominence both nationally and within the staff makes him the object of some deference on the part of his colleagues. A third is the expert staff person who has defined his area of competence, and who does not easily change his patterns of understanding and work.

The CC Board of Home Missions staff as a whole appears to have a strong loyalty to its chief executive officer. His vision of a mission to America provides both ideas and a strong motivation to both experimental work and effective work within establishd patterns. Yet the power of his person and ideas does not absolutely dominate the actions of particular agencies in the board and their staffs. A member of the Urban Church Advisory Committee in the CC Board of Home Missions indicated how programs develop in the board. It begins with "someone howling in the wilderness"; then a few people gather to talk about it. In a few years it comes to the attention of the Board's chief executive, who makes a very effective speech about it. Then it becomes a project for a committee on program, and finally it is a program for the whole denomination. One of the key steps in the process is the vitalization of an idea by the chief executive's thought and speech, and the ensuing support that the staff finds in executing it. The imagination, sense of direction in the church's mission, and sense of support within the freedom of the staff, that characterizes much of the CC work, cannot be understood apart from the impact of this man. Further, his personal interest in imaginative programs has led to the employment of personnel who do not fit the ordinary conceptions of the bureaucratic personality.

Agencies of both churches have influential staff members whose authority rests heavily on their years of work within ecclesiastical administration. Such men are not noted for their creativity, nor for any flashing brilliance in communication of ideas. Rather they represent a continuity of tradition within the staffs. By virtue of their knowledge of the work of the agencies, their influence through the years in general denominational meetings, and their relations with conference, synodical and other personnel, these men have an important effect on specific policy and ways of work. Some restiveness among other staff members centers around the power that senior staff personnel seem to have. In union negotiations there is reason to believe that such persons represent the continued interests of the established denominational policies and procedures.

Finally, there is the staff expert. In at least one instance the staff expert has such a fixed conception of his task and its implications that it is difficult for his counterpart in the other church to see how agency functions can be united. In other instances men are experts in their offices, but appear to be open to a revision of their jobs in the light of developments in the union. It is clear generally that staff persons tend to feel a proprietary interest in particular programs that they have created, nursed, and brought into wide use. In such a case any threat to a particular type of program is a threat to the person.

Changes in staff personnel will affect the union even as negotiations proceed. In the CC Board it is characteristic to move men from position to position within the staff. A man hired as an expert in one field may find himself in a few years working in a very different field because of general administrative competence. As the work of the agencies is united, there is bound to be a new configuration of the dominant persons in the determination of staff policies and ways of work. Because of the importance of personal authority, there will be tensions and new possibilities emerging as the negotiations proceed.

Differences in Understanding of Function

The manner in which personnel with the same job title can differ in the substance of their work and the way in which they function has already been alluded to. It is important enough to cite as a special difficulty in the union processes. The differences are not merely those of interpretation by the staff, however. There are significant differences in procedures that are set by the rules of the agencies involved. One example will illustrate this.

The comparable departments for the establishment of new congregations clearly have a common purpose. But the procedures for the selection of property, granting of loans, and continuing relation to new congregations differ widely. The CC building fund has a capitalization of $8 million; the E and R of $3.5 million. The CC agency will take second mortgages; the E and R will take first mortgages only. The amortization of loans is over a ten-year period in both denominations, but the CC administration requires monthly payments and the E and R annual payments. The CC churches pay a 4 per cent interest rate on all loans; the E and R pay 2 per cent on churches and 3 per cent on parsonages. (After the research was completed, the E and R Board of National Missions raised its rates to 4 per cent in part to facilitate the union, in part for other reasons.) Only missionary churches are eligible for loans in the E and R Church; in the CC denominations all churches are eligible. The E and R Church usually does not loan over $50,000-$60,000 to any one congregation; the CC Board has no set limit, and determines its amount in the light of "needs and potential." In the CC arrangements more responsibility is taken at the conference level, and there is less detailed supervision of the local expenditure once the sum has been granted. Both denominations provide literature to local churches on how to proceed in getting aid from the national church agency. The CC staff members believe that the staff supervision of the E and R Church is too detailed to be administratively practical, and for the health of the new congregation.

In the building loan policies there is a clearer reflection of the traditional polity structures than in many other areas of the Boards. The CC program, involving not only the Building Loan Fund staff, but others in Church Extension as well, tries to maintain the traditional autonomy of the local church. The staff self-consciously seeks to delegate responsibility to the conference and to the local congregation, and seeks to maintain an advisory relationship rather than a supervisory one. On occasion a national staff member exerts influence and power beyond "advice" in some local situations in which there is a significant financial investment , but in the main this is guarded against. The E and R Church, on the other hand, maintains a much more detailed supervisory relationship to its mission churches until they have achieved self-support. This is possible in part because of a traditional

338

recognition that authority and power in the Church can be institutionalized at echelons above the local congregation.

Differences in definitions of functions occur in other areas as well. The E and R secretary for urban church work, for example, avidly uses a procedure of self-study that he has found an effective aid to city congregations. The CC city church secretary is primarily interested in problems of inner-city churches, and the development of means to sustain and improve the Protestant witness in metropolitan centers. In the area of research, the E and R Church has limited its activities to research that will be of immediate practical value for the mission program. The Research Director of the CC Board of Home Missions, though he is administratively part of the Division of Church Extension and Evangelism, conceives of his task in wider terms. For example, he also works with the staff in the Christian Education division, and initiates a variety of research projects which may be of only incidental utility in the immediate range of work. The Town and Country secretaries appear to be in general agreement on the types of work they ought to do, though this does not resolve the administrative problems of relating the staffs to each other.

Important questions that pertain to all church unions are implied from the differences in understanding of functions. To what extent does agreement on procedures and organization have to precede joint work? Or to what extent can procedural and organizational unity develop out of work in which the staffs are engaged in common confidence? Clearly where such factors as rates of interest are involved, there must be a rational-legal arrangement prior to common action. In other areas, such as Town and Country agencies, it may be possible for the appropriate administrative forms to arise out of the consensus that already exists on mission and practical tasks. But it is unlikely that the latter process can ever take place in any pure sense. Each agency brings to the negotiations a defense of its procedures, its administrative arrangement, and its personnel. The concern for the *preservation of present functions and structures* seems to enter into the negotiations on the part of those staff members who are self-consciously alert to the issues in the union. The degree of self-consciousness about the implications of the union for the present staffs varies from person to person on each side. It appears, however, that the Congregational Christians are more aware of the implications of the union for their ways of work than are the E and R staff members. They are more sensitive to what they are going to have to give up and to accept. This is true in spite of the fact that according to the *Basis of Union* the over-all pattern of the new Board for Homeland Missions is to follow more closely the CC Board of Home Missions structure than the E and R Board of National Missions.

Differences in Intra-Staff and Staff-Board Relations

The *freedom* of the staff members in the CC Board of Home Missions is a notable feature. Power and authority are delegated to the staff by the Board, so that the staff has great independence in thinking and action. It can initiate programs and policies, all of which must be approved by proper committees from the Board, and sometimes by the total Board. The CC staff is not in a narrow sense the agent of action and decisions taken by denominational committees and boards. Selection of personnel for staff positions manifests this concept of responsibility. Personnel are selected often on the basis of their independent and creative ideas, rather than their ability to fulfill compliantly the directives imposed upon them by a supervisory policy-making body. The staff consists of many persons with distinctively nonbureaucratic personality characteristics. The conception of a "collegiate staff" is manifest; members are equals, with separate functions and areas of competence, and all are consulted on major policy decisions. To be sure, there are official and more important informal status patterns within the staff. In the main, however, policy is discussed by the whole staff. The independence and freedom of the staff, resting in confidence in the *person* rather than the job definition, also leads to changing of responsibilities within the staff. For instance, a staff member trained in geography moved recently from the post as Town and Country secretary to a position of responsibility for higher education.

The delegation of power and authority to the staff of the CC Board of Home Missions leads to the accusation that the CC staff and board relationship is less democratic than that of the E and R staff and its relation to its board. The E and R staff members believe that they have a greater sense of immediate responsibility to the congregations than the CC staff has, and thus the democratic controls are exercised more clearly in their administration. There is evidence that in the main this is the case. The Board members of the E and R Board of National Missions, and the members of the committees for various aspects of its program are clearly "working committees." They are probably better informed about the details of policy and program than are their counterparts in the CC Board and committees. Less initiation of policy begins with the staff in the E and R administration; more of it begins with the committees. The Board is responsible for many decisions which the staff has the power to make in the CC administration.

A comparable pattern exists at the regional level. CC conference staffs are more professionalized than most E and R synodical staffs, and thus the work of the CC Board of Home Missions staff is often related directly to the staffs of state conferences. The E and R staff works with working committees at the synodical level. The E and R staff is anxious about the future of this arrangement in the united Board for Homeland Missions. They fear that the Board will be so large that authority and power must be delegated to the staff. Thus the working committee arrangement that they now find to be satisfactory will deteriorate into "rubber stamp" committees, approving the decisions of the staff, and acting as its public relations arms in getting support for the program. The E and R staff members do not object to the limits set upon their work by their responsibility to boards and committees for minor as well as major matters of work. At least in reaction against the clearly different CC pattern, they defend their present arrangement. Some CC staff members, however, express a strong dislike for the inefficiency and the sense of control that comes in the E and R working order.

Insofar as the progress of bureaucracies involves the increasing power and authority of professional staff, and the decreasing function of democratically elected representatives, the CC Board of Home Missions is more advanced in the bureaucratic development than the E and R agencies. This implies no value judgment on either, for strong arguments can be brought to the defense of each. The CC arrangement fosters high morale in the staff; it encourages staff members to be imaginative and creative; it decreases the waste of both staff and board members' time, and is in some respects economically more efficient. But it does weaken the significance of boards and committees as deliberative bodies which initiate as well as approve policy and programs. It also relies upon staff rather than working committees at regional levels to relay matters to local churches. The E and R arrangement brings more persons into the processes of deliberation and supervision (although, as we have noted, in some areas staff supervision is very detailed). The Congregational Christians face the same embarrassment that Baptists and the International Convention of the Disciples of Christ do with a growing bureaucracy that seems to develop in a direction opposite to that which the congregational doctrine of the church would suggest. The E and R Church manifests a strength of presbyterian polity; the lines of representation and the delegation of power and authority are not only clear, but are legitimated by its doctrine of the Church. It may be that in the long run the democratic process is best exercised through presbyterian arrangements duly followed through in action. It may also be that the bureaucratic developments, so common to our time, have not affected the E and R Church as deeply because of its smaller size and its more limited resources. Whatever the causal factors may be, this difference in staff-board relationships, and in the intra-staff relationships is bound to be a major obstruction in the processes of institutional unification.

Relations Between Staffs and Congregations

The tendency of the CC staff to work co-operatively with state conferences, and less directly with local churches has been noted. There are exceptions to this, of course. Generally, however, the staff works through the conference ministers and other members of state conference staffs. National staff members also work with committees at the state level, though these committees are not considered to be effective working units in most instances. Evangelism work, for example, has been concentrated on the writing of documents, and the leadership of conferences of ministers in various parts of the country, rather than any supervision of local lay evangelism or mass evangelism programs.

The E and R staff also works with synod committees, but in many functions works directly with congregations and their ministers. Some members of the E and R staff feel that they have a pastoral relationship with local pastors. Indeed, two staff members report that one of the most rewarding aspects of their work is the personal friendship and pastoral relation with congregations and ministers. In some areas the E and R personnel work as local "trouble shooters," whereas the CC staff members generally avoid such assignments. Work with synodical committees in the E and R Church is generally more significant than in the CC arrangement, for the synodical committees have through the years taken more responsibility than their CC counterparts. The E and R Church has not developed professional staffs in the synods comparable to the conference staffs of the CC churches. This may be the result of the strength of their committees, or it may be due to a lag in the general institutionalization and professionalization that has affected most voluntary associations in the United States. In either case, the lines of authority and responsibility are fairly clear, and in many cases the relationship within these lines is pastoral and personal. In the CC churches one is impressed with the absence of a definition of the structure of relationships between staff and churches, and with the impersonality of the congregation/staff relations.

The looseness of the CC pattern makes it difficult to find a place in which a national program can be integrated into the life of a congregation. Some staff members see themselves as members of the denomination's "theological faculty"; they have a teaching function at least one step removed from the work of the local church. The literature from the Department of Evangelism, for example, cannot easily be passed to an established conference committee or directly to the Board of Deacons of a congregation. In effect, the staff must make itself wanted, rather than function through sustained established relationships. If a conference has a strong Town and Country committee, the work of the national department is not difficult. If it has a weak committee, the task of joining staff and congregation is difficult. The conference ministers or superintendents play an increasingly important role as mediators between congregations and conferences on the one hand, and the national staff and boards on the other.

Some members of the E and R staff are loath to lose their present personal relations with synodical committees and congregations. The men who work directly with congregations have a sense of the immediacy and complexity of practical problems. In the light of this sustained intimate relation, some E and R staff members believe much of the CC work is abstract, impractical, and not very significant. There is consequently some anxiety about the effects of a larger staff, a larger denomination, and a much larger board.

Administrative developments on the CC side illustrate the way in which the functioning polity of a church is derived from many sources. The CC pattern is clearly not a simple embodiment of historic congregational principles of the doctrine of the Church. Such simple embodiment is not possible in our contemporary society. The CC administration has developed in the light of the size of the denomination, the wide geographical spread of its work, the necessity for specialization of knowledge of particular problems and issues, and many more factors. There may be more consistency between E and R principles of ecclesiology and the E and R administration. But this consistency is not necessarily

344   CASE STUDIES

the result of a doctrinal determination of the political order; social factors have contributed as well.

The union is to take place between equals, in confidence and trust; yet the economic and political power is actually stronger on the CC side. This weighting of power creates vague but important difficulties. The E and R Board of National Missions exists almost entirely on annual contributions from the churches; the CC Board of Home Missions has assets of over $40 million for its various agencies. One cannot discern precise places where the CC power affects the discussions, yet there appears to be more certainty on the part of its staff that they will have things their way. Complete confidence does not exist, for in fact the two agencies are not equals in power. The E and R staff, for example, noted how a crucial appointment was made in the CC staff without proper consultation. The CC staff notes how two appointments in the E and R staff were made without proper consultation. Confidence will have to grow, and in the light of the imbalance of power special care must be taken in the negotiations.

The absence of two things is notable when an institutional process of church union is studied. One is any clear implication from an accepted oneness in Christ for the political ordering of the church. Matters of administration and policy, though governed in part by a conception of the nature and mission of the Church, are in details subject to processes and procedures as characteristic of politics and the market place as they are of the Church. The other is the absence of any euphoria or even enthusiasm about the union, for the staffs of both denominations are deeply involved in their present commitments. This is no doubt in part healthy, for a realism about specific institutional problems reigns. But to a great extent the process of unification is bothersome to personnel from both churches. It takes time and energy away from present duties and opportunities. Yet in spite of the lack of noticeable enthusiasm there is much in common between the staffs in purpose, in involvement in American society, and in procedures. Many of these points of common life have been ignored in this paper in order to indicate present and potential difficulties. The staff member who thinks that institutional administration will fall into its due place of secondary importance when the churches have a living sense of their mission is probably correct. But institutions already existing embody a sense of mission, and it is doubtful whether an inspired sense of purpose can subdue the stubbornness and importance of tables of organization, fiscal procedures, personalities, and joint committee and staff meetings. All this is inexorably a part of the process of the unification of identifiable historical churches in the oneness of the people of God.

Implications

This study of one segment of the United Church shows that the problems raised by the institutional unification of the churches differ from the problems raised by differences in doctrine, ways of worship, and "church order," conceived in a nonsociological sense. The issues of institutional unification are not primarily matters of consensus and dissensus on dogma, liturgy, and even polity. In institutional integration doctrine and formal church order are of limited importance. The issues cannot be resolved by direct implication from either the doctrine of the Church or from an ideal form of congregational or presbyterian church order. Institutional procedures have their own autonomy, their own reality and stubbornness. There may well be theological explanations of such factors; for example, they may be the effects and means of God's creative activity, or part of the disorder of an unfaithful people of God. A theological explanation, however, does not solve the problems. Indeed, there is no clear implication from a theological explanation to the bases upon which responsible church leaders can make their judgments on institutional problems.

Nor does a deep commitment to church unity and enthusiasm for its actualization dissolve the problems of institutionalism. All the leaders who work in the agencies studied are committed to the United Church; none have opposed its consummation, and many have worked hard to bring the union into being. But even when union has become a fact of history at one level, it still must be worked out in political negotiations. Shape must be given to the ways in which agencies make decisions about what they ought to do, who is responsible for acting, how policy will be expedited, and how resources will be allocated among various needs.

From the study of the United Church some hypotheses can be formulated which are probably true in other church unions as well. The factors that create difficulty in the United Church of Christ are potentially present in other church unions.

The unification of churches at the institutional level is created and takes place in the context of tension. Differences in conception of purpose and "style of life" exist which reflect differences in doctrinal conviction, institutional tradition, dominant social and cultural affiliation of the denominations, and convictions about what cultural values can be placed in the service of the church. Differences in economic resources, size and social status of denominations, create an imbalance in social power, and will be interpreted in this way in spite of pledges to ignore them. Staff members of the uniting churches represent the interests of previous patterns of organization, traditional ways of work and personal loyalties. The necessary changes in both the formal table of organization and the informal status and communication patterns become a far reaching source of tension. A period of uncertainty and experimentation is bound to take place for several reasons. Denominational agencies differ in their official and informal understandings of the focus of power and authority for initiating policy and action and for making administrative decisions. These patterns are important factors for the differences in the self-images of staff members (of who they are and what they can do). Professional staffs differ in their patterns of work with their governing boards, synods and conferences, and congregations. The general conception of the nature and purpose of a national denominational agency in the minds of staff members is affected by the informal and formal status and communications patterns.

Certain requirements for the facilitation of institutional unity emerge from this analysis. Unions of church institutions require attention at various points: the development of consensus by the merging staffs and boards on their purpose and mission; agreement on the official administrative organizational pattern, with its ordering of responsibility, authority, and power; and agreement on detailed procedures of administration (for instance, how loans are made to churches). These institutional issues are settled by processes of negotiation that are frankly political and business in character. Consensus on religious conviction affects the understanding of purpose and guiding principles of policy, and thus has implications for the organizational pattern, but it does not of itself solve the institutional issues. At least as much time and energy is required for business and political processes as for discussions about doctrine and purpose.

When the formal agreements are made, institutional union is not yet a social fact. Uniting churches need to have faith and confidence in each other and in the united church which permit a climate of patience and freedom in the merging of staffs and ways of work. Patience and freedom are needed during this period, and authority and power must be granted for the appropriate revisions in organization and ways of work. Negotiating churches need to recognize that the effectiveness of the staff—their creativity, enthusiasm, resourcefulness, and sense of purpose—depends to a great extent upon the formal and informal patterns of the new relationships between the staff and its governing board, and between the staff and the synods and congregations. Positive co-operation and integration at the institutional level will come only through years of working together. Many aspects of the new church—its particular tasks and patterns of work—will take shape as the patterns or forms of organization are revised according to the purpose and functions that develop in the course of institutional unification. Charismatic leaders, professional experts, efficient organizers, and "idea men" all must revise their modes of work in relation to the rationally established lines of authority and responsibility, and to the emerging new community of work.

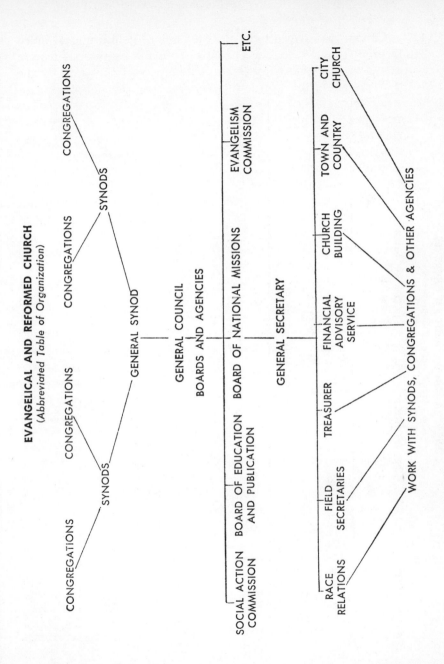

EVANGELICAL AND REFORMED CHURCH
(Abbreviated Table of Organization)

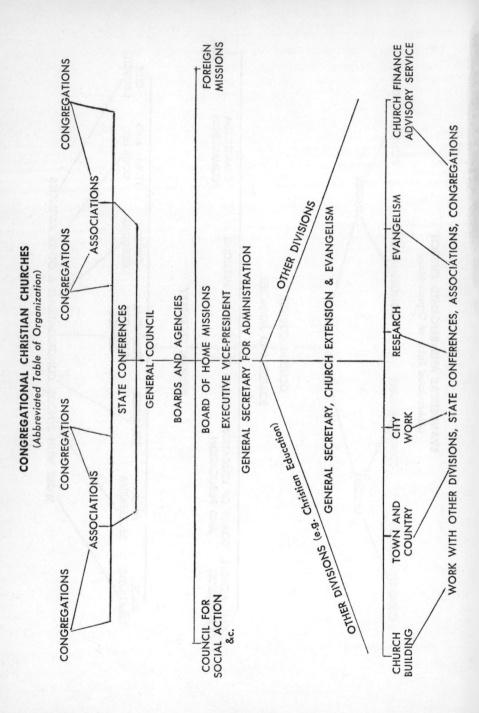

CONGREGATIONAL CHRISTIAN CHURCHES
(Abbreviated Table of Organization)

CONGREGATIONS — CONGREGATIONS — CONGREGATIONS — CONGREGATIONS — CONGREGATIONS

ASSOCIATIONS — ASSOCIATIONS

STATE CONFERENCES

GENERAL COUNCIL

BOARDS AND AGENCIES

COUNCIL FOR SOCIAL ACTION &c.

FOREIGN MISSIONS

BOARD OF HOME MISSIONS
EXECUTIVE VICE-PRESIDENT

GENERAL SECRETARY FOR ADMINISTRATION

OTHER DIVISIONS (e.g. Christian Education)

GENERAL SECRETARY, CHURCH EXTENSION & EVANGELISM

OTHER DIVISIONS

CHURCH BUILDING — TOWN AND COUNTRY — CITY WORK — RESEARCH — EVANGELISM — CHURCH FINANCE ADVISORY SERVICE

WORK WITH OTHER DIVISIONS, STATE CONFERENCES, ASSOCIATIONS, CONGREGATIONS

Changes in personnel will be as influential in this process as changes in formal procedure.

NOTES FOR ESSAY 15

1. Department of Research Memorandum, 1958:03, Board of Home Missions, The CC Churches. Further statistical information can be found in this document.
2. Such was the situation as of the early spring of 1959 when this study was completed.
3. The hypothetical character of this assertion must be emphasized. The key factor may well be the cultural orientation of staff leadership rather than the denomination as a whole.

16.
INSTITUTIONALISM AND ECUMENICAL CO-OPERATION IN THE LOCAL COMMUNITY

The purpose of this essay is to study how institutionalism affects ecumenical communication in a local community as illustrated in the experience of the Council of Churches in the city of New Bedford, Massachusetts.[1]

The Context of the Study

In New Bedford forty-six local churches representing fourteen denominations constitute the council of churches. Only a half-dozen small marginal churches are not members of the council, although they participate in a few areas of activity. Since 1944 the council has had a full-time paid executive secretary and at present maintains an annual budget of $24,500.

The New Bedford area has a population of approximately 140,000 people, of which 64 per cent are Roman Catholics, 32 per cent are Protestant and the remaining 4 per cent consist of Jewish people. The Roman Catholic population is composed largely of Portuguese, French-Canadian and Polish people who immigrated to work in the cotton mills in New Bedford around the turn of the century. The majority of the Protestants, which includes the

by **WILLIAM B. CATE**

Episcopal Church, consist primarily of old-stock Yankees and immigrant English mill-workers and their children.

In the late nineteenth century New Bedford was a world-famous whaling center. With the advent of fuel petroleum this economic activity was displaced by cotton mills, and now the city has a diversified industry since the cotton mills went South in the mid-thirties. The city has not progressed industrially with the rest of the United States and is one of the depressed industrial areas in the country, although new signs of life are taking place. Over the past thirty years the city has lost more than twenty thousand in population. This, combined with the large influx of Roman Catholic immigrants, has left the city with too many local Protestant churches for the Protestant population. The resulting weakness has contributed to the felt need for Christian co-operation in New Bedford.

The following chart gives a conception of the large number of Christian denominations to be found in an average American city. These are the churches that are members of the New Bedford council:

Denominations	Churches in New Bedford
Advent Christian	1
African Methodist Episcopal	1
African Methodist Episcopal Zion	1
American Baptist Convention	6
Episcopal	5
Friends	3
Greek Orthodox	1
Methodist	8
Primitive Methodist	2
Presbyterian	1
Salvation Army	1
Undenominational	3
Unitarian	3
United Church of Christ (Congregational)	9
United Lutheran	1
	46

New Bedford has few numerically strong churches, as witnessed by the following chart of church membership:

Size of Membership	Number of Churches
1600	1
1000	1
600-400	14
400-200	9
200-0	21
	46

It is the task of the executive of the council of churches to administer the program of the council through its various committees. The council consists of the elected delegates of the member local churches. They set up an executive committee and other program committees which do the work of the council throughout the year. It is from this administrative vantage point that the writer makes his observations on the institutionalism of the church in the local community.

The Institutionalization and the Institutionalism of the Local Church

Each local church is a complete social institution which has arisen to fulfill a given religious need and has developed stability and permanence in its structure. The development of this persistent pattern of activity is what is meant here by the institutionalization of a local church. Usually a church will become institutionalized to the particular religious needs of a particular group of people in a community. It also becomes institutionalized to some theological conception or self-image of what a Christian church should be. There exists throughout the life of a church a dynamic tension between these two social forces. We are most concerned, however, when this institutionalized process deviates from its given purpose and becomes an end in itself—what we term institutionalism.

For the purposes of this study, the local church as an institutional structure has among many components at least these four elements: (1) an organization of roles, (2) a symbol sphere which is its tradition and theology, (3) status in the class and social structure of the community, and (4) informal power organization. In other words, the local church is an institutionalized association.

Each local church has an organization of roles or status system which is determined to a high degree by its polity, position in the class structure, resulting personnel composition, and numerous other conditioning environmental factors. This organization of roles, which is to be found in the local church, is characterized by a high degree of stability and permanence.

The local church has a symbol sphere which includes its particular interpretation of Christian theology and the Christian tradition. The symbol sphere gives direction to the life of the church. Usually the interpretation of Christian theology and tradition will be in general agreement with the concepts of its parent denominational body. However, schools of theological thought increasingly cut across denominational boundaries. Because of great social mobility people move easily from denomination to denomination; doctrine is usually the last reason they join a local congregation.

It is the minister who is the interpreter of the theology and the general tradition of the church. He strongly influences the religious perspective of his people. Actually a process of mutual influencing takes place between a minister and his people.[2] Not only does the minister affect the people but soon he will find himself reflecting the outlook and the attitudes of his congregation. If his concepts are in too great a contrast to those of his people he will tend to water them down or minimize them on an expedient basis.[3]

As a part of its institutional life a church holds a position in the class structure of a community. Certain denominations in a city tend to minister to particular social and economic groups, although local congregations of the same denomination will often serve differing social classes of people in the same city. Not all the people in a local congregation are of a particular social class. Usually, however, the majority or a dominant minority belong to a particular social stratum. The people of the community have a clear image of the social status of a particular church. Community leaders know what clergyman representing what church brings the most social prestige to their affairs.

Each local church has a power structure. The power arrangement that maintains the unity and functioning of the church may actually have little correlation with the actual organization structure of a church.[4] The true guidance of a congregation very often rests in the hands of a person or group of persons who hold no office at all in the church.

Although the clergyman seldom holds the dominant position of power in the local church, he does represent the power in the local church in its relationship to other churches and to the community. In interchurch relations a minister will often feel slighted and think his prerogative usurped if he is bypassed in any way or contacts are made with laymen in his church without first receiving his permission. In the more episcopally ordered churches the clergyman has a more significant position of power because the power structure seems to adhere more closely to the organizational structure of the church. In a congregationally oriented parish the relationship of the power structure to the formal organizational structure of the church seems to be more free. Here the power of the clergyman depends mainly on his own ability to obtain it. At any rate the power structure of the church gives certain people who have little status in the world feelings of importance and positions of power and prestige. Whenever the local church power structure is threatened their prestige position is challenged.

The phenomenon of group life which is called an in-group occurs when institutional structures interact with each other. In a local community this phenomenon appears when churches come in contact with each other in the course of their operations. Members of a church see themselves as participants in a group which is different from all other church groups in the community. As a result there is a never-ending process of comparing themselves with other groups; finding reasons why they are better; building up group morale and loyalty which involves pride in self and traditions. There occurs then the group phenomenon of ethnocentrism, that is, the preferential feeling which individuals have for their own group.

Co-operation in a council of churches poses certain threats to the institutional and group loyalty of an in-group. Through interchurch contacts convenient stereotypes are dispelled. The ministry and laity of other churches are known to be concerned Christians. The real threat to the institutional structure of the local church comes, however, from the divided loyalty of its leaders who become involved in the work of the council. Through their council experience these leaders develop a new loyalty to a religious structure other than the local church and its denominational affiliation. As these people find a certain degree of Christian fellowship in this supraparochial fellowship, the new loyalty becomes a threat to the in-group solidarity of the local church. Some ministers even say that the council is stealing the loyalty of some of their people.

In New Bedford a communion breakfast was once held for all the men of the member churches of the council. Two communion services, an Episcopal one for the Episcopalians and an open Congregational service for all the other men, were held in their respective churches prior to the breakfast. One Episcopal clergyman objected to the arrangement on the ground that Episcopalian laymen did not yet appreciate the distinctiveness of Holy Communion as being the chief service of the Episcopal Church. He declared that although his church was trying to teach the uniqueness of its Holy Communion Service, by this simultaneous communion event they were giving "a sign to the people of New Bedford of unity which does not in fact exist" and were running "the risk of teaching the very thing we are opposing, namely, that there is no very great difference between the services, and

358

also that preparation for Holy Communion is not of very great importance."

Thus a council program can seem to be a dilution of Christianity to a local church and a threat to the group loyalty of the members of a local church who are involved in the work of a local council. A council program can minimize those very differences which the local churches emphasize as what makes them unique and justifies their existence.

The in-group nature of a local church can easily degenerate into self-pride and self-absorption. In a council of churches the typical question asked by the people of a local church when confronted with their financial responsibility to the program of the council is, "How much does it cost?" and "What is there in it for my church?" This type of comment typifies the concern of a local church to clearly demarcate its boundaries and to set itself off from other religious groups and institutions in the community.

The role of the minister in the organizational structure of the local church merits special consideration because he is the employed leader who influences the attitude of the church toward itself. It is the minister who brings the theological perspective into the life of the congregation and influences its total life more than any other one person does.

First of all, it appears that the ministry selects and develops men of an individualistic bent. Especially is this apparent where the prophetic function of the ministry and the importance of the pulpit is emphasized in the church. A premium is placed on individual initiative because the minister is the designated and employed leader of the local church. The minister's leadership position may give him the occupational disease of desiring to be the center of attention and conversation. Clergymen of this type tend to be poor harmonizers and equalizers. They do not work well in a co-operative church venture. They often exploit the natural predisposition of the local church to parochialism. In the competitive swing of church life many ministers may indulge in pettiness and professional jealousy in their relationships with other clergymen.

In the second place, the clergyman has a vested interest in his own church, which is the world of his primary activity and concerns. Here he earns his salary. The type of program and response he can enlist in his church will influence the financial rewards he will receive. Twenty years ago H. Paul Douglass observed that "what the churches want in a minister is essentially a successful salesman for their enterprise. A striking feature of the analysis of the ministerial qualifications desired, is the virtual absence from them of any doctrinal specification." [5] The local church in its most crassly institutional forms is the enterprise over which the clergyman presides. The success or failure of the program of the church will directly affect the future of his professional life.

It is in his church that the minister gains prestige and influence for vocational advancement. The co-operative activity of a council of churches does not have this type of appeal to him. Roswell Barnes has said that "the co-operative work for ministers can have a pull if it offers inspiration and vocation satisfaction." This pull, however, is in the realm of Christian values more than in the area of the church's institutional life. Few clergymen put the same kind of effort into a co-operative church program that they put into their own local church program. "According to an extensive collection of work records, the average minister actually gives very little time to extra parochial service of any sort. While a few gifted and influential ministers are much in evidence in these fields, they stand in striking contrast with the average." [6]

In the third place, co-operative activity in a council of churches can become a threat to the minister in his work. He faces a dilemma in loyalties. Is his first responsibility in the allocation of time and money to his local church and denomination or to the council of churches? At this stage of co-operative development in New Bedford, this does not present a serious dilemma; clergymen solve it in favor of their church and denomination. However, as co-operative work in our city develops it can become an increasingly important source of tension for the minister in his work. A minister often feels that the impact of Christian co-operation minimizes his opportunity to stress his church's uniqueness. Furthermore, a minister cannot mislead his people through misrepresentation of other religious groups if many of his parishioners know about these groups from firsthand acquaintance. Probably the greatest threat that many a minister feels is the money and manpower which a council takes away from his own church. In New Bedford the money for the council is raised through direct local church budget contributions or through a special solicitation of a local church's members. It has been the conviction of the finance committee of the council that most ministers do not put as much effort into raising money for the council as they should. The minister, in most cases, will try to protect what he thinks is for the highest good of the local church's financial interests. Occasionally ministers will imply that council activity is taking away local church leadership. Usually those local church delegates who are sent to the council are not the best leaders in the local church. An analysis of delegates to the New Bedford council over the years shows this to be true. There is a tendency for a minister to be protective of the manpower his church supplies to co-operative work.

Denominational Institutionalism as It Affects the Local Churches

Nearly every local church in a community is related to a larger denominational institution. The administrative top of the denomination serves the local church by various ways of strengthening its work. According to Douglass and Brunner the denominations are steadily becoming stronger as institutions: "Like it or not, denominations have come to mean more than they used to. They exercise wider functions and their functioning is more necessary to the well-being of the local churches than ever before. Denominations increasingly supply the competent planning for their subordinate units and furnish the technical experts." [7]

Our concern here is with the manner in which the institutionalism of the denominations affects the developing unity among the churches in an average American community. Institutional cohesiveness in a denomination is created by many factors such as the corporate nature of a communion, lay loyalty, the ordination vows of the clergy, the influence of seminaries or the pressure of other threatening bodies. The most important cohesive force in the life of a modern denomination, however, comes from the institutional thrust of the administrative power group.

Each denomination persistently pushes upon the local church the fact of its uniqueness in tradition, polity, doctrine, and program. The thrust comes primarily from the administrative offices and from the clergyman, who is the denominational representative in the local church and who is expected to represent the denomination in the local church in a dynamic way. In spite of growing ecumenical interchange, each denomination operates on the basis that its existence is based on doctrinal necessity. Much programing in the denominations now originates from specialized departments. Program suggestions and helps in religious education, youth work, stewardship, mission, and similar areas of concern come in a steady stream across the desk of the minister of the local church. Most of this programing stresses the denomination's particular slant.[8]

The thrust of the denominations to stress their institutional uniqueness is more obvious in the episcopally ordered churches, although it can be just as vigorous in a supposedly congregational-type polity. The drive comes from the power structure of the denomination, and the informal power structure might depend very little on the formal polity pattern of the denomination. Much of it is to meet needs, but at the same time a good amount is an institutional drive for self-preservation or expansion.

The denomination by its very nature must exert a certain amount of discipline over its members in order to maintain unity and stability in the structure. The heads of the denomination must maintain the unity and relative permanence of the total structure. The head role is usually played by a bishop, denominational executive, a board or a committee. In the local church it is a board, the minister, or a few individuals who serve the same function there.

The controls which the denomination exerts over its members are partly external and partly internal. The external constraints are those of ordination, professional advancement, control of property, and economic and psychological sanctions of various sorts. The internal constraints are those which are unconsciously built into the members by membership in the group. We shall consider them here merely as they relate to the minister.

It is the denominational fellowship that admits a minister into the profession, either through ordination or by transferring from some other group into the fellowship. Baptist and Congregational groups may feel that the local church installs pastors, but the ministerial fellowship of the denomination has within its hands powerful means of control. Every professional group sets up standards to which its members must conform before admittance. These standards serve the purpose of protecting the rights and privileges of the fellowship. Clergymen tend to talk one way when they are in denominational circles and another way when they are in ecumenical circles. Within the sphere of the denominational fellowship a minister feels strongly the compulsion to conform to the expected standards of that group, but in an ecumenical gathering there are pressures to be more responsive to other Christian bodies.

The most powerful controls the denomination has over its ministers are economic and professional. Professional advancement for the clergy is almost exclusively through denominational channels. The channels in the more episcopally ordered churches are more formal, whereas in the congregationally oriented denominations the avenues of advancement are more informal. Yet, these means of advance are still controlled to a great extent by the denominational leaders. Awards for efforts rest in the hands of the denominations. It is hard to get better churches if the leaders of a denomination are not in sympathy with a minister. Letters of recommendation or the right word at the right time all play a role. Each minister is under a great compulsion to raise his missionary quota to the denomination. This quota becomes the minister's bargaining power in getting recommendations for bigger churches. By contrast, money given to the budget of a council of churches will not help the minister professionally. It is not strange, therefore, that ambitious young clergymen will see their own church as an end in itself and not as just a part of the work of the kingdom of God in the community. There will be little concern for the total community responsibility of the church except as such community recognition helps to advance them and their church. Co-operative Christian effort does not benefit them in any way personally or professionally.

Being a self-perpetuating institution, a denomination has tendencies—which also is institutionalism—toward using a local church and a minister for its own good rather than the consideration of what is best for the Cause of Christ in the community in which the church is located. Its program is determined at the top levels of the denomination and then forwarded to the local church. In many denominations administrative checks and counterchecks are set up to make sure that this program is carried out at the local level. Co-operation or nonco-operation by the local church clergymen is noted by the denominational leaders. One of the awards for program co-operation is usually a news feature in the denominational house organ.

The real problem for a city council of churches comes in the lack of unity in program planning at the top denominational levels. This lack of unity makes a co-operative program in the local community almost an impossibility in many areas of church life. As the denominations are becoming more institutionalized and self-sufficient in every phase of church life they push their program more vigorously. In recent years, the denominations have taken over areas in which there had formerly been interchurch co-operation. Some examples in New Bedford are youth work, missions, teacher training, and the whole area of Christian education. The reason given is that interchurch affairs are too general and do not give the proper denominational orientation that is needed. It is true that much interchurch activity in the past has been weak in doctrinal teaching. It is also true that if a denomination feels it is being threatened by united programs it may increase activity in the area threatened. Certainly the minister finds himself in a position of divided loyalty when he wants to be a good minister of his denomination and also a co-operative clergyman in his local community.

The second type of social control exerted by the denomination over its minister is internal constraints. A great amount of social control takes place in the life of a minister through the fellowship he has with his fellow clergymen, "his significant others," in the denomination. The conception of the minister's role as held by the leaders and colleagues in his denomination and in his local church helps him to create his own self-image, thereby creating his "generalized other" or his conscience and conception of role.

If a minister's total experience is largely in his own local church or denominational fellowship, he will have little conscience about ecumenical work. His conception of his role as a minister will be in full accord with the denominational self-image. Clergymen not only get this limited point of view from their circumscribed denominational association but also through their seminary training. Without contacts with other clergy in some degree of intimacy, it is virtually impossible for the blinders to be removed, stereotypes and prejudice dispelled, and understanding generated. Much of the institutional structure of denominations works against an increased ecumenical communication in the local community. It is especially pronounced where institutionalism sets in and the denominational structure becomes dedicated to its own preservation and extension at any cost. It is not any secret malevolent purpose in the denomination that tends to make it divisive in the local community, but rather the nature of its institutional life.

The Institutionalization and Institutionalism
of a City Council of Churches

Similar social forces are at work in the institutional life of a council of churches. It is the intention of this section to see how these forces manifest themselves in a council of churches. A council of churches is the developing product of an institutionalizing process emanating from a felt need among the churches. The needs from which councils have developed are twofold. The first is an effort to overcome the handicap of a divided church in a complex world. The second is the theological conviction that the Church of Jesus Christ is but one Church. At any rate there are throughout the United States of America degrees of institutionalization which endeavor to relate, through established roles, the co-operative action of the various local churches in a community.

A council of churches, therefore, becomes a new and more inclusive in-group for the churches in a community. A city council may well set itself off against the suspected infringements of a state council of churches, a state denominational organization or a group of separatist fundamentalists, if there is such a group in the area. On the Eastern Seaboard a council of churches usually becomes an institutional defender of the rights of Protestants against the Roman Catholics. In New Bedford on several occasions the author has seen the Protestants rally together against what they thought was an infringement of their rights by the Roman Catholic majority.

The council establishes a new institutional loyalty in a community. For example, council loyalty sometimes exceeds loyalty to a minister of a local church when that minister does not have an ecumenical attitude toward other churches. After the experience of several years some churches now ask this question of a prospective minister: "What is your attitude toward Christian co-operation?" This takes place, however, only in those churches which have been actively involved in the program of the council of churches over many years.

In New Bedford, a city having a good history of co-operation and a fairly homogeneous group of churches in culture and theology, most ministers work with the program of the council. This is because the council has a comprehensive program and is of some value to almost every minister and church. Therefore, they are eager to take advantage of services that help them in their work. They also see the Christian impact on the community which is possible through the council.

Co-operation on the part of new ministers is sometimes due to the pattern of church life which has already been established. People in the church criticize a minister if he does not conform to the pattern of co-operation already functioning. Therefore, some clergymen are co-operative in New Bedford, not out of conviction but rather out of convenience and willingness to go along with established patterns of activity. On the other hand, a minority of the clergy are impelled to work in the council by a real conviction about the theological and biblical judgment on the divisiveness of the churches.

The council in New Bedford has achieved for itself a certain amount of social prestige in the community, as a result of its history of achievement and the caliber of church people who hold offices in it. By and large, the leaders of the churches are the leaders in the council, and this makes for a happy situation in developing a strong and effective program. A council of churches with paid executive leadership is more effective than council with volunteer leadership. Yet a more effective council program means the development of a more expanded institutional structure. When a council program becomes quite vigorous there arises the problem of conflicts of interests and loyalties. Paid, bureaucratic leadership in a council of churches means rapid institutionalization and often a rigid institutionalism.

The great value of the institutionalization in a council of co-operative patterns of church activity is that once they have become institutionalized in the life of a community they are difficult to dislodge. Established channels of communication are set up among the churches whereby intimacy of association across denominational boundaries develops and new areas of the churches' mission in a community are undertaken. Just as a local church is the institutionalized process to do the task of the Church in the world, so a council is the institutionalization of the need for greater Christian unity and effective responsibility of the Church for the total community.

Church councils in the United States stand in great peril of becoming rigid institutional structures at superficial levels of co-operation. Most councils of churches are involved in "life and work" concerns and do little or nothing in the realm of "faith and order" conversations. If the councils are limited to this level of the Church's life and institutionalize themselves on this plane, they can become obstacles to Christian unity rather than means to deeper unity.

The greatest danger is for a council to fail to be the representative agent of the churches. To avoid this pitfall two-way channels of communication must be kept open between the churches and the council. If the member churches feel that their will is not being expressed through the council and that too much program is being forced on them from another authoritative source similar to the denomination, they usually react adversely and ecumenical communication is stifled. A council can set itself off as an institution separate from the churches, and may seek to preserve its own life, whether serving the purpose of the churches or not.

The executive of the council of churches may become a bureaucrat with all the dangers that ensue. It is his job to make the council program a success. He may have too little feeling for the problems of the ministers and the churches and be concerned only for professional success. He can fall into the danger of measuring his success in terms of the business world which is usually activity, money, and big program. The real test is the degree of Christian unity that is engendered in and among the churches, and the fashion in which the mission of the Church is advanced.

One of the dangers apparent is excessive activity. A council of churches has various committees to do specific jobs. It is easy for these committees to think principally of their own program and not of the total church life of the community. If too many committees begin to operate in this parochial manner without the co-ordinating impact of a strong executive committee or board of directors, the council may become an organization which competes with the churches rather than serving as a vehicle of co-operation. It is possible for the council executive, because of his employee status, to find himself competing with clergymen for the time and money of their people rather than working with and for them.

Conclusions and Questions

- A local church is part of a larger institutional structure which is the denomination. Each denomination has a self-image or conception of what the Church should be. This self-image seems to become more emphasized and the structure of the institution more rigid through co-operative interchurch contact in a council. However, this is only part of the reaction. In many instances the self-image of the denomination through interchurch encounter softens into a more ecumenical conception of the Church. What combinations of factors in the ecumenical contact contribute to rigidity on one hand and ecumenical growth on the other?
- The study indicates that the lack of unity on the community level is to a great degree created and continued by the institutional rigidity of the modern denomination. It has also indicated how the clergyman in most cases is the denominational representative and preserver of denominational loyalty and interest in the local church. Does the study indicate how laymen who have become ecumenically minded can be the source of real growth in unity? The clergyman is sensitive to the attitude of the laity. Perhaps new institutional loyalties and structures can be developed at the local level where the drive for institutional self-preservation is the weakest. As the laity gain a new vision

of the one Church through a local council will they not influence the minister and the denominational heads?

- The study depicts the natural disposition of a local church group to become self-absorbed and involved in institutionalism. We have called it ethnocentrism or the "in-group" phenomenon. How does a local church transcend its institutional form to become a church which is obedient to the demands of the Christian gospel? We have said that only a minority of ministers and laity seem to catch the ecumenical vision and carry the work of a local council. We have also said that it is the leaders of the local church who can make a council effective. Are genuinely consecrated Christian people, who understand the Christian gospel in its fullest terms, the only final answer to parochialism and institutionalism in the local church?

NOTES FOR ESSAY 16

1. The data of the study are based on the experience of the author as executive secretary of the New Bedford Council of Churches for five years. His essay has been critically examined by other council of churches executives and has been rewritten in the light of these critical comments and three years of subsequent council experience in another locality. The author wishes to acknowledge help from the Reverend Alan A. Brash, General Secretary, The National Council of Churches in New Zealand; Mr. Korula Jacob, Secretary, The National Christian Council of India; the Reverend Harvey L. Perkins, General Secretary, Australian Council for the World Council of Churches; Dr. T. Ross Paden, Executive Secretary, the Spokane Council of Churches; the Reverend B. Bruce Whittemore, Executive Director, Cleveland Area Church Federation; Dr. J. Quinter Miller, Assistant General Secretary, National Council of Churches in the U.S.A.; and the Reverend Sheldon Rahn, Former Director of Social Service, the Detroit Council of Churches.
2. Sidney E. Mead, "The Rise of the Evangelical Conception of the Ministry in America (1607-1850)," *The Ministry in Historical Perspective*, H. Richard Niebuhr and D. D. Williams, eds. (New York: Harper & Brothers, 1956), p. 218. Joseph H. Fichter, S. J., *Social Relations in the Urban Parish* (Chicago: The University of Chicago Press, 1954), p. 136.
3. Richard T. LaPierre, *A Theory of Social Control* (New York: McGraw-Hill Book Company, Inc., 1954), p. 285.

4. Murray H. Leiffer, *The Effective City Church* (New York: Abingdon-Cokesbury Press, 1949), p. 160.
5. H. Paul Douglass and Edmund deS. Brunner, *The Protestant Church as a Social Institution* (New York: Harper & Brothers, 1935), p. 105.
6. *Ibid.*, p. 189.
7. *Ibid.*, p. 99.
8. Alan Brash writes: "I have found it very difficult to fight in all denominational missionary propaganda the assumption that the body producing the propaganda is the only one in existence. This is just as true of the major churches as of the sectist bodies."

BIBLIOGRAPHY FOR ESSAY 16

Allport, Gordon W., *The Nature of Prejudice* (Boston: The Beacon Press, 1954).

Angell, Robert Cooley, *Free Society and Moral Crisis* (Ann Arbor: The University of Michigan Press, 1958).

Boulding, Kenneth E., *The Organizational Revolution* (New York: Harper & Brothers, 1953).

Fichter, Joseph H., *Social Relations in the Urban Parish* (Chicago: The University of Chicago Press, 1954).

Gerths, Hans, and Mills, C. Wright, *Character and Social Structure* (New York: Harcourt, Brace and Company, 1953).

LaPierre, Richard T., *A Theory of Social Control* (New York: McGraw-Hill Book Company, 1954).

Leiffer, Murray H., *The Effective City Church* (New York: Abingdon-Cokesbury Press, 1949).

Yinger, J. Milton, *Religion, Society and the Individual* (New York: The Macmillan Company, 1957).

General Bibliography

GENERAL BIBLIOGRAPHY

(See also the titles listed following the individual essays.)

REPORTS AND ARTICLES which reflect the concern of the Faith and Order movement with social, cultural, and institutional factors.

Clark, Elmer T., "Nontheological Factors in Religious Diversity," *The Ecumenical Review* III:4 (July, 1951), pp. 347-356.

Dodd, C. H., Cragg, G. R., and Ellul, Jacques, *Social and Cultural Factors in Church Divisions* (London: SCM Press); American ed., *More Than Doctrine Divides the Churches* (New York: World Council of Churches, 1952).

Ehrenstrom, Nils, and Muelder, Walter G., "Reports on Institutionalism," *Minutes of the Faith and Order Commission*, 1956-1960.

"Institutionalism." A special issue of the *Bulletin of the Division of Studies*, World Council of Churches, Vol. VI, No. 1 (Spring, 1960).

"Institutionalism and Unity," Interim Report of the Faith and Order Study Commission on Institutionalism, *The Old and the New in the Church* (London: SCM Press, 1961; Minneapolis: Augsburg Publishing House, 1961).

Jenkins, Daniel, "The Ecumenical Movement and Its Nontheological Factors," *The Ecumenical Review* III:4 (July, 1951), pp. 339-346.

Marsch, W. D., "Kirche als Institution in der Gesellschaft," *Zeitschrift für evangelische Ethik* 4 (1960), pp. 73-92; English version in *The Student World*, 1959, No. 1.

Minear, Paul S., ed., *The Nature of the Unity We Seek, Official Report of the North American Conference on Faith and Order, September 3-10, 1957*, Oberlin, Ohio (St. Louis: Bethany Press, 1958), pp. 206-272.

Muelder, Walter G., "Institutional Factors Affecting Unity and Disunity," *The Ecumenical Review* VIII:2 (January, 1956), pp. 113-126.

Muelder, Walter G., "Institutionalism in Relation to Unity and Disunity," *The Nature of the Unity We Seek, Official Report of the North American Conference on Faith and Order, September 3-10, 1957, Oberlin, Ohio*, Paul S. Minear, ed. (St. Louis: Bethany Press, 1958), pp. 90-102.

Pickering, W. S. F., ed., *Anglican-Methodist Relations: Some Institutional Factors*, Papers presented to the Study Commission on Institutionalism (London: Darton, Longman and Todd, 1961).

Schrey, Heinz-Horst, "Die nicht-theologischen Faktoren der Kirchentrennung," *Monatsschrift für Pastoral-Theologie* 48 (März, 1959), pp. 84-93.

Sperry, W. L., ed., *The Non-theological Factors in the Making and Unmaking of Church Union*, Report No. 3 prepared by the Commission on the Church's Unity in Life and Worship, Edinburgh, 1937 (New York: Harper & Brothers, 1937).

The Third World Conference on Faith and Order, Lund, 1952, Oliver S. Tomkins, ed. (London: SCM Press, 1953), pp. 32, 44-48, 174-203.

GENERAL WORKS

Allen, A. V. G., *Christian Institutions* (Edinburgh: T. & T. Clark; New York: Charles Scribner's Sons, 1897).

Becker, Howard, and Boskoff, Alvin, eds., *Modern Sociological Theory in Continuity and Change* (New York: Dryden Press, 1957).

Bell, G. K. A., ed., *Documents on Christian Unity*, I-IV (London: Oxford University Press, 1924, 1930, 1948, 1958).

Dombois, Hans, *Das Recht der Gnade: Oekumenisches Kirchenrecht I* (Witten: Luther-Verlag, 1961).

Dombois, Hans, ed., *Recht und Institution* (Witten: Luther-Verlag, 1956).

Douglass, H. Paul, *A Decade of Objective Progress in Church Unity, 1927-1936* (New York: Harper & Brothers, 1937).

Douglass, H. Paul, and Brunner, Edmund deS., *The Protestant Church as a Social Institution* (New York: Harper & Brothers, 1935).

Flew, R. Newton, ed., *The Nature of the Church* (London: SCM Press; New York: Harper & Brothers, 1952).

Gustafson, James M., *Treasure in Earthen Vessels: The Church as a Human Community* (New York: Harper & Brothers, 1961).

Harrison, Paul, *Authority and Power in the Free Church Tradition: A Social Case Study of the American Baptist Convention* (Princeton: Princeton University Press, 1960).

Hertzler, Joyce O., *Social Institutions* (New York: McGraw-Hill Book Company, 1929).

Lee, Robert, *The Social Sources of Church Unity* (New York and Nashville: Abingdon Press, 1960).

Merton, Robert K., *Social Theory and Social Structure* (Glencoe, Ill.: The Free Press, 1957).

Merton, Robert K., et al., eds., *Sociology Today: Problems and Prospects* (New York: Basic Books, 1959).

Moberg, David O., *The Church as a Social Institution* (Englewood Cliffs, N.J.: Prentice-Hall, Inc., 1962).

Neill, Stephen, *Towards Church Union, 1937-1952*, Faith and Order Commission, Paper No. 11 (London: SCM Press, 1952).

Niebuhr, H. Richard, *The Social Sources of Denominationalism* (New York: Henry Holt and Co., Inc., 1929).

Nottingham, E. K., *Religion and Society* (New York: Doubleday & Co., Inc., 1954).

Panunzio, Constantine, *Major Social Institutions* (New York: The Macmillan Company, 1939).

Schelsky, H., Goldschmidt, D., and Greiner, H., eds., *Soziologie der Kirchengemeinde* (Stuttgart: F. Enke-Verlag, 1959).

Schweizer, Eduard, *Church Order in the New Testament* (London: SCM Press; Naperville, Illinois: Alec R. Allenson, Inc., 1961).

"Surveys of Church Union Negotiations," *The Ecumenical Review*, VI:3 (April, 1954); VIII:1 (October, 1955); IX:3 (April, 1957); XII:2 (January, 1960); XIV:3 (April, 1962).

Wach, Joachim, *Sociology of Religion* (Chicago: University of Chicago Press, 1944). G.T. *Religionssoziologie* (Tübingen: I. C. B. Mohr–Paul Siebeck–Verlag, 1951).

Weber, Max, *The Theory of Social and Economic Organization*, tr. by A. M. Henderson and Talcott Parsons (New York: Oxford University Press, 1959).

Welch, Claude, *The Reality of the Church* (New York: Charles Scribner's Sons, 1958).

World Council of Churches, Commission on Faith and Order, *One Lord, One Baptism* (London: SCM Press; Minneapolis: Augsburg Publishing House, 1960).

Yinger, J. Milton, *Religion, Society and the Individual: An Introduction to the Sociology of Religion* (New York: The Macmillan Company, 1957).